Frommer's

Paris
day BY day®

6th Edition

by Anna Brooke

FrommerMedia LLC

Contents

Published by:

Frommer Media LLC

Copyright © 2024 Frommer Media LLC. All rights reserved. No part of this publication may be reproduced, stored in a retrieval system or transmitted in any form or by any means, electronic, mechanical, photocopying, recording, scanning or otherwise, except as permitted under Sections 107 or 108 of the 1976 United States Copyright Act, without the prior written permission of the Publisher. Requests to the Publisher for permission should be addressed to Support@FrommerMedia.com.

Frommer's is a trademark or registered trademark of Arthur Frommer.

ISBN: 978-1-628-87567-6 (paper); ISBN 978-1-628-87568-3 (ebk)

Editorial Director: Pauline Frommer
Editor: Melinda Quintero
Production Editor: Erin Geile
Photo Editor: Alyssa Mattei
Cartographer: Roberta Stockwell
Compositor: Lissa Auciello-Brogan
Indexer: Kelly Dobbs Henthorne

Front cover photos, left to right: Sandwiches from Chambelland Bakery © Aldo Sperber. Le Consulat in Montmartre © anshar/Shutterstock.com. The Eiffel Tower from the Seine River © Viacheslav Lopatin.

Back cover photo: Enjoying an afternoon in the Jardin du Luxembourg. © nito/Shutterstock.com.

For information on our other products and services, please go to Frommers.com.

Frommer's also publishes its books in a variety of electronic formats. Some content that appears in print may not be available in electronic formats.

Manufactured in China

5 4 3 2 1

About this Guide

Organizing your time. That's what this guide is all about.

Other guides give you long lists of things to see and do and then expect you to fit the pieces together. The Day by Day guides are different. These guides tell you the best of everything, and then they show you how to see it *in the smartest, most time-efficient way.* Our authors have designed detailed itineraries organized by time, neighborhood, or special interest. And each tour comes with a bulleted map that takes you from stop to stop.

Hoping to follow Hemingway's footsteps, or to tour the highlights of the Louvre? Planning a walk through Montmartre, or a whirlwind tour of the very best that Paris has to offer? Whatever your interest or schedule, the Day by Days give you the smartest routes to follow. Not only do we take you to the top attractions, hotels, and restaurants, but we also help you access those special moments that locals get to experience—those "finds" that turn tourists into travelers.

The Day by Days are also your top choice if you're looking for one complete guide for all your travel needs. The best hotels and restaurants for every budget, the greatest shopping values, the wildest nightlife—it's all here.

Why should you trust our judgment? Because our authors personally visit each place they write about. They're an independent lot who say what they think and would never include places they wouldn't recommend to their best friends. They're also open to suggestions from readers. If you'd like to contact them, please send your comments our way at Support@FrommerMedia.com, and we'll pass them on.

Enjoy your Day by Day guide—the most helpful travel companion you can buy. And have the trip of a lifetime.

About the Author

Anna Brooke has authored multiple guidebooks on Paris and France for Frommer's, and her work has appeared in international publications such as *The Sunday Times Travel Magazine*, *Time Out*, and the *Financial Times*. She is also an author of children's fiction and composes lyrics and music for film and stage. She can be found at @AE_Brooke and instagram.com/annabrookewriter.

Advisory & Disclaimer

Travel information can change quickly and unexpectedly, and we strongly advise you to confirm important details locally before traveling, including information on visas, health and safety, traffic and transport, accommodations, shopping, and eating out. We also encourage you to stay alert while traveling and to remain aware of your surroundings. Avoid civil disturbances, and keep a close eye on cameras, purses, wallets, and other valuables.

While we have endeavored to ensure that the information contained within this guide is accurate and up-to-date at the time of publication, we make no representations or warranties with respect to the accuracy or completeness of the contents of this work and specifically disclaim all warranties, including without limitation warranties of fitness for a particular purpose. We accept no responsibility or liability for any inaccuracy or errors or omissions, or for any inconvenience, loss, damage, costs, or expenses of any nature whatsoever incurred or suffered by anyone as a result of any advice or information contained in this guide.

The inclusion of a company, organization, or website in this guide as a service provider and/or potential source of further information does not mean that we endorse them or the information they provide. Be aware that information provided through some websites may be unreliable and can change without notice. Neither the publisher nor author shall be liable for any damages arising herefrom.

Star Ratings & Icons

Every hotel, restaurant, and attraction listing in this guide has been ranked for quality, value, service, amenities, and special features using a **star-rating system.** Hotels, restaurants, attractions, shopping, and nightlife are rated on a scale of zero stars (recommended) to three stars (exceptional). In addition to the star-rating system, we also use a **kids icon** to point out the best bets for families. Within each tour, we recommend cafes, bars, or restaurants where you can take a break. Each of these stops appears in a shaded box marked with a coffee-cup-shaped bullet ☕.

Frommers.com

Now that you have this guidebook to help you plan a great trip, visit our website at **www.frommers.com** for additional travel information on more than 4,000 destinations. We update features regularly to give you instant access to the most current trip-planning information available. At Frommers.com, you'll find scoops on the best airfares, lodging rates, and car rental bargains. You can even book your travel online through our reliable travel booking partners. Other popular features include:

- Online updates of our most popular guidebooks
- Vacation sweepstakes and contest giveaways
- Newsletters highlighting the hottest travel trends
- Podcasts, interactive maps, and up-to-the-minute event listings
- Opinionated blog entries by Arthur Frommer himself
- Online travel message boards with featured travel discussions

A Note on Prices

In the "Take a Break" (coffee-cup icon) and "Best Bets" sections of this book, we have used a system of dollar signs to show a range of costs for 1 night in a hotel (the price of a double-occupancy room) or the cost of an entree at a restaurant. Use the following table to decipher the dollar signs:

Cost	Hotels	Restaurants
$	under $130	under $15
$$	$130–$200	$15–$30
$$$	$200–$300	$30–$40
$$$$	$300–$395	$40–$50
$$$$$	over $395	over $50

How to Contact Us

In researching this book, we discovered many wonderful places—hotels, restaurants, shops, and more. We're sure you'll find others. Please tell us about them, so we can share the information with your fellow travelers in upcoming editions. If you were disappointed with a recommendation, we'd love to know that, too. Please write to: Support@FrommerMedia.com.

13 Favorite
Moments

13 Favorite Moments

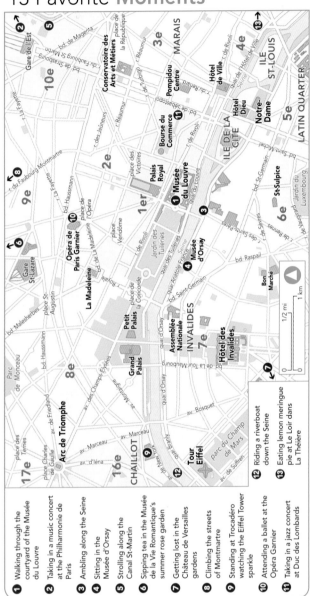

① Walking through the courtyard of the Musée du Louvre

② Taking in a music concert at the Philharmonie de Paris

③ Ambling along the Seine

④ Sitting in the Musée d'Orsay

⑤ Strolling along the Canal St-Martin

⑥ Sipping tea in the Musée de la Vie Romantique's summer rose garden

⑦ Getting lost in the Château de Versailles gardens

⑧ Climbing the streets of Montmartre

⑨ Standing at Trocadéro watching the Eiffel Tower sparkle

⑩ Attending a ballet at the Opéra Garnier

⑪ Taking in a jazz concert at Duc des Lombards

⑫ Riding a riverboat down the Seine

⑬ Eating lemon meringue pie at Le Loir dans La Théière

Previous page: I.M. Pei's iconic glass pyramid dominates the courtyard of the Musée du Louvre.

Waiting for the Eiffel Tower to light up after dark, strolling along the Seine on a warm summer night—these could become your favorite moments in the world, not just in Paris. This is an electric city—a "moveable feast" (as Ernest Hemingway so aptly called it). The list of wonderful experiences to be had here is endless. Here are 13 of my favorites.

❶ Walking through the courtyard of the Musée du Louvre early in the morning, hurrying to join the line, and catching the sun glinting off the glass pyramids in the center—it only heightens the excitement of seeing the masterpieces inside. *See p 32.*

❷ Taking in a concert at the Philharmonie de Paris. The main auditorium is futuristic, like the inside of a wooden spaceship—all sinuous lines and floating "clouds" (sound-reflecting surfaces designed to perfectly disperse the sound waves). The eclectic program is fab too, covering everything from classic symphonic works to fusion jazz. *See p 146.*

❸ Ambling along the Seine toward the islands, watching the tour boats cruise slowly by, the lights from their windows reflecting on the river. On summer nights, the riverside is packed, even after 10pm; sometimes it seems as if everybody in Paris is here. Bands play, lovers kiss, children frolic, everybody smiles—this is how life should be all the time. See p 8 for a good starting point.

❹ Sitting in the Musée d'Orsay in the center sculpture court, down below the entrance, looking up at the huge, ornate clock on the wall far above. Through the frosted glass around it, you can see the shadows of people passing by on invisible walkways. The sheer scale is astounding; the look is pure drama. And all around you, the works of history's most talented sculptors lounge, leap, and laugh silently. *See p 7.*

The light-filled sculpture hall in the Musée d'Orsay.

❺ Strolling along the Canal St-Martin, passing delicate iron bridges, locks, and people sitting at the water's edge. You could spend the better part of a day losing yourself in the bohemian boutiques, stopping at a cafe, and then continuing along to the Parc de la Villette for a picnic in the park or a trip around the *Cité des Sciences.* *See p 75.*

❻ Sipping tea in the Musée de la Vie Romantique's summer rose garden. The pink, ivy-clad house once frequented by George Sand and Frédéric Chopin feels like Paris's best-kept secret. Visit the museum and then wind down in the garden over a Darjeeling tea and a *tarte du jour,* with just the buzzing of bees and the clinking of teacups for company. *See p 40.*

❼ Getting lost in the Château de Versailles gardens. This opulent

The Seine winds its way through Paris.

château of the Sun King, Louis XIV, was the *bijou* (jewel) in the royal crown. Nowadays it is the glittering highlight of any visit to the Île-de-France. Nothing can beat a day spent ambling through the terraced gardens, admiring the fountains and Marie Antoinette's hamlet. Classical music extravaganzas take place during the warmer months. *See p 167,* ❷.

❽ **Climbing the streets of Montmartre.** This hilly, hopelessly romantic neighborhood is my favorite in all of Paris. A sweeping view of the city spreads out before you from every cross street. Every corner reveals another evocative stone staircase too steep to see all the way down, but at the bottom you know you'll find sweet old buildings and streets of old paving stones. *See p 70.*

❾ **Standing at Trocadéro, watching the Eiffel Tower sparkle** at nightfall. It's the best place in town to take in the tower's elegant, filigree proportions, and that moment when somebody, somewhere, flicks the button to light it up is matchless. *See p 26.*

❿ **Attending a ballet at the Opéra Garnier.** Whether you're seeing a traditional rendition of Tchaikovsky's *The Nutcracker* or a contemporary version of Prokofiev's *Romeo and Juliet,* the Charles Garnier–designed grande dame of performance spaces provides a breathtaking backdrop for ballet. Climb the majestic central staircase, order champagne for the *entr'acte* (intermission), and then sink into your red velvet chair and admire Chagall's famous ceiling fresco before the lights go down. *See p 146.*

⓫ **Taking in a jazz concert at Duc des Lombards.** This is one of the most renowned jazz clubs in Paris, and for good reason. Some of the genre's most famous musicians come to play in this small, intimate space. I love coming here for dinner and making a night of it. On Fridays and Saturdays there are even free jazz sessions after midnight. *See p 143.*

⓬ **Riding a riverboat down the Seine,** where all the buildings are artfully lighted so they seem to glow from within. On warm nights, take an open-top boat and feel as if you can reach up and touch the damp, stone bridges as you pass beneath them. *See p 11.*

⓭ **Eating lemon meringue pie at Le Loir dans la Théière.** The tearoom—decorated in old posters and Alice in Wonderland frescos—serves what is easily the biggest slice of lemon pie I've ever tasted. It's the most delicious too—with a crispy pastry base, smothered in tangy lemon cream, offset by sweet, fluffy meringue. *See p 68.* ●

1 The Best **Full-Day Tours**

The Best **in One Day**

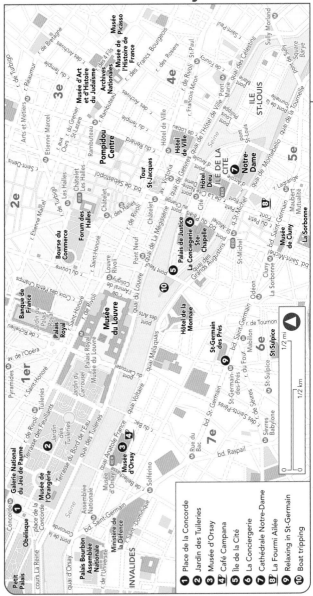

1. Place de la Concorde
2. Jardin des Tuileries
3. Musée d'Orsay
4. Café Campana
5. Île de la Cité
6. La Conciergerie
7. Cathédrale Notre-Dame
8. La Fourmi Ailée
9. Relaxing in St-Germain
10. Boat tripping

Previous page: The iconic Eiffel Tower.

This whirlwind 1-day tour covers everything I would want to see if I had only 24 hours in the City of Light. Start at the stately Place de la Concorde, then spend some time with the Musée d'Orsay's 19th-century masterpieces. Enjoy strolling the narrow cobblestone streets of Paris's islands before admiring the iconic Cathédrale de Notre-Dame. Relax at a cafe in Saint-Germain for pre-dinner drinks and end the day with a moonlit Seine cruise. It's an ambitious itinerary, so start early. You'll need to reserve a time slot for all your museum visits and the evening cruise. START: **Métro to Concorde.**

A fountain in Place de la Concorde, with the ancient Luxor Obelisk in the background.

❶ ★★ Place de la Concorde.
From the city's largest square, you get immediate Paris gratification. First, admire the view of the Eiffel Tower, and then position yourself to see down the Champs-Élysées to the Arc de Triomphe, a monument to Napoleon's conquests. Behind you are the Tuileries gardens and the Louvre. In the center of the square stands the 3,300-year-old Luxor Obelisk (a gift from Egypt in 1829), placed near the spot where Queen Marie-Antoinette was guillotined in 1793 during the Revolution. To your left, you'll see the Madeleine Church (see p 16)—a mirror image of the Assemblée Nationale across the Seine (home to the lower house of the French Parliament). This lovely viewpoint is your own instant postcard. Welcome to Paris. ⏱ *10 min. Go early in the morning to avoid crowds or just after sunset to see the buildings aglow. Free admission. Métro: Concorde.*

❷ Jardin des Tuileries. Place de la Concorde ends where the Louvre's stately sculpture-strewn gardens begin. Throughout an area about the size of two football fields, chestnut trees shade winding paths. It's a beautiful place to walk, read, or admire works by such greats as Rodin and Maillol. See also the "Jardin des Tuileries" tour on p 98. ⏱ *20 min. Late Mar–May & Sept daily 7am–9pm, June–Aug daily 7am–11pm, Oct to early Mar 7:30am–7:30pm. Métro: Tuileries or Concorde.*

❸ ★★★ Musée d'Orsay.
Across the Seine on the Left Bank is the Gare d'Orsay. Built for the 1900 Universal Exhibition, this Belle Epoque train station now houses a museum devoted to works created from 1848 to 1914. Fans of Impressionism will swoon at masterpieces by Manet, Renoir, Degas, Cézanne, and Monet. The Post-Impressionist collection includes pieces by van

The Tuileries gardens, between Place de la Concorde and the Louvre.

Gogh, Rousseau, and Gauguin. A huge, ornate clock and a 3m (9½-ft.) model of the Statue of Liberty by the French sculptor Frédéric-Auguste Bartholdi (1834–1904) dominate the light-filled central hall. Where train tracks once lay, statues of robust maidens and eager men now stand, including the original of Carpeaux's *La Danse* (once controversial for its frolicking nude women), taken from the facade of Paris's Opéra Garnier (see p 146). ⏲ *2–3 hr. Esplanade Valéry Giscard d'Estaing, 7th. www. musee-orsay.fr.* ☎ *01-40-49-48-14. Admission 16€ ages 26 & over, 13€ ages 19–25, free for children 18 & under and visitors 25 & under from EU countries. Tues–Wed & Fri–Sun 9:30am–6pm, Thurs 9:30am–9:45pm. Métro: Solférino & Assemblée Nationale. RER C: Musée d'Orsay.*

☕ **Café Campana.** Near the Impressionist galleries, the Musée d'Orsay's Art Nouveau–inspired restaurant serves tasty brasserie-style meals. At teatime, indulge in coffee and delicious cream-filled pastry puffs. *$$.*

❺ ★★★ **Île de la Cité.** One of the most quintessentially Parisian experiences you can have is a stroll along the Seine to the Île de la Cité, the birthplace of Paris. Take a right as you leave the Musée d'Orsay. It's about a 15-minute walk to this island, home to **Notre-Dame Cathedral.** Cross onto the island at the **pont Neuf** (New Bridge), which despite its name is the oldest bridge in the city; note the statue of Henri IV, who commissioned the *pont* in 1578. To your right will be the pretty pink Place Dauphine, which opens onto the west wing of the **Palais de Justice,** Paris's law courts (Rue de Harlay). This is an active court building, so unfortunately tourists are not welcome. But you can admire the majestic east facade (the main entrance) behind gilded gates, between the Conciergerie and Sainte-Chapelle (see the next stop of this tour). ⏲ *30 min. Métro: Pont Neuf.*

❻ ★★ **La Conciergerie.** The fairy-tale towers that soar above the north end of the island near the pont Neuf mark the fortress where Marie Antoinette was imprisoned before her execution. Its intimidating look is courtesy of an 1850s makeover, but most of the building is much older—several parts date to the 12th and 13th centuries, when it was a royal palace (the monarchs moved to the Louvre at the end of the 14th century). During the French Revolution, torture and execution were commonplace here, and it became a symbol of terror. You can get a good feel for what the building looked like in Medieval and Revolutionary times—notably the vast former banquet halls and guardrooms—thanks

Marie Antoinette awaited her execution in the foreboding Conciergerie.

to the museum's excellent "Histo-pad," a smart device with augmented reality functions. Next door is the 13th-century **Sainte-Chapelle** (buy a dual ticket via the Sainte-Chapelle website: www.sainte-chapelle.fr), a Flamboyant Gothic masterpiece built by Saint Louis (King Louis IX). It's famous for the breathtaking "light show" cast on the interior when the sun shines through its jewel-like stained-glass windows, which recount the stories of the Bible and King Louis. ⏱ *1 hr. 2 bd. du Palais, 1st. www.paris-conciergerie.fr.* ☎ *01-53-40-60-80. Admission 11.50€ (18.50€ dual ticket, via www.sainte-chapelle.fr only) adult, free for children 18 & under and visitors 25 & under from EU countries. Daily 9:30am–6pm. Métro: Cité.*

❼ ★★★ Cathédrale Notre-Dame. As you approach the island's eastern tip, you'll see the familiar silhouette of one of the world's best-known cathedrals. Founded in 1160, Notre-Dame stood through wars of religion and centuries of kings (Napoleon also crowned himself emperor here in 1804) before losing its riches to plunderers during the Revolution. By the 19th century, it had fallen into disrepair and was scheduled for demolition until author Victor Hugo, who wrote *The Hunchback of Notre-Dame*, led a successful campaign for its restoration. In 2019, a vast fire consumed its spire and gutted the entire roof—though it didn't bring it down (thanks to 400 firefighters). At the time of writing, it was set to re-open at the end

The Notre-Dame in the process of rebirth after the 2019 fire.

Outside Les Deux Magots cafe on Boulevard Saint-Germain.

of 2024, so hopefully you'll see the cathedral, pretty much as it was before the fire—which means as follows:

At the far end of the cathedral is the nave, with three elaborately sculpted 13th-century portals: on the left, the Portal of the Virgin; in the center, the Portal of the Last Judgment; and on the right, the Portal of St. Anne. Above them all glow the ruby hues of the West Rose Window, its beauty surpassed only by the North Rose Window. The colors are especially vivid in the late afternoon. Near the altar, the 14th-century statue *Virgin and Child* was near the altar before the fire and survived the destruction. Many other priceless objects that were locked in the treasury during the fire also survived, including a collection of crosses and ancient reliquaries and the Crown of Thorns (brought from the Sainte-Chapelle). If it's open, get an up-close look at the cathedral's famous gargoyles by climbing the 422 steps up the towers' stone staircases to the top. The non-acrophobic will love the views of the fanciful and detailed hobgoblins and chimeras. ⏱ *1 hr. 6 Parvis Notre-Dame/Place Jean Paul II, 4th. www.notredamedeparis.fr.* ☎ *01-42-34-56-10. Free admission to cathedral. Check the website for up-to-date information on opening times and prices for the tower. Métro: Cité.*

🔟 ★ **La Fourmi Ailée.** Escape the crowds around Notre-Dame by crossing the pont au Double to the Left Bank. A 5-minute walk past Square René Viviani brings you to the "Flying Ant" tearoom, an institution, practically unchanged by the passing of time. Sticky cakes and excellent hot dishes, such as veal blanquette (19€), are served in a library-like dining room. *8 rue du Fouarre, 5th. www.parisresto.com.* ☎ *01-43-29-40-99. $$.*

🟡 ★★ **Relaxing in Saint-Germain.** Head right as you leave the cafe and go up Rue Dante to join Boulevard Saint-Germain (turning right) and, after 5 minutes, the bustle of Saint-Germain-des-Prés. This area was the incubator for artistic creativity in the 1920s, Nazi resistance in the 1940s, and student revolution in the 1960s. These days, you can get a great cup of coffee, drop a wad of cash on high-fashion clothes, or spend a night on the town. The best way to experience the neighborhood is to weave your way through glittering, tree-lined Boulevard Saint-Germain and its narrow side-streets, soaking up the atmosphere and stopping at shops and bars that strike your fancy. The district is also the realm of Paris's historic literary cafes: the stylish **Café de Flore,** 172 bd. St-Germain (cafedeflore.fr; ☎ 01-45-48-55-26), a favorite of the philosopher Jean-Paul Sartre; and the more touristy **Les Deux Magots,** 6 place St-Germain-des-Prés (lesdeuxmagots. fr; ☎ 01-45-48-55-26), a regular haunt of both Sartre and Hemingway. At either spot, you can linger over a *café* or enjoy a complete meal. Prices are high, but you can stay at your table and people-watch as long as you like.

🔟 ★★ **Boat Tripping.** After dinner, walk down to the riverside at the pont Neuf and catch one of Vedettes du Pont Neuf's long, low boats. As the boats navigate the river by night, the city's lights reflect in the Seine's inky waters like diamonds. Magical. ⏱ *1 hr. Square du Vert Galant, 4th. www. vedettesdupontneuf.com.* ☎ *01-46-33-98-38. Tickets 15€ adults, 9€ children 4–12, free for children 3 & under. Apr–Oct daily 10:45am–10:45pm, about every 30 min.; Nov–Early Mar 10:30am–9:30pm (10pm on weekends), about every 45 min.*

Budget Paris in 1 Day

Believe it or not, it is possible to spend a day in Paris with just 30€ in your pocket. Start your morning amid an extensive collection of Chinese art at the fabulous and free **Musée Cernuschi,** 7 av. Vélasquez, 8th (www.cernuschi.paris.fr; ☎ 01-53-96-21-50; free admission to the permanent collection; Tues–Sun 10am–6pm; Métro: Villiers or Monceau). The collection ranges from Neolithic terra cottas and Wei dynasty funeral statues (A.D. 386–534) to Sung porcelain and rare gold Liao dynasty objets d'art (A.D. 907–1125). Then, if the weather is fair, find a place in the sun for an early picnic lunch at the **Parc Monceau** next door. This elegant oasis ringed with stately mansions was designed by writer, artist, and architect Louis Carrogis Carmontelle in 1778 as a hideaway for the duke of Chartres. Admire the Roman columns and a small Egyptian pyramid as you tuck into your baguette. You'll find picnic provisions at the street market on Rue de Lévis by the Villiers Métro stop (access on bd. de Courcelles, av. Vélasquez, av. Van Dyck & av. Ruysdaël; Métro: Monceau or Villiers). If it's cold or rainy, opt for lunch at Les Caves Populaires, at 22 rue des Dames, 17th (☎ 01-53-04-08-32; Mon–Sat 8am–2am, Sun 11am–2am; Métro: Place de Clichy). This rustic local haunt on one of Paris's most bohemian streets is the perfect spot for coffee or a glass of wine (a steal starting at just 2.50€), with snacks from about 7€. After your meal, while away the afternoon amid the arty streets of **Montmartre** (p 70). At the highest point in Paris, this village within the city affords incomparable views. For dinner, you'll find some of the best no-frills French cuisine in town at **Bouillon Pigalle,** 22 bd. de Clichy, 18th (https://bouillon lesite.com; ☎ 01-42-59-69-31; daily noon to midnight; Métro: Pigalle). Reserve ahead or be prepared for very long queues.

The Best **in Two Days**

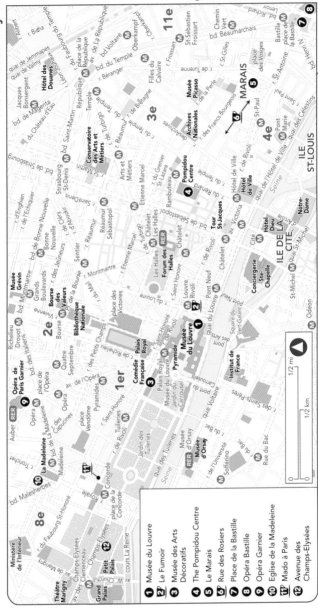

1. Musée du Louvre
2. Le Fumoir
3. Musée des Arts Décoratifs
4. The Pompidou Centre
5. Le Marais
6. Rue des Rosiers
7. Place de la Bastille
8. Opéra Bastille
9. Opéra Garnier
10. Eglise de la Madeleine
11. Mado à Paris
12. Avenue des Champs-Elysées

If you followed the **1-day tour of Paris,** you've already had a good introduction to the city—and a hint that there's so much more to see. Start early with coffee and fresh croissants. **Le Nemours** (2 Galerie de Nemours, 1st), nestled behind graceful columns opposite the Louvre and the historic Comédie Française theater (p 147), is an atmospheric spot that's perfect for people-watching. START: **Métro to Palais Royal–Musée du Louvre.**

❶ ★★★ Musée du Louvre.
Book ahead for a time-stamped ticket to make sure you can get into what is arguably the world's greatest art museum. The Louvre is so humongous you could easily spend a day in each wing and still not see everything. Avoid overdosing on culture by deciding what you want to see in advance. For help navigating the museum, opening times, and ticket prices, see the **Louvre tour** on p 32. ⏲ *2 hr.*

❷ ★★ Le Fumoir. This chic cafe with a convenient location near the Louvre and Arts Décoratifs museums has a faithful following among Paris's literary and media crowds. Sink into a Chesterfield armchair and order a refreshing fruit cocktail, or fill up on French classics with a Scandinavian twist. *6 rue de l'Amiral de Coligny, 1st. www.lefumoir.com.* ☎ *01-42-92-00-24. Métro: Louvre-Rivoli. $$$.*

The vast wings of the Louvre contain some of the world's greatest works of art.

❸ ★★★ Musée des Arts Décoratifs. This excellent museum (set inside the Louvre palace but separate from the Louvre) contains one of the world's most important collections of design and decorative art. It covers a breathtaking range of pieces, from medieval liturgical items, Art Nouveau and Art Deco furniture, and Gothic paneling to Renaissance porcelain and 1970s psychedelic carpets. Period rooms show how the museum's collections would have looked in a real house. The most memorable are couturière Jeanne Lanvin's purple early–Art Deco boudoir and a grandiose Louis-Philippe bedchamber. If you have time, check out the rotating exhibitions at both the Fashion and Textile and Advertising and Graphic Design departments. The former comprises some 152,800 items of clothing and accessories (many by world-famous designers such as Yves Saint Laurent and Christian Dior), while the latter covers the evolution of advertising from the 18th century to today. ⏱ *1–1½ hrs. 107 rue de Rivoli, 1st. https://madparis.fr.* ☎ *01-44-55-57-50. Admission 14€ adults, free for children 18 & under & visitors 26 & under from EU countries. Tues–Wed & Fri–Sun 11am–6pm, Thurs until 9pm. Métro: Palais-Royal Musée du Louvre.*

❹ ★★ The Pompidou Centre. If the Louvre's classic artworks leave you craving modernity, walk eastward to Paris's most avant-garde building, the Pompidou Centre—one of the world's leading modern and contemporary art museums, famed for its bold, "exoskeletal" architecture, with brightly painted pipes. **Note:** The museum is closed for renovations until 2027. **See p 44.**

❺ ★★ Le Marais. After so much culture, I find nothing more relaxing than strolling around the winding medieval streets of the Marais district—traditionally the city's old Jewish quarter and home to magnificent 17th- and 18th-century mansions (called *hôtels*). You can spend hours perusing its charming boutiques and tiny Jewish bakeries and absorbing museums if you take the Marais tour (p 66). One of its most picturesque squares is the **Place des Vosges**—Paris's oldest square, remarkable for its perfect symmetry, formed by 36 red-brick–and–stone arcades with sharply pitched roofs. In 1615, a 3-day party was held here celebrating Louis XIII's marriage to Anne of Austria. ⏱ *2 hr. Most Jewish shops and restaurants close Fri evening through Sat, the Jewish Sabbath. Many boutiques open Sun. Métro: St-Paul.*

❻ ★ Rue des Rosiers, 4th. Two places on this street serve the best falafel sandwiches in town (from 5€): L'As du Falafel, no. 34 (www.asdu fallafel.com; ☎ 01-48-87-63-60) and Chez Hanna, no. 54 (chez-hanna-restaurant.fr; ☎ 01-42-74-74-99). Choose the one with the shortest queue; both serve soft pitas bursting with tahini sauce, pickled cabbage, and, of course, tasty chickpea balls. Unless it's raining, eat on a bench in nearby Place des Vosges. (See previous stop.) *$.*

❼ ★★ Place de la Bastille. From Place des Vosges, it's a short walk to Place de la Bastille, the site of one of the most famous moments in French Revolutionary history. Here stood the Bastille prison, a massive building that loomed ominously over the city as a symbol of royal authority. On July 14, 1789, a mob attacked it, and its fall marked the beginning of the people's uprising that eventually led to the founding of the first French republic in 1792. Today, the site is home to the modern Bastille Opera House. The central column, the Colonne de Juillet, honors the casualties of the 1830 revolution, which ironically put Louis-Philippe on the throne after the upheaval of the Napoleonic wars. In the 1848 revolution, Louis-Philippe's throne was burned below the column and the rioters' remains were entombed in the vault, which you can visit on a 90-minute guided tour (in French; www.colonne-de-juillet.fr; admission 13€ adults, 6€ children 7–17, free for children 6 & under; most Sat & Sun 2:30pm and 4:30pm). ⏱ *15 min. Métro: Bastille.*

❽ ★★ Opéra Bastille. This impossible-to-miss behemoth,

The ceiling of the Opéra Garnier and its distinct Chagall painting.

which opened in 1989 as part of President Mitterrand's "Grand Travaux" (large-scale monument program), is the home of the Opéra National de Paris (together with the Opéra Garnier; see the next stop). Designed by Canadian-Uruguayan architect Carlos Ott, the building infamously ran over budget and had structural issues that took years to resolve. Today, however, the 80m-tall (262-ft.) monument has found its place in the landscape, and the operas performed in its 2,745-seat auditorium are of the highest standard. Tickets are sold online, or try your luck 40 minutes before the performance, when remaining tickets are sold off at a discount. Or buy a visitor's ticket to explore the building on a guided tour (17€) ⏱ *15 min. 2 place de la Bastille, 4th. www.operadeparis.fr.* ☎ *08-92-89-90-90 (0.35€/min.) or 33-1-71-25-24-23 from abroad. Tickets 10€–215€. Métro: Bastille.*

❾ ★★★ Opéra Garnier. On your second day (or third, if you followed the 1-day tour), start by seeing Charles Garnier's architectural explosion. His 1875 opera house goes beyond baroque and well into the splendors of rococo, and is hailed as one of most spectacular Italian-style theaters in the world. Today it shares its program with the Opéra Bastille, though ballet performances are more common here than opera. An elaborate ceiling painted by Marc Chagall in 1964 and an 8-ton chandelier dominate the main theater, while the facade is a riot of marble and flowing sculpture, with gilded busts and multihued pillars. This is where the Phantom did his haunting (a man-made lake below the opera house inspired novelist Gaston Leroux to create his tragic antihero). Even if you don't see a show, buy a visitor's ticket (14€, 9€ ages 13–25) to admire the flamboyant gilded interior, including the grand staircase where a salamander sculpture serves the double function of hiding electric cables and protecting the opera from fire: Paris's previous opera houses burned down, so Garnier included the salamander as a luck charm (according to legend, the creatures are fire-resistant). ⓘ *20 min. Place de l'Opéra, 9th. www.operadeparis.fr.* ☎ *08-92-89-90-90 (0.35€/min.) or 33-1-71-25-24-23 from abroad. Tickets 10€–215€. Visiting hours daily 10am–5pm; until 1pm on matinee performance days. Métro: Opéra, RER A: Auber).*

⑩ ★★ Eglise de la Madeleine. Tear yourself away from the Art Nouveau–style department stores behind the opera house on Boulevard Haussmann (**Galeries Lafayette** and **Au Printemps,** p 91), and head west down Boulevard des Capucines to this neoclassical church, designed by Barthélémy Vignon in 1806 as a "temple of glory" for Napoleon Bonaparte. The exterior, which mirrors the Assemblée Nationale on the other side of Place de la Concorde, is marked by fluted Corinthian columns, while interior highlights include a wonderful frieze of the Last Judgment and a painting of the history of Christianity by Jules-Claude Ziegler. The square around the church, **Place de la Madeleine,** is known for its top-end restaurants and luxury food shops like avant-garde chocolatier Patrick Roger (no. 3). ⓘ *30 min. Place de la Madeleine, 8th. lamadeleineparis.fr.* ☎ *01-44-51-69-00. Free admission. Daily 9:30am–7pm. Métro: Madeleine.*

The neoclassical Eglise de la Madeleine, built in 1806.

The Arc de Triomphe at the end of the Champs-Élysées.

11 ★★ Mado à Paris. After a long day traversing the city, coffee and cakes might be in order. In a handy spot off Place de la Concorde, little shell-shaped sponge gateaux called madeleines fill this modern café's counter like exquisite gourmet jewels. Sidle up to a table and try the different flavors—salted caramel, lemon, chocolate, pistachio, and raspberry, or just plain "nature" (with hints of vanilla)—they're all delicious paired with an espresso or piping hot tea. *252 rue de Rivoli, Castellane, 1st. madoaparis.com.* ☎ *09-54-65-87-02. Wed–Fri 8:30am–7pm, Sat–Sun 9:30am–7pm. Métro: Concorde. $.*

12 ★★ Avenue des Champs-Élysées. Although not as beautiful as most of us imagine, this bustling 2km (1¼-mile) avenue—the symbolic gathering place for national parades and sports victory celebrations, largely centered around Napoleon's early-19th-century **Arc de Triomphe** (p 25)—is inseparable from Paris in the minds of most people. It is also part of the city's **Golden Triangle** (along with av. Georges V and av. Montaigne), where Chanel, Louis Vuitton, and other designer boutiques stand alongside lavish palace hotels, such as the Hôtel Georges V. You'll find plenty for tighter budgets, too, such as H&M and Zara, along with cinemas and bars.

The Best **in Three Days**

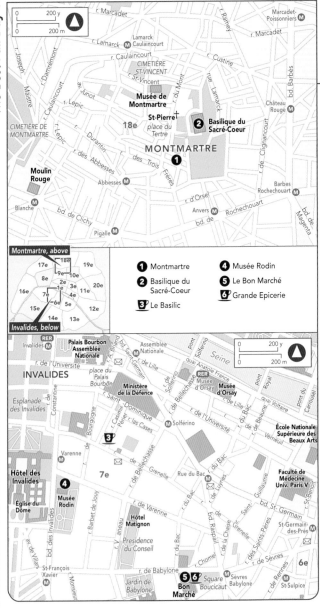

- **1** Montmartre
- **2** Basilique du Sacré-Coeur
- **3** Le Basilic
- **4** Musée Rodin
- **5** Le Bon Marché
- **6** Grande Epicerie

After 2 jam-packed days, you may want to slow down a bit. A good way of getting a leisurely feel for two very different parts of the city is to spend the morning amid the cobblestones and windmills of Montmartre on the Right Bank before heading to the throng of boutiques in the Saint-Germain district, south of the Seine, in the afternoon. If you fancy slackening the pace even more, choose one of these two areas and follow the full-day tours on p 70 or p 58. START: **Métro to Abesses or Blanche.**

❶ ★★★ Montmartre. With its steep hills, staircase streets, quaint windmills, and sweeping views, this is, for some, the most romantic neighborhood in Paris, and many would say the most beautiful. Unfortunately, it's not exactly a secret—prepare yourself for some tacky souvenir shops and the ever-present tourist onslaught around the Sacré Coeur. Still, spending a morning wandering around the streets of Montmartre is enough to make the heart flutter (and not just from the exertion of climbing all those stairs). Take the Métro to Abbesses or Blanche and head upward. Fall in love with such streets as Rue des Abbesses, Rue des Trois Frères, or Rue des Martyrs. Find the windmills on Rue Lepic or the famous one atop the titillating Moulin Rouge on the boulevard below. For more guidance, try the Montmartre walking tour on p 70. ⏲ *2 hr. Métro: Abbesses or Blanche.*

❷ ★★★ Sacré Coeur. You can either take a funicular from the end of Rue Berthe or, better still, wander up to Sacré Coeur via the bustling Place du Tertre; however you get here, this white wedding-cake basilica will draw a gasp from you when it first hovers into view. Construction began in 1876 and didn't end until 1919—the whole thing was paid for by donations from the faithful to thank God for freeing Paris from the invaders of the 1870–71 Franco-Prussian War. The mosaics inside—on the ceiling, walls, and floors—are dizzying, and the panoramic view from the steps out front is almost as splendid as the one from its dome (300 steps higher), where a panorama unfolds 50km (30 miles) into the distance. The Sacré Coeur's bell, called La Savoyarde, is 3m (10 ft.) wide and weighs 18,835 kg (19 tons), making it the biggest working swinging bell in the world. ⏲ *1 hr. Place Saint-Pierre, 18th.*

The Basilica Sacré Coeur crowns the highest hill in Paris.

www.sacre-coeur-montmartre.com.
☎ 01-53-41-89-00. Free admission
to basilica, 7€ to dome. Daily 6am–
10:30pm (dome 10am–7pm). Métro:
Abbesses or Anvers.

3 ★★ **Le Basilic.** On Rue Lepic,
north of the Café des Deux Moulins
(no. 15), where Amélie worked in
the film of the same name, an
honest two-course lunch of hearty
French staples costs just 15€.
Dishes—think Rossini-style beef with
creamy potato gratin and a velve-
teen mousse au chocolat—are fresh
and hearty, and the atmosphere is
wholly Montmartrois. 33 rue Lepic,
18th. https://lebasilic.fr. ☎ 01-46-
06-78-43. Daily 11:45am–12:45am. $.

The Thinker in the courtyard of the
Musée Rodin.

4 ★★ **Musée Rodin.** A short
Métro ride will bring you to this
peaceful museum, where the sculptor Auguste Rodin once had his
studio. Today his works are scat-
tered inside and outside a somber
18th-century mansion of gray stone.
The Thinker perches pensively in
the courtyard, while the lovers in
The Kiss embrace in perpetuity
inside. There's also a room devoted
to the oft-overlooked works of
Rodin's talented mistress, Camille
Claudel. It's rarely crowded, so it's
a good option when things are
overwhelming at the Louvre.
⏱ 1 hr. Hôtel Biron, 79 rue de
Varenne, 7th. www.musee-rodin.fr.
☎ 01-44-18-61-10. Admission 13€,
free for children 18 & under & visitors
25 & under from EU countries. Tues–
Sun 10am–6:30pm. Métro: Varenne
or Invalides. RER C: Invalides.

5 ★ **Shopping at Le Bon
Marché.** If you haven't found everything you hoped to yet, and you're
tired of walking from boutique to
boutique, do what the chic locals do
and come to this swank department
store. If you fancy an extra treat,
book online for a free personalized

shopper at "Le Personal Shopper"
or opt for the "Styliste Privé,"
where professional stylists and
beauty experts give you tailored
advice (150€ for 2 hours). The place
is all very designer-label oriented,
which may put some strains on the
holiday budget. But this is Paris's
oldest department store, and even
the central escalators are worth
photographing, so you should at
least take a look. ⏱ 2 hr. 24 rue de
Sèvres, 7th. www.lebonmarche.com.
☎ 01-44-39-80-00. Mon–Sat 10am–
7:45pm, Sun 11am–7:45pm. Métro:
Sèvres-Babylone.

6 ★ **Grande Epicerie.** In the
building next to the Bon Marché,
this grand food hall contains all the
pâtés and cheeses your heart could
desire. You can build yourself a
gorgeous picnic, or take a seat in
one of the excellent eateries
(there's a brasserie, a tapas spot, a
truffle-themed counter, and more)
and let someone else do all the
work. 38 rue de Sèvres, 7th. www.
lagrandeepicerie.com. ☎ 01-44-39-
81-00. Mon–Sat 8:30am–9pm, Sun
10am–8pm. $$. ●

Monumental Paris

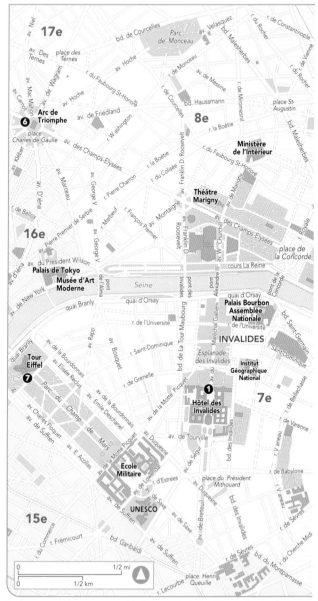

17e

av. Niel

bd. de Courcelles

Parc de Monceau

av. Velasquez

bd. Malesherbes

r. du Rocher

r. de Constantinople

av. Des Ternes

place des Ternes

av. Hoche

r. de Monceau

av. de Messine

r. de Miromesnil

r. de Vienne

r. du Rocher

av. Mac Mahon

av. de Wagram

r. du Faubourg St-Honoré

bd. Haussmann

place St-Augustin

av. Carnot

av. Hoche

av. de Friedland

8e

Arc de Triomphe ➏

r. W. Washington

av. des Champs-Elysées

r. la Boétie

r. du Faubourg St-Honoré

Ministère de l'Intérieur

bd. Malesherbes

place Charles de Gaulle

av. Kléber

av. d'Iéna

av. Marceau

r. la Boétie

r. du Colisée

Franklin D. Roosevelt

r. de Marigny

Théâtre Marigny

16e

av. Pierre Premier de Serbie

av. George V

r. Pierre Charron

r. Marbeuf

av. François Premier

av. Montaigne

Franklin D. Roosevelt

av. W. Churchill

av. des Champs-Elysées

r. Royale

place de la Concorde

av. d'Iéna

av. du President Wilson

av. George V

Palais de Tokyo

Musée d'Art Moderne

pont de l'Alma

cours La Reine

pont de la Concorde

av. de New York

quai Branly

Seine

quai d'Orsay

pont des Invalides

pont Alexandre III

quai d'Orsay

Palais Bourbon Assemblée Nationale

bd. Saint-Germain

r. de l'Université

av. Rapp

r. de l'Université

r. Saint-Dominique

av. Bosquet

Maréchal Gallieni

INVALIDES

r. Saint-Dominique

quai Branly

av. de la Bourdonnais

r. Saint-Dominique

bd. de La Tour Maubourg

Esplanade des Invalides

Institut Géographique National

r. de Bellechasse

Tour Eiffel ➐

av. Elisée Reclus

av. de la Bourdonnais

av. Emile Deschanel

r. de Grenelle

av. de la Motte Picquet

➊

Hôtel des Invalides

7e

r. de Varenne

Parc du Champ de Mars

av. Charles Floquet

av. de Suffren

av. E. Acollas

Ecole Militaire

av. Duquesne

av. de Tourville

bd. des Invalides

r. V. aneau

av. de Ségur

av. de Lowendal

av. d'Estrées

place du Président Mithouard

av. Duquesne

r. de Babylone

15e

r. Frémicourt

r. du Commerce

av. de Suffren

UNESCO

av. de Saxe

av. de Breteuil

bd. des Invalides

r. de Sèvres

bd. du Montparnasse

av. de Saxe

av. de Suffren

bd. Garibaldi

place Henri Queuille

r. Lecourbe

r. de Sèvres

bd. du Cherche Midi

0		1/2 mi
0		1/2 km

Previous page: Make sure you can visit the Louvre by buying tickets online in advance.

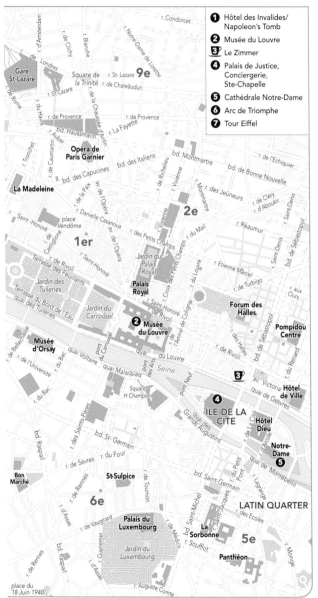

1. Hôtel des Invalides/Napoleon's Tomb
2. Musée du Louvre
3. Le Zimmer
4. Palais de Justice, Conciergerie, Ste-Chapelle
5. Cathédrale Notre-Dame
6. Arc de Triomphe
7. Tour Eiffel

This tour covers a lot of ground, so be prepared for lots of walking and, when your feet ache, Métro-hopping. For your efforts, you'll see the city's most glorious edifices in one giant sweep. If you get an early start and keep moving, you should be able to make it to the Eiffel Tower (the last stop) by sunset. Just remember to buy your timed-entry tickets in advance for any museums you decide to stop in. START: **Métro to Invalides.**

① ★★★ Hôtel des Invalides/ Napoleon's Tomb. The imposing Les Invalides complex, with its symmetrical corridors and beautiful Dôme church (Libéral Bruand and Jules Hardouin-Mansart's golden-domed masterpiece), was built in 1670 by Louis XIV as a military hospital and a showpiece of the Sun King's military power. Approach it from the cherub-clad pont Alexandre III to see it as intended, from the end of its perfectly balanced gardens, lined with cannons. Inside is the Musée de l'Armée, with enough historic weaponry (vicious battle-axes, clumsy blunderbusses) to mount another revolution. Among the collection's gems are a German Enigma machine, used by Hitler's army to encrypt messages, and suits of armor worn by the kings and dignitaries of France, including one worn by Louis XIV and François I's exquisite "armor suit of the lion," inspired by Classical war heroes. The complex also contains a section on military history from the Sun King to Napoleon; the Historial Charles de Gaulle, a high-tech audiovisual attraction covering the whole of de Gaulle's life, particularly his role in World War II; the Musée des Plans Reliefs, the collection of scale-model cities Vauban, Louis XIV's military engineer, used for planning military attacks; and of course, Napoleon's beautiful, over-the-top tomb, set inside the Dôme church, featuring giant statues that represent his victories. You can also see his death mask and an oil painting by Paul Delaroche, painted at the time of Napoleon's first banishment in 1814. ⏱ *1 hr. 129 rue de Grenelle, 7th. www.musee-armee.fr.* ☎ *01-42-44-38-77. 14€, free for children 17 & under & visitors 25 & under from EU countries. Daily 10am–6pm (first Fri of month until 10pm). Métro: Invalides, Varenne or La Tour Maubourg; RER C: Invalides.*

② ★★★ Musée du Louvre. The home of da Vinci's *Mona Lisa* is one of the world's largest and best museums, set in Paris's former royal palace. It's worth spending a day here (see "Exploring the Louvre," p 32), but for this tour, admire it from the outside. ⏱ *20 min.*

③ ★ Le Zimmer. Jules Verne, Marcel Proust, and Igor Stravinsky once frequented this storied, 19th-century brasserie. During WWII, the "Honneur de la Police" (underground police Résistance) secretly occupied its cellars. Today, it's an atmospheric spot—all mirrors and red velvet—for lunch with terrace views onto your next stop, the Conciergerie. The 28€ menu is good value. *1 place du Châtelet, 1st. www. lezimmer.com.* ☎ *01-42-36-74-03. Métro: Châtelet. $$.*

④ ★★★ Palais de Justice, Conciergerie & Sainte-Chapelle. Take the Pont au Change to the Île de la Cité and walk down boulevard du Palais. Immediately on your right is the complex made up of the Conciergerie (formerly a prison,

The Palais de Justice, a working judicial building.

now a museum), the Palais de Justice (law courts, not open to visitors), and the exquisite Sainte-Chapelle church. Once a palace, the Conciergerie was converted to a prison during the Revolution and became a symbol of terror—Paris's answer to the Tower of London. Carts once frequently pulled up to the Conciergerie to haul off fresh victims for the guillotine. Among the few imprisoned here who lived to tell the tale was American political theorist and writer Thomas Paine. Inside, you can learn about the bloody history of the Conciergerie and visit some of the old prison cells, including a re-creation of Marie Antoinette's. The Palais de Justice is still the center of the French judicial system and thus doesn't accept tourists, but you can peek through its grand, gated entrance as you make your way to the Sainte-Chapelle—stunning in afternoon light. It was built in the 13th century to hold a crown of thorns that King Louis IX believed Christ wore during his crucifixion (the crown, saved from Notre-Dame at the time of the fire, was temporarily moved to the Louvre). The chapel's stained-glass windows comprise more than 1,000 scenes depicting the Christian story from the Garden of Eden through to the

Apocalypse, shown on the great Rose Window. (Read them from bottom to top and from left to right.) The stained glass of Sainte-Chapelle is magnificent in daylight, glowing with reds that have inspired the saying "wine the color of Sainte-Chapelle's windows." ⏱ 1 hr. 2–6 bd. du Palais, 1st. ☎ 01-53-40-60-80. Conciergerie, www.paris-conciergerie.fr. 11.50€, free for ages 18 & under & visitors 25 & under from EU countries. Sainte-Chapelle, www.sainte-chapelle.fr. 11.50€, free for children 18 & under & visitors 25 & under from EU countries. Combined ticket Conciergerie & Sainte-Chapelle 18.50€ (on www.sainte-chapelle.fr only); free entry, as above. Daily 9:30am–6pm (Sainte-Chapelle daily Oct–Mar 9am–5pm, Apr–Sep 9am–7pm). Métro: Cité or Châtelet (exit place du Châtelet).

❺ ★★★ Cathédrale Notre-Dame. For a good view of the repair work on the buttresses, take the short bridge—pont de l'Archevêché—just behind the cathedral to Île Saint-Louis. ⏱ 1 hr. See p 9, ❼.

❻ ★★★ Arc de Triomphe. Napoleon commissioned the world's largest triumphal arch in 1806 to commemorate the victories of his Grande Armée. The

Standing within the Arc de Triomphe.

monument is engraved with the names of hundreds of generals (those underlined died in battle) who commanded French troops in Napoleonic victories. The arch was finished in 1836, after Napoleon's death. His remains, brought from St. Helena in 1840, passed under it on the journey to his final resting place at the Hôtel des Invalides. These days, the arch is the focal point of state funerals, Bastille Day celebrations, and the site of the Tomb of the Unknown Soldier, in

whose honor an eternal flame burns. It's also a huge traffic circle, representing certain death to pedestrians, so you reach the arch via an underground passage (well-signposted). The constant roar of traffic can ruin the mood, but the view from the top (accessible via elevator or stairs) makes enduring the din worthwhile. The last leg of your tour is a 20-minute walk away. You can also hop back on the Métro to Trocadéro or flag down a taxi on the Champs-Élysées. ○ *45 min. The Arc de Triomphe is open late at night, so if you prefer a nighttime view, you can put this off until after dinner. Place Charles de Gaulle–Etoile, 8th. www.paris-arc-de-triomphe.fr. ☎ 01-55-37-73-77. Admission 13€, free for children 17 & under & visitors 25 & under from EU countries. Apr–Sept daily 10am–11pm; Oct–Mar 10am–10:30pm. Métro/RER: Charles de Gaulle–Etoile.*

❼ ★★★ Tour Eiffel. At last. It's the Eiffel Tower to English speakers and the *Tour Eiffel* to the French-speaking world, but whatever you

The base of the graceful Eiffel Tower.

Taking in the view over Paris from the Eiffel Tower.

call it, it is synonymous with Paris. The tower was meant to be temporary, built by Gustave-Alexandre Eiffel (who also created the framework for the Statue of Liberty) in 1889 for the Universal Exhibition. It weighs 7,000 tons but exerts about the same pressure on the ground as an average-size person sitting in a chair. Praised by some and denounced by others, the tower created as much controversy in the 1880s as I.M. Pei's glass pyramid at the Louvre did in the 1980s. The tower, including its antenna, is 324m (1,062 ft.) high, and from the top you can see for 65km (40 miles). But the view of the tower is just as important as the view from it. If you go to Trocadéro on the Métro and then walk from the Palais de Chaillot gardens across the Seine, you'll get the best view (not to mention photo opportunities). I always come right at sunset or just after dark when the tower's 20,000 bulbs sparkle for 5 minutes every hour on the hour from nightfall to 11:45pm. Inside the tower's lacy ironwork are restaurants, bars, and historic memorabilia. Take your time, take selfies over the new transparent floor on the 1st level, or even book a table at Frédéric Anton's pricey restaurant **Le Jules Verne** (reserve 3 months in advance for an evening meal; www.restaurants-toureiffel. com; ☎ 01-83-77-34-34), and enjoy sweeping views from the second level as you dine. If your pockets aren't that deep, Madame Brasserie, on the first floor, is a panoramic compromise. Or opt for a glass of bubbly from the tiny top floor champagne bar—no more than a barman behind a hatch. ⏱ *2 hr. Champ de Mars, 7th. www.tour-eiffel. fr. ☎ 01-44-11-23-23. Admission via lift to 1st or 2nd floor 18.10€ adults, 9€ ages 12–24, 4.50€ ages 4–11; lift to top floor 28.30€ adults, 14.10€ ages 12–24, 7.10€ ages 4–11; stairs to 1st and 2nd floors 11.30€ adults, 5.60€ ages 12–24, 2.60€ ages 4–11; stairs & lift 21.50€ adults, 10.70€ ages 12–24, 5.40€ ages 4–11; free for children 3 & under. Daily 9:15am–10:45pm (but times may vary with season, so check the website). Métro: Trocadéro, Ecole Militaire, or Bir-Hakeim. RER: Champs-de-Mars-Tour-Eiffel.*

Paris with Kids

La Villette

- Porte de la Villette Ⓜ
- Maison de la Villette
- Cité des Sciences et de l'Industrie
- Corentin Cariou Ⓜ
- Géode
- Zénith
- ❸
- allée du Belvédère
- Parc de la Villette
- Grande Halle
- Pavillon P. Delouvrier
- Théâtre Paris–Villette
- Cité de la Musique
- Conservatoire de Paris
- Porte de Pantin Ⓜ
- 19e

- quai de la Charente
- quai de la Gironde
- r. de Barbanègre
- quai de l'Oise
- quai de la Marne
- r. de Metz
- r. de Thionville
- galerie de la Villette
- Canal de l'Ourcq
- Canal Saint-Denis
- bd. MacDonald
- boulevard Périphérique
- bd. Sérurier
- allée du Zénith
- av. Jean Jaurès
- r. Danielle Casanova

- r. St-Lazare
- r. de Chateaudun
- Notre-Dame-de-Lorette Ⓜ
- r. de Maubeuge
- Cadet
- r. du Faubourg Montmartre
- r. La Fayette
- r. Richer
- Le Peletier Ⓜ
- r. de Provence
- Richelieu-Drouot Ⓜ
- bd. Haussmann
- bd. Montmartre ❺
- bd. des Italiens
- r. de Richelieu
- Grands Boulevards
- r. Montmartre
- Quatre Septembre Ⓜ
- Bourse Ⓜ
- r. Vivienne
- place des Victoires
- r. du Mail
- **Bibliothèque Nationale**
- r. Croix des Petits Champs
- r. du Louvre
- **Banque de France**
- **Palais Royal**
- 1er
- place de la Concorde
- Concorde Ⓜ
- Pyramides Ⓜ
- r. de Rivoli
- Terrasse des Feuillants
- Tuileries Ⓜ
- r. Saint-Honoré
- **Jardin des Tuileries**
- Terrasse du Bord de l'Eau
- quai des Tuileries
- **Jardin du Carrousel**
- Palais Royal-Musée du Louvre Ⓜ
- **Musée du Louvre**
- r. de Rivoli
- St-Honoré Ⓜ
- Louvre-Rivoli Ⓜ
- r. de l'Amiral de Coligny
- pont de la Concorde
- **Assemblée Nationale** Ⓜ
- Seine
- quai Anatole France
- bd. Saint-Germain
- **Ministère de la Défence**
- r. Saint-Dominique
- r. de Bellechasse
- **Musée d'Orsay**
- quai Voltaire
- quai Malaquais
- pont du Carrousel
- quai du Louvre
- Pont Neuf
- Solférino Ⓜ
- r. du Bac
- square du Vert-Galant
- quai de Conti
- quai des Grands Augustins
- **Palais de Justice**
- **Ecole Nationale Supérieure des Beaux Arts**
- INVALIDES
- r. de Bellechasse
- Rue du Bac Ⓜ
- bd. St-Germain
- **St-Germain-des-Prés**
- St-Germain-des-Prés Ⓜ
- St-Michel Ⓜ
- **Musée Rodin**
- r. de Varenne
- **Hôtel Matignon**
- bd. Raspail
- des Saints-Pères
- r. du Four
- Mabillon Ⓜ
- Odéon Ⓜ
- bd. Saint-Germain
- Cluny-La Sorbonne Ⓜ
- r. de Babylone
- **Bon Marché**
- Sèvres-Babylone Ⓜ
- St-Sulpice Ⓜ
- **St-Sulpice**
- r. de Tournon
- **Musée National du Moyen Age**
- r. de Sèvres
- r. de Rennes
- **La Sorbonne**
- Vaneau Ⓜ
- r. d'Assas
- 6e
- **Palais du Luxembourg**
- bd. St-Michel
- r. de Médicis
- 0   1/4 mi
- 0   0.5 km
- bd. du Montparnasse
- r. de Vaugirard
- **Jardin du Luxembourg**
- Luxembourg RER
- ❶
- Montparnasse Bienvenüe Ⓜ
- place du 18 Juin 1940
- Notre-dame Des Champs Ⓜ
- r. d'Assas
- Luxembourg RER
- r. Guy Lussac
- Falguière Ⓜ
- ❻

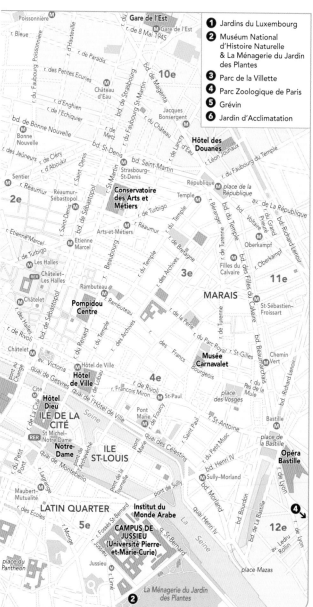

1 Jardins du Luxembourg

2 Muséum National d'Histoire Naturelle & La Ménagerie du Jardin des Plantes

3 Parc de la Villette

4 Parc Zoologique de Paris

5 Grévin

6 Jardin d'Acclimatation

et's face it: **Many kid-approved attractions are outdoors,** which means you're dangerously reliant on good weather. But this tour has been designed for you to pop into a museum or two at will (though you will require advance tickets to the museums), to keep the brood smiling come rain or shine. Look for the "kids" icon throughout the book for more sights and in chapter 6 to find family-friendly dining options around the city. And if the best-laid plans fail, you can always rush them off for a day at Disneyland Paris (p 170). START: **Métro to Odéon or RER to Luxembourg.**

Toy boats in the Jardins du Luxembourg.

1 Jardins du Luxembourg. Kids can run amok in these elegant gardens, which are done in classic French style, with urns and statuary and trees planted in patterns. Statues peek out everywhere as children sail toy boats on the ponds, ride the ponies, or catch a puppet show, if you get lucky with timing. Kids can also watch the locals play *boules* (lawn bowling), but are unlikely to be invited to join in. Don't miss the swings in the play area, the old-fashioned merry-go-round, and (if you're with toddlers) the sandpits. ⏱ *1 hr. Métro: Odéon. RER: Luxembourg.*

2 Muséum National d'Histoire Naturelle & La Ménagerie du Jardin des Plantes. The giant whale skeleton that greets you at this natural history museum lets you know right off the bat that the kids are going to be fine here. Beyond those bones in the Galerie de l'Evolution are more skeletons and stuffed animals, lined-up like a queue for Noah's Ark. To see the dinosaurs, you'll need a separate ticket for the Galérie de Paléontologie. Ditto for the adjacent galleries, filled with sparkling minerals, and hothouses of rare plants. In the surrounding gardens (the Jardin des Plantes), there's also a wonderful little zoo—La Ménagerie—with small animals, birds, crocodiles, and wild cats. ⏱ *90 min. 56 rue Cuvier, 5th. www.mnhn.fr. ☎ 01-40-79-54-79. Admission 13€ adults, 10€ ages 3–25, free for children 2 & under (1 full-price ticket gives reduced price access to the other galleries and the Ménagerie). Daily 10am–6pm. Métro: Jussieu or Gare d'Austerlitz.*

3 ★★★ Parc de la Villette. In the rejuvenated northeast part of town, this retro-futurist, canal-side succession of gardens is a fab place for kids to run around. There's a wonderful children's science museum, **La Cité des Sciences,** home to a planetarium, a submarine, and the **Cité des Enfants** gallery with hands-on science activities for 2- to 7-year-olds and 5 to 12s (30 av. Corentin-Cariou; www.cite-sciences.fr; ☎ 01-85-53-99-74; admission 12€ adults, 9€ ages 6–25, 3€ for children ages 2–5; joint tickets 16€). And the **Philharmonie Paris** (p 146), a post-modernist philharmonic hall, has a brilliant interactive music museum—**La Philharmonie des Enfants**— aimed at 4- to 10-year-olds (221 av. Jean-Jaurès, 19th; https://philharmoniedeparis.fr/en/philharmoniedesenfants; ☎ 01-44-84-44-84, admission 14€, free for visitors age 2 and under; family ticket 2 adults & 1 child 33€). ⏱ *3 hr. 19th. 211 av. Jean Jaurès, 19th.* www.lavillette.com. ☎ *01-40-03-75-75. Daily 6am–1am. Métro: Porte de la Villette or Porte de Pantin.*

❹ Parc Zoologique de Paris. Created as a temporary exhibition for the 1931 Colonial Fair, the Paris Zoo was so successful it became permanent in 1934. Today's park is a zoo of the future, dedicated to endangered species, and split into five conservation areas, called "biozones," corresponding to habitats in Patagonia (South America), the Sahel (Africa), Europe, Madagascar, and tropical French Guiana. For something special, treat the kids to breakfast with the giraffes; it's a splurge, but it's magical (reservations by email only, resa museum@mnhn.fr; 60€ adults, 45€ ages 3–12). ⏱ *2 hr. Intersection of av. Daumesnil and the route du Lac, 12th.* www.parczoologiquede paris.fr. ☎ *08-11-22-41-22 (0.06€/min). Admission 20€ adults, 15€ children 3–12, free for ages 2 and under.*

Mid-Oct to mid-Mar daily 10am–5pm; Mid-Mar to mid-May & Sept to mid-Oct Mon–Fri 10am–6pm, Sat–Sun 9:30am–7:30pm; Mid-May to end of Aug daily 9:30am–8:30pm (Thurs until 11:30pm). Métro: Porte-Dorée.

❺ Grévin. At this waxworks museum, kids will enjoy wandering among stars—both French (Edith Piaf) and international (Ryan Gosling). Among the hundreds of wax figures, you'll find heads of state, artists, writers, and historical figures—at times, the museum even verges on educational. ⏱ *1 hr. 10 bd. Montmartre, 9th.* ☎ *01-47-70-85-05.* www.grevin.com. *Admission 19€ adults, 16.50€ children 6–18, free for children 5 & under. Daily 10am–7pm. Times may vary seasonally. Métro: Grands-Boulevards.*

❻ ★★ Jardin d'Acclimatation. Let the kids while away a sunny afternoon here. You can start with a ride on a narrow-gauge train from porte Maillot to the entrance (daily, roughly every 30 min. from 10am–7pm; Fri & Sun until 8pm). Inside are water rides, fairground rides (think flying chairs and small rollercoasters), a puppet theater, playgrounds, shooting galleries, and eating spots galore. Kids can ride ponies and paddle about in boats—they can even drive little cars. Bear in mind that it's only for young kids (most rides are open by height: over 80cm or over 120cm); teenagers will hate it. ⏱ *2–3 hr. Bois de Boulogne, 16th.* www.jardin dacclimatation.fr. ☎ *01-40-67-90-82. Admission 7€ to enter, then around 4.90€ for each attraction or 50€ for a pack of 15 tickets, or opt for the Pass Illimité around 33€ for unlimited access to rides; free for 80cm and under. Mon–Tue & Thurs–Fri 11am–6pm; Wed and Sat–Sun and school holidays 10am–7pm. Métro: Sablons or Porte Maillot.*

Exploring the Louvre

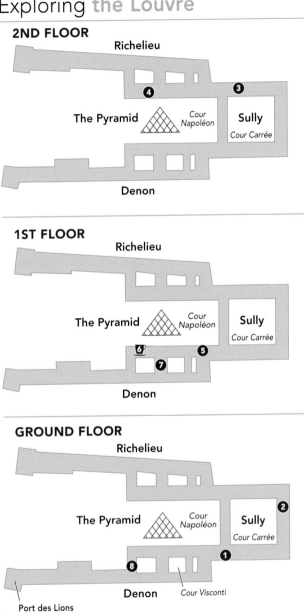

2ND FLOOR

Richelieu

The Pyramid

Cour Napoléon

Sully

Cour Carrée

4

3

Denon

1ST FLOOR

Richelieu

The Pyramid

Cour Napoléon

Sully

Cour Carrée

6

7

5

Denon

GROUND FLOOR

Richelieu

The Pyramid

Cour Napoléon

Sully

Cour Carrée

2

8

1

Cour Visconti

Denon

Port des Lions

1 *Venus de Milo*
2 *Outer coffin of Tamutnefret*
3 *The Card Sharper*
4 *The Lacemaker*
5 *Winged Victory of Samothrace*
6 Café Mollien
7 *Mona Lisa*
8 Italian Sculpture
9 European Sculpture
10 Cour Visconti

THE PYRAMID

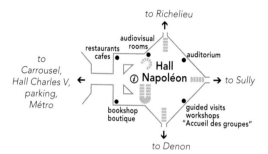

to Richelieu

audiovisual rooms

restaurants cafes

auditorium

to Carrousel, Hall Charles V, parking, Métro ←

ⓘ **Hall Napoléon** → *to Sully*

bookshop boutique

guided visits workshops "Accueil des groupes"

↓ to Denon

LOWER GROUND FLOOR

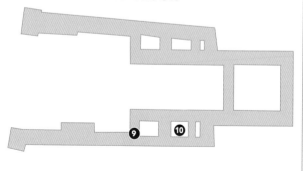

9   10

Before becoming a museum, the Musée du Louvre was France's main royal palace. In 1527, François I demolished most of the old castle to build a new one, which makes up part of the building you see today. (François also inadvertently founded part of the museum's collection—the *Mona Lisa* and *Virgin of the Rocks* once hung in his bathroom.) The rest of the building was completed over the centuries, particularly by Henri II and Napoleon, whose apartments may be visited on the 1st floor (if you're from the U.S., remember that the French first floor is your second floor). More recent additions include the glass pyramids designed by I. M. Pei (in 1989) and the Cour Visconti extension, which houses a wonderful Islamic art collection. START: **Métro to Palais Royal–Musée du Louvre.**

Travel Tip

Laid out end to end, the Louvre would be the size of several football fields, so put aside at least 3 to 4 hours to get a general feel for the place and browse a bit between stops. Pick up a map when you arrive at the museum and use it to find my suggested selection of works—the floor and rooms are marked for each entry. Or you'll find themed, self-guided tour maps at the information point under the Pyramid.

❶ ★★★ Venus de Milo. Begin your tour in Greek Antiquities, where *Venus* stands alluringly, her drapery about to fall to the floor. The statue dates to 100 B.C. Myths about her abound—one story maintains that her arms were knocked off when she was hustled onto a French ship. Another claims she was rescued from a pottery kiln. Both are untrue—she was found buried as you see her now, along with part of an arm, a hand holding an apple, and a pair of small columns, one of which fit neatly into her base and bore the inscription ALEXANDROS, SON OF MENIDES, CITIZEN OF ANTIOCH, MADE THIS STATUE. Sadly, those parts were all lost over time. *Ground floor, Room 345.*

❷ ★★★ Outer coffin of Tamutnefret. On the same level, enter the Ancient Egypt department, where you'll see this intriguing sarcophagus (1295–1069 B.C.) from the Ramesside period. It belonged to Tamutnefret, singer of Amun, and one of two gloriously decorated wooden coffins shows Tamutnefret crossing her arms amid gilded depictions of gods like

After all these millennia, Venus de Milo still manages to work the crowd.

Osiris (Falcon), Thot (Ibis), and Anubis (dog). It's stunning. *Ground floor, Room 321.*

❸ ★★★ **The Card Sharper.** In Room 912, on the second floor, you'll find Georges de la Tour's sensational *Tricheur (The Card Sharper)*, painted around 1630. In this gorgeous work, complex relationships play out in shimmering colors. In the center, a courtesan holds her hand out for a glass of wine poured by a servant. Her cheating friend holds cards behind his back as he casts a colluding glance at him. The chubby-cheeked youth in the embroidered shirt is the victim of a plot. A cruel tale, playfully told. *2nd floor, Room 912.*

❹ ★★★ **The Lacemaker.** *The Lacemaker* (around 1664) is one of Johannes Vermeer's most famous paintings. It shows a young woman bent over her work, her shape forming a subtle pyramid, and her face, hair, and rich yellow blouse aglow. The book in the foreground is probably the Bible and sets the moral and religious tone of the painting. This work, which is usually surrounded by a crowd of admirers, exemplifies Vermeer's unique use of color and light. *2nd floor, Room 836.*

❺ ★★★ **Winged Victory of Samothrace.** Head toward the Denon Wing, where at the top of the Daru stairs stands Nike, the goddess of victory, her wings flung back in takeoff, and the fabric of her skirts swirling around her, as fine as silk. The statue's origins are uncertain. Most scholars date it to somewhere between 220 and 190 B.C. The statue was discovered on the Greek island of Samothrace In 1863, and its base was discovered in 1879. In 1950, one of the statue's hands was found; it's on display in a glass case near the statue. An inscription on the statue's base includes the word RHODHIOS (Rhodes)

and this, along with the fact that the statue stands on the prow of a ship, has led some scholars to theorize that the piece was commissioned in celebration of a naval victory by Rhodes. Others believe it was an offering made by a Macedonian general after a victory in Cyprus. Regardless of its origins, this glorious work is considered one of the best surviving Greek sculptures from that period. *Top of the Daru staircase, Room 703.*

☕ ★★ **Café Mollien.** Ready for a break? Café Mollien, by the French painting department, is particularly enjoyable in the summertime, when the outdoor rooftop terrace is open. Choose between sandwiches, salads, and hot dishes such as pasta. The lemon cake is tasty for an afternoon snack. *$.*

❼ ★★★ **Mona Lisa.** This lady's enigmatic smile and challenging eyes draw scores of admirers daily. Though the identity of the subject has long been under debate (Was she the wife of an Italian city official? Is she meant to be in mourning? Is "she" a man—perhaps even a self-portrait of da Vinci himself?), many specialists say she is Lisa Gherardini, wife of 16th-century Florentine cloth merchant Francesco del Giocondo (hence the work's alternative title, *La Gioconda*).The painting has been through a lot over the years. It was stolen in 1911 (by a Louvre employee who simply put the painting under his coat and walked out with it) and wasn't recovered until 1913. During World War II, it was housed in various parts of France for safekeeping. In 1956, the painting was severely damaged after someone threw acid on it. In 1962 and 1963, it toured the United States, and was shown in New York City and Washington,

The Mona Lisa *once hung over François I's bathtub.*

D.C. In 1974, it was shown in Tokyo and Moscow. In 2022 a man smeared cake all over her transparent, bullet-proof case in an apparent protest about climate-change (the painting was untouched). All the hype and history aside, some find actually seeing Leonardo da Vinci's *Mona Lisa* (painted between 1503 and 1507) a disappointment. It's a very small painting (just 77cm tall, 53cm wide) and has been kept behind glass since it was attacked by a vandal in the 1990s. That, along with the crowds surrounding it, makes it difficult to connect with. Despite these shortcomings, few come to the Louvre without stopping by. *1st floor, Room 711.*

❽ ★★★ Italian Sculpture.
Make your way down to the ground floor of the Denon Wing and head to Room 403, which is filled with exquisite Italian sculptures. Michelangelo's two statues are among the most dramatic in the room—the muscular arms of his *Rebellious Slave* are tensed furiously against his bindings, while the *Dying Slave* seems resigned to his fate. Both were commissioned in 1505 by Pope Julius II as funerary art. Look across the room for the delicate

wings of Cupid, who clutches the breast of Psyche in a pas de deux in pure white marble in Antonio Canova's *Psyche Revived by Cupid's Kiss* (1793). It is love carved in stone. *Ground floor, Room 403; the collection continues on the lower-ground floor immediately below.*

❾ ★★★ European Sculpture.
Head into room 169, filled with late-Gothic Christian religious statues from Germany and the Netherlands, many dripping in glorious color and gilding. Amid the statues depicting the heads of saints and the Virgin and Child, lies the mesmerizing, life-size carving of Sainte Marie-Madeleine (Mary Magdalene) in lime tree wood and polychromy. It was made by Gregor Erhart (1470–1540) of the Ulm School, and the way Mary's hair tumbles down her naked skin is both magnificent and otherworldly. The story goes that after Jesus' death, repentant Mary lived secluded in a cave in Saint-Baume in France, clothed only by her hair. This statue was probably suspended from a church vault and would once have included angels. Though the angels are gone, Mary is no less beautiful. *Lower-round floor, Room 169.*

The Louvre: Practical Matters

The main entrances to the Musée du Louvre, 1st (www.louvre.fr; ☎ 01-40-20-53-17) are at 99 rue de Rivoli, inside the Carousel du Louvre underground shopping mall, and the glass pyramid in the main courtyard. Check online beforehand to see which entrance you should use; they differ according to whether or not you have pre-booked your ticket (www.louvre.fr/en/visit/map-entrances-directions#museum-entrances). I wholly recommend you buy your ticket in advance. If you don't, you may be turned away (no more than 30,000 people are allowed into the museum per day). The good news is that tickets are time-stamped, so lines for people with tickets shouldn't be too long.

The museum is busy all the time, but you may find smaller crowds if you book to arrive shortly after opening at 9am or after 6pm Friday when it's late-night opening. Admission is 17€, free for children 18 and under and visitors 25 and under from EU countries, and free for everyone the first Sunday of the month (Oct–Mar). Hours are Wednesday to Monday 9am to 6pm (Fri until 9:45pm), closed Tuesday. Métro: Palais Royal–Musée du Louvre and Louvre Rivoli.

❿ ★★★ Cour Visconti.

Opened in 2012, the Cour Visconti section provides the Louvre's more than 2,000 pieces of Islamic art with an appropriately prominent setting. The fascinating collections (including many lavish pieces made for heads of state) highlight the development of Islamic art from its beginnings in the 7th century up until the early 19th, showing the differences in artistic styles according to culture, geography, and era. *Lower-ground floor, Room 186.*

The Cour Visconti showcases the Louvre's Islamic art collection.

Paris for Museum Lovers

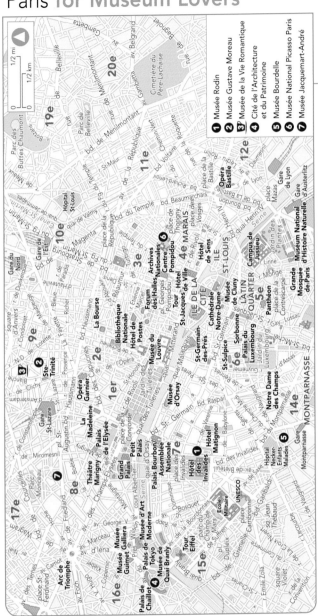

1 Musée Rodin
2 Musée Gustave Moreau
3 Musée de la Vie Romantique
4 Cité de l'Architecture et du Patrimoine
5 Musée Bourdelle
6 Musée National Picasso Paris
7 Musée Jacquemart-André

You'd need a lifetime to fully explore the hundreds of museums in Paris. Once you've visited the behemoths (the Louvre and Musée d'Orsay), you'll have dozens of beautiful, more intimate addresses dedicated to sculpture, inventions, and architecture to explore. This section is not a tour per se, but a list to find what suits your fancy. For some of the following, you may need to book in advance to avoid disappointment. START: **Métro to Varennes.**

The Thinker *strikes a contemplative pose outside the Musée Rodin.*

1 **kids** **★★★ Musée Rodin.** This peaceful museum, housed in the building that was once sculptor Auguste Rodin's studio, can't help but inspire thoughts of romance. *The Thinker* ponders in the sublime gardens, while the lovers in *The Kiss* are locked in a permanent embrace inside. ⏱ *1 hr. Hôtel*

Biron, 79 rue de Varenne, 7th. www. musee-rodin.fr. ☎ *01-44-18-61-10. Admission museum 13€; free for children 18 & under & visitors 25 & under from EU countries. Tues–Sun 10am–6:30pm. Métro: Varenne or Invalides. RER C: Invalides.*

2 **★★ Musée Gustave Moreau.** Painter Gustave Moreau

Save on Admission Fees

The permanent collections of 12 of Paris's 14 municipal museums are free (see www.parismusees.paris.fr/en for a full list), and many museums are free of the 1st Sunday of the month. If you plan to visit several nonmunicipal museums outside of this date, and combine them with other activities like a boat trip or a cabaret show, consider the **Paris Passlib': Mini** (45€ for 3 activities from 32 offered), **City** (99€ for 5 attractions from 56 offered), **Explore** (169€ for 6 attractions from 76), and **Prestige** (249€ for 7 attractions from 76). However, you'll probably only save money if you select the most expensive activities on the list, so do your homework first (https://en.parisinfo.com).

was around at the same time as the Impressionists, but he worked against the prevailing mood, drawing inspiration from the Bible, Greek mythology, Leonardo da Vinci, and Indian miniatures. This atmospheric museum, where he lived and worked, reveals Moreau's obsession with knickknacks and furniture, which are displayed alongside his fabulous mythical beasts and fantasy worlds. ⏱ *1 hr. 14 rue de la Roche-foucauld, 9th. www.musee-moreau.fr.* ☎ *01-48-74-38-50. Admission 7€ adults, free for ages 18 & under & visitors 25 & under from EU countries. Wed–Mon 10am–6pm. Métro: Trinité.*

3 ★★★ **Musée de la Vie Romantique.** Hidden from the rest of the world is this charming, green-shuttered 18th-century mansion that once housed composers Gioachino Rossini and Frédéric Chopin, novelist George Sand, and painter Eugène Delacroix. But what really takes the gâteau (cake), quite literally, is the rose garden, which doubles as a tearoom. Decadence is yours for the price of your *café* and *tarte au abricots* (apricot tart). *16 rue Chaptal, 9th. https://museevieromantique. paris.fr.* ☎ *01-55-31-95-67. Tues–Sun 10am–6pm. Free admission. Métro: Pigalle, St-Georges, or Blanche.*

4 kids ★★ **Cité de l'Architecture et du Patrimoine.** Comprising 8 sq. km (3 sq. miles) of space in the east wing of the Palais de Chaillot, the City of Architecture and Heritage contains more than 850 breathtaking full-size copies of French architectural treasures, including molded portions of churches, châteaux, and great French cathedrals, such as Chartres. There are also reconstructions of modern architecture, the centerpiece of which is an apartment by Le Corbusier. ⏱ *2 hr. Palais de Chaillot, 1 place du Trocadéro, 16th. www.cite delarchitecture.fr.* ☎ *01-58-51-52-00. Admission 9€ adults; free for ages 18 & under & visitors 25 & under from EU countries. Wed & Fri–Mon 11am–7pm, Thurs 11am–9pm. Métro: Trocadéro.*

5 ★★ **Musée Bourdelle.** Hidden away from the hustle and bustle of Montparnasse is the workshop where Rodin's star pupil, sculptor Antoine Bourdelle (1861–1929), lived and worked. The sumptuous array of statues, many inspired by Greek mythology, includes Centaure Mourant (The Dying Centaur) writhing in agony; Penelope, Ulysses' wife, who waited 20 years for her husband to return; and, in the gorgeous walled garden, the colossal General Alvear

The Cité de l'Architecture et du Patrimoine is a must-see for architecture buffs.

Greek mythology inspired many of the sculptures at the Musée Bourdelle.

horse statue (part of an allegorical monument that was never finished). ① *90 min. 18 rue Antoine-Bourdelle, 15th. www.bourdelle.paris.fr.* ☎ *01-49-54-73-73. Free admission. Tues–Sun 10am–6pm. Métro: Montparnasse-Bienvenüe.*

❻ kids ★★★ Musée National Picasso Paris. This shrine to all things Picasso is set in the stunning Hôtel Salé in the Marais, a 17th-century mansion built by salt-tax farmer Pierre Aubert, whose position gave the mansion its name—*salé* means "salty." Inside you'll find hundreds of the genius's paintings, sculptures, collages, and drawings, presented in more or less chronological and thematic order, covering his eclectic style, from neoclassicism to surrealism via his own flamboyantly abstract inventions. On the 2nd floor (1st floor for U.S. visitors) is Picasso's private collection, which includes works by artists he admired like Courbet and Cézanne, as well as paintings by his friends, who included masters like Braque and Matisse. ① *2 hr. 5 rue de Thorigny, 3rd. www.museepicassoparis.fr.* ☎ *01-85-56-00-36. Admission 14€, free for ages 18 & under & visitors 25*

& under from EU countries. *Tues–Fri 10:30am–6pm & Sat–Sun 9:30am–6pm. Métro: Chemin Vert or Saint-Paul.*

❼ kids ★★ Musée Jacquemart-André. This decorative-arts museum, set in the stately former home of the collectors it's named for—Nélie Jacquemart and Edouard André—houses an array of rare 18th-century French paintings and furnishings, 17th-century Dutch and Flemish paintings, and Italian Renaissance works fit for a king. The salons drip with gilt and the ultimate in fin-de-siècle style. Works by Bellini, Carpaccio, Uccello, van Dyck, Rembrandt, Tiepolo, Rubens, Watteau, Boucher, Fragonard, and Mantegna hang on almost every wall. If you fancy a decadent snack, Mme. Jacquemart's high-ceilinged tearoom complies, with delicious sticky cakes, light meals, and piping-hot tea. ***Note:*** At time of writing, the museum was set to close for renovations until September 2024. ① *1 hr. 158 bd. Haussmann, 8th. www.musee-jacquemart-andre. com.* ☎ *01-45-62-11-59. Admission 12€ adults, 7.50€ ages 7–25, free for children 6 & under. Daily 10am–6pm (until 8:30pm on Mon during temporary exhibitions). Métro: Miromesnil or St-Philippe du Roule.*

A sumptuous salon in the Musée Jacquemart-André.

Paris's Best Modern & Contemporary Art

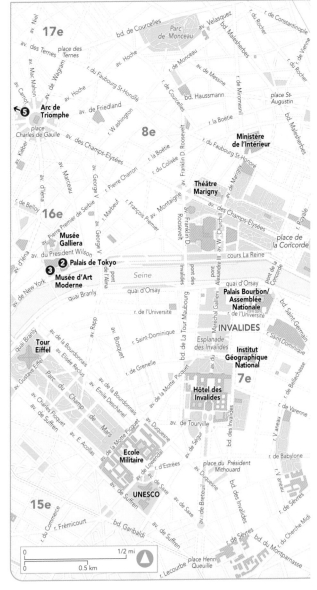

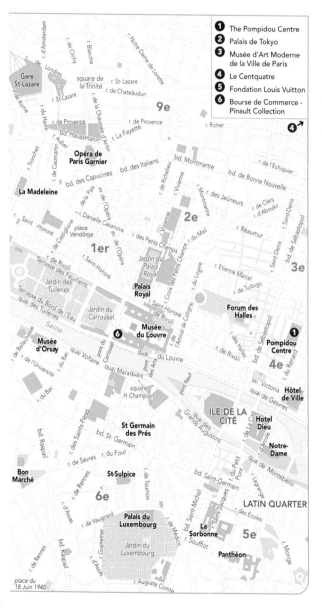

1 The Pompidou Centre
2 Palais de Tokyo
3 Musée d'Art Moderne de la Ville de Paris
4 Le Centquatre
5 Fondation Louis Vuitton
6 Bourse de Commerce - Pinault Collection

You only have to look at the Louvre's glass pyramid or the Pompidou Centre's madcap exterior to realize that Parisians can be unconventional when they put their minds to it—something that's also reflected in the city's art scene, which includes everything from edgy art squats to sleek museums and galleries. Here's where to find Paris's most exciting modern and contemporary art venues, both big and small. Métro: Champs-Élysées Clemenceau).

START: **Métro to Rambuteau.**

The Pompidou Centre houses Europe's biggest collection of modern art.

① kids ★★★ The Pompidou Centre. This benchmark art venue, designed by Richard Rogers and Renzo Piano, is one of the best-known sites in Paris, holding the largest collection of modern art in Europe. The permanent collections cover 20th- and 21st-century art, with some 40,000 rotating works. It is closed for renovations until 2027, however. ⏱ 2 hr. Place Georges Pompidou, 4th. www.centre pompidou.fr. ☎ 01-44-78-12-33. Métro: Rambuteau or Hôtel de Ville. RER A & B: Châtelet-les-Halles.

② ★ Palais de Tokyo. This "Site de Création Contemporaine" is a showcase for experimental art on a big scale. Inside its stripped-back interior, international artists fill the space with temporary exhibitions of whatever weird eccentricities they can muster. It also wows with two good eateries: Bambini, an Italian canteen (Mon–Fri noon–3pm &

7pm–2am, Sat–Sun noon–3:30pm) and Monsieur Bleu, a posh neo–Art Deco brasserie with a cocktail bar and an Eiffel Tower–view terrace (noon–2am). ⏱ 2 hr. 13 av. du President Wilson, 16th. www.palaisde tokyo.com. ☎ 01-81-97-35-88. Admission 12€ ages 26 & over, 9€ ages 19–26, free for children 18 & under. Wed & Fri–Mon noon–10pm, Thurs noon to midnight. Métro: Alma-Marceau or Iéna. RER C: Pont d'Alma.

③ ★★ Musée d'Art Moderne de la Ville de Paris. Take yourself on a journey through 20th-century "isms": Fauvism, Cubism, Surrealism, realism, expressionism, and neorealism to be exact, with works by such artists as Braque, Dufy, Picasso, Léger, and Matisse, all presented in chronological order. In addition to the permanent collection, expect fascinating retrospectives on major 20th-century artistic movements, plus thematic exhibitions on the best of today's artistic pickings. *11 av. du Président Wilson, 16th. www.mam.paris.fr.* ☎ *01-53-67-40-00. Free admission for permanent collections. Tues–Sun 10am–6pm (Thurs until 9:30pm for temporary exhibitions). Métro: Alma-Marceau or Iéna. RER C: Pont d'Alma.*

❹ kids ★★ Le Centquatre. What was once the municipal morgue is now a vast space dedicated to all things artistic and fun. You'll find food for both the soul and the stomach here: contemporary theater, dance, music, and edgy visual arts, as well as a gourmet grocery, cafes, and restaurants. Along with concerts and dance parties for grown-ups are activities for families and little ones (musical events, art workshops, and so forth), and a bookstore. *5 rue Curial, 19th. www.104.fr.* ☎ *01-53-35-50-00. Free admission (temporary exhibitions & other events may charge). Tues–Sun noon–7pm. Métro: Riquet.*

❺ ★ Fondation Louis Vuitton. Sydney's opera house meets a space-age galleon in this vast, whimsical art space (built by American architect Frank Gehry) in the Bois de Boulogne. Amid its glass sails, sunken water-features, and clever lighting are big, stark spaces spattered with world-class temporary exhibitions, a state-of-the-art auditorium used for concerts, and an excellent bookshop on art and architecture. Should hunger strike, you can sample contemporary French cuisine at Le Frank, a chic restaurant with giant fish-shaped light fixtures. *8 Ave du Mahatma Gandhi, 16th. www.fondationlouis vuitton.fr.* ☎ *01-40-69-96-00. Admission 16€ adults, 10€ ages 18–26, 5€ artists and children 3–17, free for children 2 and under. Mon, Wed–Thurs noon–7pm, Fri noon–11pm, Sat–Sun 11am–8pm. Métro: Les Sablons or by electric shuttle from Place Charles de Gaulle (corner of Ave Friedland).*

❻ ★★ Bourse de Commerce—Pinault Collection. At the western tip of the Les Halles gardens, the stunning former Chamber of Commerce building (on the site of an 18th-century corn exchange) is the city's newest contemporary art space. This museum/art gallery houses the Pinault Collection, the personal 3,000-piece contemporary art holding of billionaire François Pinault (the honorary chairman of Kering, the luxury group that owns YSL, Gucci, and Alexander McQueen). The third-floor restaurant offers sweeping views over Paris's rooftops and St-Eustache church (www.halleauxgrains.bras.fr). *2 rue Viarmes, 1st. www.pinault collection.com.* ☎ *01-83-75-10-00. Admission 14€ adults, 10€ ages 18–25, free for children 17 and under. Wed–Sun 11am–7pm (until 9pm Fri). Métro: Louvre-Rivoli or Les Halles. RER: Châtelet-des-Halles.*

The Gehry-designed Fondation Louis Vuitton houses exhibition space, an auditorium, and Le Frank restaurant.

Hemingway's Paris

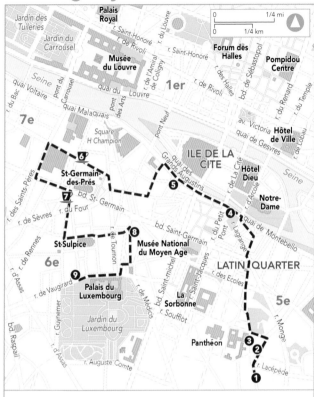

1. Marché Mouffetard
2. Ernest & Hadley's Apartment
3. Hemingway's Writing Apartment
4. Shakespeare & Company
5. Booksellers along the quai des Grands Augustins
6. Café Pré aux Clercs
7. Les Deux Magots
8. Shakespeare & Company's Original Site
9. Hemingway's Last Apartment

For fans of Papa Hemingway, a trip to Paris is a pilgrimage. This is where Hemingway honed his craft, bullied F. Scott Fitzgerald, and charmed Gertrude Stein. Here he married more than once and had countless mistresses, not the least of which was Paris herself. Oh sure, he cheated on her with Cuba and Spain, but we all know Paris is the one he *really* loved. This tour follows his spectacular rise and charts the beginning of his fall. START: **Métro to Censier Daubenton.**

❶ ★ Marché Mouffetard. At the beginning of his memoir, *A Moveable Feast*, Hemingway describes spending time on Rue Mouffetard's "wonderful narrow crowded market street." That description still fits—it's narrow, crowded, and wonderfully Parisian.

❷ Ernest & Hadley's Apartment. Several blocks up Rue Mouffetard, Rue du Cardinal-Lemoine branches off to the right. A few houses down, on the fourth floor of no. 74, a 22-year-old Hemingway and his wife Hadley rented their first Parisian apartment together in 1921. This wasn't, however, where Hem worked—that was around the corner, on Rue

Descartes. (See the next stop.) *74 rue du Cardinal-Lemoine, 5th.*

❸ Hemingway's Writing Apartment. When he first moved to Paris as a writer for the *Toronto Star* newspaper, Hemingway took a grimy, cheap room on the top floor of a hotel on Rue Descartes to write in peace. The building—as a small wall plaque says—was also where French poet Paul Verlaine died in 1896. *39 rue Descartes, 5th.*

❹ ★ Shakespeare & Company. Walk toward the river for about 15 minutes, first on Rue Descartes (which joins Rue Montagne St-Geneviève) through Place Maubert, then down Rue F. Sauton, and then take a sharp left onto Rue de

Rue Mouffetard.

la Bûcherie to reach Paris's best expat bookstore (just on the other side of Square René Viviani). In the 1920s, it was at 12 rue de l'Odéon (see stop **8** on this tour) and belonged to American publisher Sylvia Beach. It was at that location that Hemingway broke a vase when he read a bad review, that Henry Miller used to "borrow" books and never bring them back, and that James Joyce's *Ulysses* was first published. The current location is still a favorite of writers for its eccentric attitude and wonderful selection of books. You may have to wait in line to get in. ○ *30 min–1 hr. 37 rue de la Bûcherie, 5th. www. shakespeareandcompany.com.* ☎ *01-43-25-40-93. Mon–Sat 10am– 8pm & Sun noon–7pm. Métro: St-Michel.*

⑤ Booksellers along Quai des Grands Augustins. Hemingway frequently shopped here among the secondhand book peddlers (called *bouquinistes*) along the edge of the Seine. Now, as then, their collections are bewilderingly

Un serveur at Les Deux Magots in Saint-Germain-des-Prés.

eclectic and somewhat hit-and-miss—like a flea market for books. I once saw the complete Harry Potter collection, in English, next to a book of French erotica. ○ *30 min–1 hr. Quai des Grands Augustins, 6th.*

⑥ Café Pré aux Clercs. Next you'll come to a series of cafes where you can take a well-deserved rest, as Hem surely would, over a whiskey or a glass of the house red. The first cafe is this charming one reached by walking down Rue des Grands Augustins (no. 7 was once Pablo Picasso's studio). Turn onto Rue St-André des Arts, and then right along Rue de Seine and left onto the antiques-shop-lined Rue Jacob, which brings you to Rue Bonaparte and this cafe. It was one of Hem's early haunts, a short walk from the Hotel d'Angleterre, where he slept (in room no. 14) on his first night in Paris. You'll get to more-famous (and more-touristy) Les

One of the secondhand booksellers along the Quai des Grands Augustins.

The 1920s—Americans in Paris

The so-called Lost Generation, led by American expatriates Gertrude Stein and Alice B. Toklas, topped the list of celebrities who "occupied" Paris after World War I. Paris attracted the *littérateur*, *bon viveur*, and drifter, including writers Henry Miller, Ernest Hemingway, and F. Scott Fitzgerald, as well as composer Cole Porter.

With the collapse of Wall Street, many Americans returned home. But not hard-core bohemians like Miller, who wandered around smoking Gauloises when not writing *Tropic of Cancer*. He eventually left in 1939, as war clouds were beginning to loom. Gertrude and Alice remained in France and are buried together (Stein died in 1946, Toklas in 1967) in the Cimetière du Père-Lachaise (p 100).

Deux Magots if you continue down rue Bonaparte. *30 rue Bonaparte, 6th.* www.restaurant-preauxclercs. com. ☎ 01-83-76-16-53. $$–$$$.

7 ★★ **Les Deux Magots.** Loop down noisy Rue des Saints-Pères to the more sophisticated hustle of boulevard Saint-Germain, and soon you'll see the glass front of this cafe, which has gotten more mileage out of the gay '20s than any flapper ever could have. It even launched its own literary award event in 1933—the Prix des Deux Magots. This was the preeminent hangout of the arty expat crowd, where Hemingway charmed the girls, picked fights with the critics, and hassled tourists. The feel today is admittedly touristy, and the food pricey, but it's still a good place to have a coffee and wonder what he'd think of it all now. *6 place St-Germain-des-Prés, 6th.* lesdeux magots.fr. ☎ 01-45-48-55-25. $$–$$$.

8 **Shakespeare & Company's Original Site.** You can get in a bit of shopping at the many posh boutiques and little jewelry stores on Rue Saint-Sulpice before turning right onto Rue de l'Odéon and passing a plaque marking the site of the original Shakespeare & Company bookstore. *12 rue de l'Odéon, 6th.*

9 **Hemingway's Last Apartment.** After turning down Rue de Vaugirard and walking past the French Senate, look for this narrow lane near the Jardins du Luxembourg. The impressive building at no. 6 was Hemingway's last Paris apartment. My, how the fallen became mighty. From the look of its ornate stonework and heavy gates, you might get the idea that he'd written a successful novel *(The Sun Also Rises)* and left poor Hadley for somebody richer (Pauline Pfeiffer). And so he had. Here, he wrote *A Farewell to Arms,* and began his descent into alcoholism. *6 rue Férou, 6th.*

The Paris of Emily in Paris

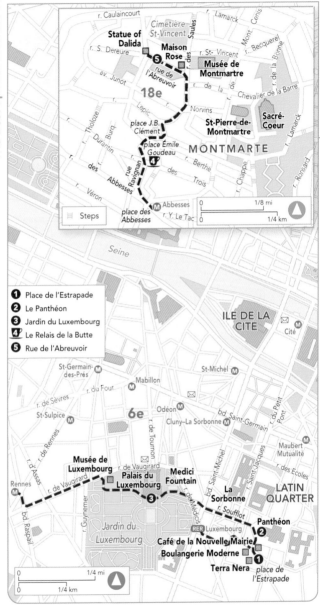

Statue of Dalida

Maison Rose

Musée de Montmartre

rue de l'Abreuvoir

18e

place J.B. Clément

St-Pierre-de-Montmartre

Sacré-Coeur

place Émile Goudeau

MONTMARTE

Abbesses

place des Abbesses

≡ Steps

| 0 | 1/8 mi |
| 0 | 1/4 km |

1 Place de l'Estrapade
2 Le Panthéon
3 Jardin du Luxembourg
4 Le Relais de la Butte
5 Rue de l'Abreuvoir

ILE DE LA CITÉ

St-Germain-des-Prés

Mabillon

St-Michel

St-Sulpice

Odéon

Cluny–La Sorbonne

6e

Musée de Luxembourg

Palais du Luxembourg

Medici Fountain

La Sorbonne

LATIN QUARTER

Jardin du Luxembourg

Rennes

Panthéon

Luxembourg

Café de la Nouvelle Mairie

Boulangerie Moderne

Terra Nera

place de l'Estrapade

| 0 | 1/4 mi |
| 0 | 1/4 km |

Who hasn't seen, or at least heard of, Darren Starr's Netflix phenomenon, *Emily in Paris*? The Parisian life of Emily Cooper (played by Lily Collins) has been such a hit that fans of the show have been flocking to the City of Light in hope of visiting the places featured onscreen. This tour lets you follow in her footsteps (minus the stilettos and designer outfits, unless you really want to), taking you to some of the series' prettiest filming locations. Even if you're not into the show, you'll see a memorable mix of iconic sights and lesser-known gems. This tour concentrates mostly on two neighborhoods, the Latin Quarter and Montmartre, both of which have their own, more classic tours on p 54 and p 70. START: RER to Luxembourg.

❶ ★ Place de l'Estrapade. You can kill several Emily birds with one stone on this pretty little square in the Latin Quarter. Not only is it where she shared an apartment with love interest Gabriel (played by Lucas Bravo), but it's also the setting for three other spots: the bakery where she tastes her first croissant (today's Boulangerie Moderne, 16 rue des Fossés Saint-Jacques), the Deux Compères restaurant where Gabriel worked (today's Terra Nera, an Italian eatery, next-door), and across the street (at no. 19), the Café de la Nouvelle Mairie, where she'd go for coffee. A far cry from the sugary show, the square takes its name from something much more sinister: a medieval form of public lynching (that took place here until the 1700s), called Strappado, whereby victims were tied, then dropped from a height so that their bodies would dislocate. Nice!

❷ Le Panthéon. Get that image out of your mind, then turn right at Terra Nera onto Rue Clotaire to see the final resting place of luminaries

The Panthéon.

The Medici Fountain in the Jardin du Luxembourg.

such as Voltaire and Rousseau, Marie and Pierre Curie, World War II heroes of the Résistance, and (since 2021) the American-born entertainer and activist Josephine Baker. The national mausoleum's neoclassical architecture was the photogenic backdrop for Emily's telephone break-up with her American boyfriend in the first season. Now head down Rue Soufflot.

❸ **Jardin du Luxembourg.** Like Emily (in episode 2), many a Parisian has been for their morning run in this former royal park—the stately, statue-strewn gardens of the Italianate Luxembourg Palace (today's French Senate). There are fountains galore, but the most splendid waterworks is the **Medici Fountain,** draped with lithe Roman gods sculptured by Auguste Ottin and topped with the Medici coat of arms, in honor of the palace's first resident, Marie de Médicis. Take the exit at Porte Férou, and walk 7 minutes to catch Métro line 12 at Rennes station to Abbesses in Montmartre.

☕ ★★ **Le Relais de la Butte.** Head right down rue des Abbesses, then right again onto rue Ravignan. At the top of the hill, in season 3, Emily, Mindy, and Emily's crush Alfie (Lucien Laviscount) had breakfast in this wood-fronted restaurant (founded in 1672), and it's not hard to see why. Its terrace is nestled amid the cobbles and trees below Place Emile Goudeau like a ready-made postcard. It's a great spot for a late lunch of cheese and charcuterie in the shade. *12 rue Ravignan, 18th. lerelaisdelabutte.fr.* ☎ *01-42-23-24-34. $$.*

❺ **Rue de l'Abreuvoir.** A further meander through Montmartre's Butte, up rue Ravignan, rue J.B. Clément and rue de Saules, and you'll find this quaint but touristy street. The pastel-pink Maison Rose restaurant (at no. 2) is where Emily had dinner with her friend Mindy (Ashley Park) in the fifth episode, and at the bottom of the street is where one of the show's most memorable scenes took place: the Hästens bed sequence (where Emily sets up an outdoor marketing campaign in front of the statue of Dalida). ●

3 The Best Neighbor-hood Walks

The Latin Quarter

The Best Neighborhood Walks

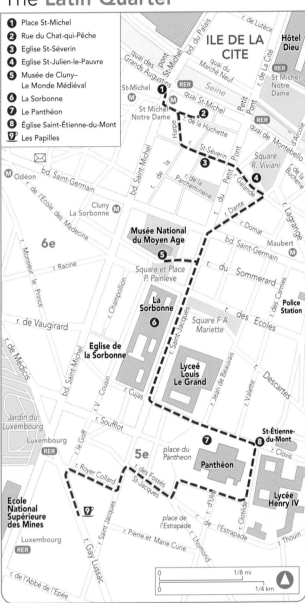

Previous page: Luxembourg Palace and Gardens, in Saint-Germain-des-Prés.

In the 1920s, this Left Bank neighborhood was the heart of Parisian cafe society. You'll still find plenty of cafes, plus universities and shops, all constantly buzzing with activity. Traditionally arty, intellectual, and bohemian, the area also has a history of political unrest. Today, it is still one of Paris's most interesting, not to mention picturesque, quarters to explore. START: **Métro to St-Michel.**

The Fontaine Saint-Michel, at the center of Place Saint-Michel.

❶ **Place Saint-Michel.** An elaborate 1860 fountain of Saint Michael presides over this bustling cafe- and shop-lined square, where skirmishes between occupying Germans and French Resistance fighters once took place. This is the beginning of busy Boulevard Saint-Michel, which was trendy long ago but is now a disappointing line of fast-food chains and standard high-street stores. It is, however, the main student quarters, and a young, lively atmosphere pervades.

❷ **Rue du Chat-qui-Pêche.** Turn left down Rue de la Huchette, bypassing its endless kabob and pizza joints to reach this street, which is one of the narrowest in Paris, at just 1.8m (6 ft.) wide. Plenty of local tales exist about the history of the name ("Street of the Cat Who Fishes"), but nobody knows for sure.

❸ **Église Saint-Séverin.** This charming medieval church was built in the early 13th century and reconstructed in the 15th. Don't miss the gargoyles projecting from the roof. Inside, linger over the rare Georges Rouault etchings from the early 20th century, and the abstract 1970s stained-glass windows in the apse chapels. ⏱ *30 min. 1 rue des Pretres St-Séverin, 5th. www.saint-severin.com.* ☎ *01-42-34-93-50. Mon–Sat 9:30am–1pm & 2–7:30pm, Sun 9am–1pm & 3–8pm.*

❹ **Église Saint-Julien-le-Pauvre.** Take Rue Saint-Séverin to Rue Galande and, after snapping photos of its quaint old houses, find this Melkite Greek church, which dates, at least in part, to 1170. Note the unusual capitals covered in carved vines and leaves. The garden contains one of the oldest trees in Paris and has one of my favorite views of Notre-Dame. ⏱ *20 min. Rue St-Julien-le-Pauvre, 5th. https://sjlpmelkite.business.site.*

Stained glass window at Église Saint-Séverin.

The Musée de Cluny–Le Monde Médiéval is home to the famous Lady and the Unicorn *tapestries.*

☎ 01-43-54-52-16. Mon–Sat 2–6pm, Sun 10am–1pm. Métro: Cluny–La Sorbonne.

❺ ★★ Musée de Cluny–Le Monde Médiéval. With one of the world's strongest collections of medieval art, this small, manageable museum is a gem. Most visitors come to see the *Lady and the Unicorn* tapestries, but there's much more here than long-haired maidens and mythical creatures: This 15th-century Gothic building sits atop 2nd-century baths. The Gallo-Roman pools are in excellent shape—the frigidarium (cold bath) and tepidarium (warm bath) can still be clearly seen (although you can no longer take a dip). ⏱ 1 hr. 6 place Paul-Painlevé, 5th. www.musee-moyenage.fr. ☎ 01-53-73-78-00. Admission 12€ adult, 10€ ages 18–24, free for ages 17 & under from EU countries & 17. Tues–Sun 9:30am–6:15pm. Métro: Cluny–La Sorbonne.

❻ ★★ La Sorbonne. France's most famous university, dating back some 700 years, has all the venerable buildings and confident, scraggly-haired students you might imagine. Teachers here have included Thomas Aquinas, and the alumni association counts Dante,

Calvin, and Longfellow among its past members. This is a sprawling place, and not open to the public, but you can book a guided tour (in French only; email visites-sorbonne@ac-paris.fr). ⏱ 30 min. 12 rue de la Sorbonne, 5th. www.sorbonne.fr. ☎ 01-40-46-23-48. Admission for guided tour adults 15€, students 7€. Métro: Cluny–La Sorbonne.

❼ ★★★ Le Panthéon. This magnificent building was built (1764–1790) by Louis XV as a tribute to Saint Geneviève. Since the Revolution, however, it's been used to honor more earthly heroes. France's great dead are entombed here,

Cafes along Place de la Sorbonne.

including Voltaire, Rousseau, Zola, and Hugo. Recent additions include Alexandre Dumas (2002) and Marie Curie (in 1995), who was one of only two women here until 2015, when WWII *résistantes* Geneviève de Gaulle-Anthonioz (de Gaulle's niece) and Germaine Tillion were accepted. Appropriately, Foucault's pendulum is here—the famous device, which proved that the Earth rotates on an axis, was said to hang from "the eye of God." Although the pendulum appears to swing, it's not moving—the Earth is. ⏱ *1 hr. Place du Panthéon, 5th. www. pantheon.monuments-nationaux.fr.* ☎ *01-44-32-18-00; Admission 7.50€ ages 26 & over, 6€ ages 18–26 from outside EU, free for ages 25 & under from EU countries & 17 & under from outside EU. Daily 10am–6pm (Apr–Sept until 6:30pm). Métro: Cardinal Lemoine. RER B: Luxembourg.*

❽ ★★ Église Saint-Étienne-du-Mont. This gem of a church, a joyous mix of late Gothic and Renaissance styles, is famed for its 16th-century chancel, home to Paris's only remaining **rood screen** (an intricately carved partition separating the nave from the chancel), inspired by the Italian Renaissance.

The church was once part of an abbey dedicated to St-Geneviève (Paris's patron saint), and stones from the saint's original sarcophagus lie in an ornate shrine here. That's about all that is left of her—the saint's bones were burned during the Revolution, and her ashes were thrown in the Seine. The remains of two other great minds, Racine and Pascal, are buried here too. ⏱ *30 min. 1 pl. St-Geneviève, 5th. www.saintetiennedumont.fr.* ☎ *01-43-54-11-79. Free admission. Tues–Fri 10am–1pm & 2–7:30pm; Sat–Sun 8:30am–1pm & 2–8pm; Mon 2:30–7:30pm (time varies during school holidays). Métro: Cardinal Lemoine. RER: Luxembourg.*

❾ Les Papilles. Ready for a break? This is just the place. The owners of this sweet Provençal-style bistro are dedicated to Southern French food and adventurous wine. The small menu changes with the seasons, and the wines change with the owners' moods. If it's available, try the excellent stewed chicken or the hearty cassoulet. *30 rue Gay-Lussac, 5th. www.lespapillesparis.fr.* ☎ *01-43-25-20-79. RER B: Luxembourg. $$.*

Le Panthéon, an 18th-century memorial hall honoring France's greatest intellectuals.

Saint-Germain-des-Prés

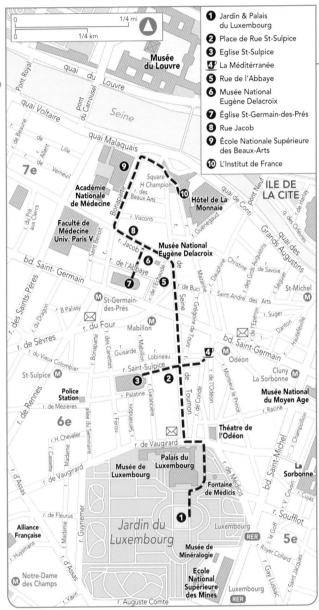

1 Jardin & Palais du Luxembourg
2 Place de Rue St-Sulpice
3 Eglise St-Sulpice
4 La Méditérranée
5 Rue de l'Abbaye
6 Musée National Eugène Delacroix
7 Église St-Germain-des-Prés
8 Rue Jacob
9 École Nationale Supérieure des Beaux-Arts
10 L'Institut de France

This neighborhood was the place to be in the 1920s. Here the literati met the glitterati and *tout* Paris marveled at the ensuing explosion of creativity and alcoholism. On these streets, Sartre fumed while Hemingway and Fitzgerald drank and quarreled. Today the bookshops have been replaced by designer boutiques, but it's still the place to go for a night on the town. START: **Métro to Luxembourg.**

Palais du Luxembourg, home to the French Senate.

❶ ★★★ kids Jardin & Palais du Luxembourg. There's a certain justice in the fact that this former palace, built between 1615 and 1627 for the widow of Henry IV, is now home to the democratically elected French Senate. The lovely Italianate building also houses the **Musée du Luxembourg,** famed for its world-class temporary art exhibitions (19 rue de Vaugirard, 6th; www.musee duluxembourg.fr; ☎ 01-40-13-62-00). Most people, however, come for the gardens. The picturesque paths of the Jardins du Luxembourg have always been a favorite of artists, although children, students from the nearby Sorbonne, and tourists are more common than painters nowadays. Hemingway claimed to have survived a winter by catching pigeons here for his supper, and Gertrude Stein used to cross the gardens on her way to sit for Picasso. The classic formal gardens are well groomed and symmetrically designed. More than 80 statues vie for your attention—a long-haired French queen, a nymph playing a

flute, and a stern effigy of poet Charles Baudelaire, to highlight a few. It's fanciful and delightful; you could spend hours here and not discover all its secrets. Particularly popular with families are the pond in which children float wooden boats, the games area, and pony rides. ◷ *1 hr. Métro: Odéon. RER: Luxembourg.*

❷ Place & Rue Saint-Sulpice. Turn down any street on the north side of the gardens and walk a few blocks to Place Saint-Sulpice and its surrounding streets. Welcome to shopping heaven (or window-shopping purgatory). This is where you'll find all the usual chic high-street fashion boutiques for your inspection—agnès b., Comptoir de Cotonniers, perfumer Annick Goutal, and more. If you want to stock up for a picnic, pop down to 8 rue du Cherche-Midi to Poilâne bakery for some of the city's best breads and sandwiches to go. Or turn onto Rue Bonaparte, where Pierre Hermé (at no. 72) makes the city's most delicious macaroons.

The Église Saint-Sulpice.

❸ ★★ Église Saint-Sulpice.

Filled with paintings by Delacroix, including *Jacob Wrestling with the Angel*, this is a wonderful church in which to meditate and take in some gorgeous frescoes. The church has one of the world's largest organs, comprising 6,700 pipes—a national treasure, especially when it's played (see www.aross.fr/en/news for a schedule). ⏱ *30 min. Rue St-Sulpice, 6th. www.paroissesaintsulpice.paris. ☎ 01-42-34-59-98. Daily 8am–7:45pm.*

❹ La Méditerranée.

A short walk away lies this restaurant, filled with murals by 20th-century stage designers Christian Bérard and Marcel Vertés and paintings by Picasso and Chagall. It was once a haunt of Jacqueline Kennedy, Picasso, and Jean Cocteau (whose work enlivens the plates and menus). The chef delivers creative interpretations of traditional dishes, including carpaccio of sea bass with herb toast, and an incredible bouillabaisse, thick with seafood. *2 place de l'Odéon, 6th. www.la-mediterranee.com. ☎ 01-43-26-02-30. Métro: Odéon. $$$.*

❺ Rue de l'Abbaye.

Saint-Germain was built around an old abbey that once towered over this street, although there's virtually nothing left of it today. With houses and churches built from brick, the street is charming, particularly Rue de Furstenberg—once the abbot's stables, it's now filled with upscale design shops and galleries.

❻ ★★ Musée National Eugène Delacroix.

The Romantic painter Eugène Delacroix lived and worked in this lovely house on Rue de Furstenberg from 1857 until his death in 1863. The museum sits on a charming square and has a romantic garden. Most of his major works are in the Louvre (you may buy a joint ticket for the Louvre, 15€), but the collection here is unusually personal, including an early self-portrait and letters and notes to such friends as Baudelaire and George Sand. You can also see his work in the Chapelle des Anges in Église Saint-Sulpice (see stop ❸ on this tour). ⏱ *1 hr. 6 rue de Furstenberg, 6th. www.museedelacroix.fr. ☎ 01-44-41-86-50. Admission 7€ adults, free for children 17 & under & visitors 25 & under from EU countries. Wed–Mon 9:30am–5:30pm. Métro: St-Germain-des-Prés.*

❼ ★★★ Église Saint-Germain-des-Prés.

This exquisite little church is the oldest in Paris, and a rarity in France—only a few buildings this old exist in such complete form. It dates to the 6th century, when Merovingian king Childebert founded a Benedictine abbey here, although little remains from that time. Its aged columns still bear their medieval paint in breathtaking detail. You can visit the tomb of the French philosopher René Descartes (1596–1650) in the second chapel. On the right as you enter, look into the Chapelle de Saint-Symphorien. It was here, during the revolution, that many clergymen were imprisoned before being executed just outside on the square. ⏱ *30 min. 3 place St-Germain-des-Prés, 6th. www.eglise-saintgermaindespres.fr. ☎ 01-55-42-81-18. Sun–Mon 9:30am–8pm, Tues–Sat 8:30am–8pm. Métro: St-Germain-des-Prés.*

The imposing Institut de France houses several government agencies.

⑧ Rue Jacob. This elegant street, with clean lines and classic 19th-century architecture, was once home to such illustrious residents as the author Colette and the composer Richard Wagner. Today, it holds charming bookstores and antiques shops and is all very posh-bohemian.

⑨ École Nationale Supérieure des Beaux-Arts. Turn onto Rue Bonaparte and walk toward the river to reach this fine-arts school, where the main attraction is the architecture. The school occupies a 17th-century convent and the 18th-century Hôtel de Chimay. Attending an exhibition (held frequently) will grant you a peek inside, but if none is on, just wander down Rue Bonaparte, lined with lovely small art galleries. ⏱ *30 min. 14 rue Bonaparte, 6th. https://beauxartsparis.fr.* ☎ *01-47-03-50-00. Open during exhibitions Tues–Sun 1–7pm (Thurs until 9pm). Métro: St-Germain-des-Prés.*

⑩ L'Institut de France. Turn right along the river and you'll see a hard-to-miss elegant domed baroque building, home to five subgovernmental agencies all lumped together as the rather ominously named L'Institut. Here the Académie Française zealously (some would say too zealously) guards the purity of the French language from "Franglais" encroachment (Jacques Cousteau was once a member), while other, lesser-known agencies (Sciences, Inscriptions et Belles Lettres, Beaux Arts, and Sciences Morales et Politiques) do . . . whatever it is they do. It's all a bit intimidating (academy members are known as "the Immortals"), and all buildings are closed to the public, but it's possible to arrange in advance for a guided tour (available in English). ⏱ *15 min. 23 Quai de Conti, 6th. www.institutdefrance.fr.* ☎ *01-44-41-44-41. Guided tours (request via website only). Métro: St-Germain-des-Prés or Louvre Rivoli.*

The elegant interior of the Ecole Nationale Supérieure des Beaux-Arts.

The **Islands**

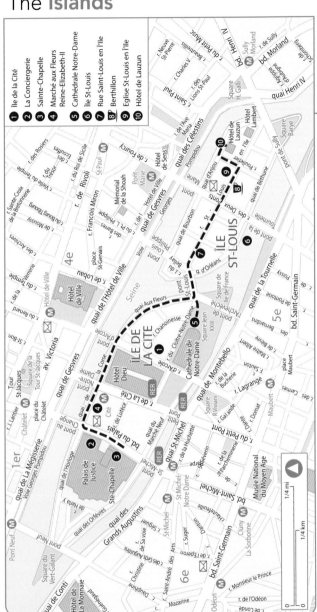

The Île de la Cité is where it all began. By the time the Romans came in 52 B.C., the Celtic Parisii tribe had been living on the Île de la Cité for about 200 years. Over the next 2 millennia, the Franks, Merovingians, and Capetian kings expanded Paris, but the city's soul remained here, around Notre-Dame cathedral. Across the pont Saint-Louis, Île Saint-Louis (former marshlands) is a coveted residential area filled with glorious 17th-century mansions. This tour takes you through both islands and along some of the loveliest stretches of the Seine. START: **Métro to Cité.**

① Île de la Cité. By medieval times, this was a thriving island town with huddles of houses and narrow streets. But it was all swept away in the 19th century by Baron Haussmann when he evicted some 25,000 people to make way for the large administrative buildings we see today, such as the law courts. Few have written more movingly about its heyday than Victor Hugo, who invites the reader "to observe the fantastic display of lights against the darkness of that gloomy labyrinth of buildings; cast upon it a ray of moonlight, showing the city in glimmering vagueness, with its towers lifting their great heads from that foggy sea." You have only to look upwards while on Pont Neuf (which links the Île de la Cité to the city at large) to see what he's talking about: On a cloudy day, dramatic skies cast eerie light over the island. The bridge is embellished by a statue of Henri IV. The name means "new bridge"—ironic considering that it's Paris's oldest bridge, dating back to the 16th

century. A staircase below leads to the Square du Vert-Galant, one of my favorite riverside picnic spots.

② ★★★ La Conciergerie. This intimidating building, originally a medieval royal palace, was converted into a prison during the Revolution and became an object of terror at a time when idle accusations could result in spontaneous executions. Marie Antoinette, Danton, and Robespierre all were held here before being guillotined. Today, you can see the cells where they were held, and thanks to "Histopad," a smart tablet with augmented reality functions, see parts of the building as it would have looked in the 14th century and during the Revolution. A strange and interesting place. *See p 8, ⑥*.

③ ★★★ Sainte-Chapelle. Tucked away among the huge Conciergerie and the vast law courts of the Palais de Justice is this tiny church—a precious place seemingly made almost entirely of dazzling stained-glass windows. One of the

Pont Neuf, at the western end of Île de la Cité.

Tiny Sainte-Chapelle is known for its dazzling stained-glass windows.

loveliest things you can do is visit at night for a classical music concert. You'll find a list of concerts on the website. *See p 24,* ④.

④ **Marché aux Fleurs Reine-Elizabeth-II.** Renamed (in 2014) after the now late Queen Elizabeth II, to commemorate the 70th anniversary of the Normandy landings in WWII, this vivid flower market must be one of the most photographed places in the city—and for good reason. It bursts with color all year round, thanks to century-old pavilions filled with orchids, house plants, and beautiful seasonal bouquets. ⏱ *30 min. Place Louis Lépine, Quai de la Corse, Quai des Fleurs, 4th. Mon–Sat 8am–7:30pm, Sun 8am–7pm. Métro: Cité.*

⑤ ★★★ **Cathédrale Notre-Dame.** This world-famous cathedral is more beautiful in person than on film. If they've re-opened, climb its towers to see snarling gargoyles and sweeping panoramas of the city. *See p 9,* ⑦.

⑥ **Île Saint-Louis.** Despite its central location, the Île Saint-Louis still feels like a tranquil backwater, removed, somehow, from the rest of the buzzing city. The 17th-century buildings lining the narrow streets are some of the city's most expensive properties, and many of them have hosted, at one point or another, French literary stars, such as Racine and Molière. A bourgeois arty crowd still frequents the many art galleries around. It's a lovely place to wander, and so tiny that it's almost impossible to get lost.

⑦ **Rue Saint-Louis-en-l'Île.** The Île Saint-Louis's central artery is gorgeous, narrow, and lined with restaurants and boutiques selling art, clothes, precious stones and minerals, food, hats, and jewelry. Hôtel Chenizot, at no. 51, has fantastic carved dragons and bearded fauns on its facade. Hôtel Lambert, at no. 2, is a glorious 17th-century mansion built by Le Vau (of Versailles and Louvre fame), soon to be turned into a cultural center by its billionaire owner, the technology mogul Xavier Niel. The end of the street closest to the Île de la Cité is a great place to get a photo of Notre-Dame.

⑧ **Berthillon.** On Île Saint-Louis, even the ice-cream stores are sophisticated. This place proves it, with polite crowds queuing outside

Climb Notre-Dame's tower and you'll be rewarded with close-ups of gargoyles and sweeping city views.

for cones to go, and others perched at the tables inside to try the lemon, hazelnut, and mango flavors favored by the locals—the chocolate is especially divine. *31 rue St-Louis-en-l'Île, 4th. www. berthillon.fr. Métro: Pont Marie. $.*

⑨ Église Saint-Louis-en-l'Île.
This 17th-century church, vastly overshadowed by Notre-Dame, has wonderful rococo-baroque architecture, including a lovely sunburst above the altar. Not as dramatic as its famous neighbor, but it's more intimate and enchanting. ⏱ *20 min. 19 rue St-Louis-en-l'Île, 4th. www.saint louisenlile.catholique.fr. ☎ 01-46-34-11-60. Tues–Sun 10am–12:30pm & 3–5:30pm. Métro: Pont Marie.*

⑩ ★★ Hôtel de Lauzun. This
astonishing place, with fantastic

drains in the shapes of sea serpents, was where poets Baudelaire and Théophile Gautier hosted famously long, hazy hashish parties. Baudelaire wrote *Les Fleurs du Mal* while living here, although it's hard to see how he could have been so depressed living somewhere so pretty. The building takes its name from a former occupant, the duc de Lauzun. He was a favorite of Louis XIV until he asked for the hand of the king's cousin, the Duchesse de Montpensier. Louis refused and had Lauzun tossed into the Bastille. Eventually the duchess convinced Louis to release him, and they married secretly and moved here in 1682. *17 Quai d'Anjou. Generally closed to the public, although guided tours are becoming more frequent. Check with the tourist office or send an email to visites.hdv@paris.fr. Métro: Pont Marie.*

Peaceful Île Saint-Louis.

The **Marais**

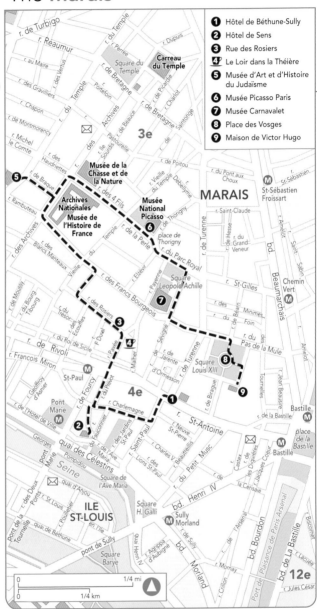

1 Hôtel de Béthune-Sully
2 Hôtel de Sens
3 Rue des Rosiers
4 Le Loir dans la Théière
5 Musée d'Art et d'Histoire du Judaïsme
6 Musée Picasso Paris
7 Musée Carnavalet
8 Place des Vosges
9 Maison de Victor Hugo

When the Île de la Cité became overcrowded in the 17th century, it was here, to what had been swampland (*marais* means swamp), that the wealthy Parisians moved, filling the streets with fashionable mansions called *hôtels*. Over the years, it became the center of the city's Jewish community, although today the gay and lesbian community has also adopted the area. Its many boutiques and diverse buildings make for excellent shopping and exploring. START: **Métro to St-Paul.**

The Hôtel de Béthune-Sully is one of the finest 17th-century buildings in Paris.

❶ Hôtel de Béthune-Sully. Out of the Métro, turn right on Rue Saint-Antoine and walk through the wooden doorway at no. 62. The relief-studded facade of this gracious mansion dazzles just as much as when it was first designed as the residence of the family of Maximilien de Béthune, duke of Sully, Henri IV's famous minister, in 1625. It stands as one of the finest Louis XIII structures in Paris and, although the building is closed to the public, there's a bookshop on heritage buildings and art, and a charming walled garden (open during office hours, and on weekends from around 9am–6pm), with a "secret" door to the Place des Vosges (see **❽**, below). *⏱ 30 min. 62 rue St-Antoine, 4th. www.hotel-de-sully.fr. Métro: St-Paul.*

❷ Hôtel de Sens. Given the leaded windows and fairy-tale turrets, you might not be surprised to find that this 15th-century mansion has a gloriously ornate courtyard in which you can wander at will most afternoons. Once a private home for archbishops and, later, queens, it now holds a fine-arts library, the Bibliothèque Forney. *⏱ 20 min. 1 rue du Figurier. www.paris.fr/lieux/bibliotheque-forney-18.*

The Hôtel de Sens once housed the archbishops of Sens.

Dining along colorful streets of the Marais.

☎ 01-42-78-14-60. Courtyard Tues–Fri 11am–7pm, Sat noon–7pm. Métro: St-Paul.

❸ Rue des Rosiers. Perhaps the most colorful and typical street remaining from the time when this was the city's main Jewish quarter, Rue des Rosiers (Street of the Rosebushes) meanders among the old buildings with nary a rose to be seen. It is jam-packed with falafel cafes and shops, though, and makes a plum spot for a cheap lunch.

④ ★ Le Loir dans la Théière. This bustling tearoom serves some of the best salads and homemade cakes in the Marais. There's usually a queue to get a table, but it's worth the wait—especially for the humongous lemon meringue pies (8€ a slice). *3 rue des Rosiers, 4th. http://leloirdans latheiere.com.* ☎ *01-42-72-90-61. $.*

❺ ★★★ Musée d'Art et d'Histoire du Judaïsme. Since 1998, MAHJ has been housed in the magnificent Hôtel de Saint Aignan, one of the many palatial 17th-century mansions that dot the Marais. This museum was created in 1948 to protect the city's Jewish history after the Holocaust. It's an important and moving place, with excellent Jewish decorative arts from around Europe—German Hanukkah lamps, a wooden sukkah cabin from Austria—and documents related to the continent's Jewish history. There's also a memorial to the Jews who lived in the building in 1939, 13 of whom died in concentration camps. ⏱ *45 min. Hôtel de St-Aignan, 71 rue du Temple, 3rd. www.mahj.org.* ☎ *01-53-01-86-60. Mon–Fri 11am–6pm (in summer Wed until 9pm), Sat–Sun 10am–7pm. Admission 10.50€ ages 26 & up, 7.50€ ages 18 to 25 (from outside EU), free for ages 18 & under. Métro: Rambuteau.*

❻ ★★★ Musée Picasso Paris. This fabulous museum's permanent collection boasts some 5,000 works by Pablo Picasso (though not all are on show at once). Pieces from his Blue period, Surrealist paintings, and Cubist sculptures sit alongside startling assemblages of Picasso's own art collection, with works by Modigliani and Renoir. A showpiece in its own right is the building—the Hôtel Salé—one of the

The meticulously manicured topiary of the Musée Carnavalet.

most extravagant 17th-century mansions in Paris, built by salt-tax farmer and advisor to Louis XIV Pierre Aubert (hence the building's name: "salé" means "salty"). The magnificent central staircase was based on Michelangelo's stair plan for the Laurentian Library in Florence. ◷ *1 hr. Hôtel Salé, 5 rue du Thorigny, 3rd. www.museepicasso paris.fr.* ☎ *01-85-56-00-36. Tues–Fri 10:30am–6pm, Sat–Sun 9:30am–6pm. Admission 14€ adults, free for ages 18 and under & visitors 25 & under from EU countries. Métro: Saint-Paul.*

❼ ★★★ Musée Carnavalet.

The Renaissance palace that houses this free museum was acquired by Mme de Carnavalet (hence its name) but is most associated with the letter-writing Mme de Sévigné, who moved here in 1677 to be with her daughter and poured out nearly every detail of her life in her letters. Several salons cover the Revolution, and others display furniture from the Louis XIV period to the early 20th century, including a collection of pieces from Marcel Proust's cork-lined bedroom. Also on view is the shoe worn by Marie Antoinette during her execution on October 16, 1793. ◷ *1 hr. 16 rue des Francs-Bourgeois, 3rd. www.carnavalet.paris.fr.* ☎ *01-44-59-58-58. Tues–Sun*

10am–6pm. Free admission. Métro: St-Paul or Chemin Vert.

❽ Place des Vosges. This is

Paris's oldest square and was once its most fashionable; today it's arguably its most adorable, with perfect brick-and-stone pavilions rising above covered arcades. Its perfect symmetry might be why so many writers and artists (Descartes, Pascal, Gautier, and Hugo) chose to live here. *See p 14,* ❺.

❾ ★★ Maison de Victor Hugo.

The writer of *Les Misérables* lived here from 1832 to 1848, and his home has been turned into a tiny shrine, with period rooms dedicated to his life and works. His "Chinese" room is particularly impressive, with an Oriental-style medley of black, green, and red panels and porcelain. The decor is based on the Chinese room at Hauteville Fairy in Guernsey, where Hugo's mistress, Juliette Drouet, lived during the couple's exile from France (after Napoleon III's coup d'état). The views from the windows offer an interesting panorama over the pink-brick Place des Vosges. There's a lovely courtyard cafe here too. ◷ *30 min. 6 place des Vosges, 4th. www.maisons victorhugo.paris.fr.* ☎ *01-42-72-10-16, Free admission. Tues–Sun 10am–6pm. Métro: St-Paul or Bastille.*

Striking Chinese-inspired decor in the Maison de Victor Hugo.

Montmartre & the Sacré Coeur

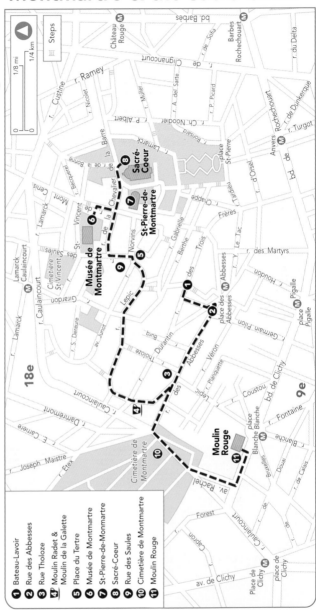

1 Bateau-Lavoir
2 Rue des Abbesses
3 Rue Tholoze
4 Moulin Radet &
   Moulin de la Galette
5 Place du Tertre
6 Musée de Montmartre
7 St-Pierre-de-Montmartre
8 Sacré-Coeur
9 Rue des Saules
10 Cimetière de Montmartre
11 Moulin Rouge

Steps

0   1/8 mi
0   1/4 km

18e

9e

Sacré-Coeur

Musée de Montmartre

St-Pierre-de-Montmartre

Cimetière de Montmartre

Moulin Rouge

Artsy, graceful, undulating Montmartre does something to your heart. From the moment you see its narrow, tilting houses, still windmills, and steep streets, you're in love. This part of town—known as the La Butte, or "the Hill" in the 18th arrondissement—was a rural village separate from Paris until 1860. Then, in the 1880s, Renoir and Toulouse-Lautrec helped make it a lair of artists—a legacy that lives on today. It all starts at the Abbesses Métro station—designed by French architect Hector Guimard—it's one of only two stations in Paris that still has its original Art Nouveau roof (the other is Porte Dauphine, in the 16th). START: **Métro to Abbesses.**

The Moulin de la Galette.

❸ Rue Tholoze. Rue des Abbesses soon brings you to this steep, narrow street, with an adorable windmill at the top. Halfway up is Studio 28 (www.cinemastudio28.fr), which was the city's first proper arthouse cinema, named after the year it opened. It showed Buñuel's *L'Age d'Or* in 1930, and outraged locals ripped the screen from the wall. Today, it still shows arty flicks and has a tiny bar.

❹ Moulin Radet & Moulin de la Galette. The Moulin Radet windmill, confusingly enough, tops a

❶ Bateau-Lavoir. This building is called the "cradle of Cubism." While living here from 1904 to 1912, Picasso painted *The Third Rose* (of Gertrude Stein) and *Les Demoiselles d'Avignon*. Today, it's filled with art studios, with some occasionally open to view. ⏱ *10 min. 13 place Emile Goudeau. Métro: Abbesses.*

❷ Rue des Abbesses. On this street, the unusual rust-red church with the turquoise mosaics is the neo-Gothic Saint-Jean-de-Montmartre, built early in the 20th century. Peek inside to see its delicately weaving arches. Many excellent cafes and dress shops line this street.

The Saint-Jean-de-Montmartre church.

Artists paint and sell their works in Place due Tertre.

restaurant called Le Moulin de la Galette, after the dance hall that once stood here, inspiring such artists as Renoir. The traditionally French food is moderately priced. *83 rue Lepic. www.moulindelagalette paris.com.* ☎ *01-46-06-84-77. $$.*

⑤ Place du Tertre. This old square would be lovely were it not for the tourists—and the artists chasing you around, threatening to draw your caricature. You can buy some very good original paintings here, but you'll have to haggle to get a reasonable price. The perpetual hubbub can be entertaining— it's charming and awful all at once.

⑥ ★★ Musée de Montmartre & Jardins Renoir. This oasis of calm will give you a good look at Montmartre's artistic history. There are pictures of 19th-century Montmartre, rural and lined with windmills, along with a few Toulouse-Lautrec posters and the like. The gardens—named after Auguste Renoir, who lived on-site from 1875 to 1877—offer heartwarming

cityscapes and views over Montmartre's vineyard (see stop ⑨), as well as a pleasant cafe. ⏱ *45 min. 12 rue Cortot, 8th. www.museede montmartre.fr.* ☎ *01-49-25-89-37. Admission 15€ ages 26 & over, 10€ ages 18–25, 8€ ages 10–17, free for children 9 & under. Daily 10am–7pm. Métro: Abbesses or Lamarck-Caulincourt.*

⑦ Saint-Pierre-de-Montmartre. Follow the winding roads ever upward to this early-Gothic Benedictine abbey, now a small church. This is one of the city's oldest churches (from 1133), and its simplicity in the shadow of the Sacré Coeur is refreshing. ⏱ *15 min. Rue du Mont-Cenis.*

⑧ ★★★ Sacré Coeur. The creamy white domes of this basilica soar high above Paris. Inside is an artistic and architectural explosion of color and form; out front are sweeping views of the gorgeous city in soft pastels. Unmissable. *See p 19, ②.*

Iconic Sacré Coeur crowns the highest summit in Paris.

Montmartre Cemetery provides a peaceful respite from the neighborhood's bustling streets and squares.

❾ Rue des Saules. Head down Rue des Saules, pausing to admire the oft-photographed cabaret Au Lapin Agile (au-lapin-agile.com), which was a favorite hangout of Picasso's back when it was called Cabaret des Assassins. It's still usually crowded with tourists, strange fans of old French music, and those seeking Picasso's muse. Opposite, notice the small patch of vines, a throwback from the days when Montmartre was a wine-growing village separate from Paris. The Clos Montmartre harvest (red wine) is celebrated annually in October over a very boozy few days (fetedesvendangesdemontmartre.com).

❿ ★★ Cimetière de Montmartre. Retrace your steps and follow Rue Lepic back down past no. 54, where van Gogh lived with his brother Theo. Turn right onto Rue Joseph-de-Maistre and then left onto Rue Caulaincourt to this quiet resting place. Get a map from the gatehouse—it will help you find the graves of Truffaut, Stendhal, Degas, and many others. But don't

follow it too closely—it doesn't list most of the graceful statues of exquisitely tragic women draped across tombs, nor does it tell you where the most beautiful trees stand, or where the light dapples through just so. You'll have to discover those treasures on your own. ⏲ 1 hr. *Access on Rue Rachel by stairs from Rue Caulaincourt, 18th. www.paris.fr/lieux/cimetiere-de-montmartre-5061.* ☎ *01-53-42-36-30. Free admission. Mon–Fri 8am–6pm, Sat–Sun 8:30am–6pm. Métro: Blanche.*

⓫ Moulin Rouge. Immortalized by Toulouse-Lautrec (and more recently, Lily Collins in *Emily in Paris*), this bright red windmill hasn't changed much with time. Just as the windmill remains outside, the cancan still goes on inside. It's all just as tawdry and tacky as it was when Toulouse-Lautrec downed one absinthe after another to endure it, but it's still the most traditional place to see real cancan in Paris. *See p 142.*

Canal Saint-Martin & Villette

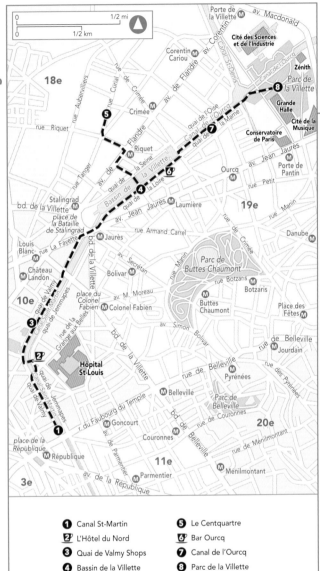

1 Canal St-Martin
2 L'Hôtel du Nord
3 Quai de Valmy Shops
4 Bassin de la Villette
5 Le Centquartre
6 Bar Ourcq
7 Canal de l'Ourcq
8 Parc de la Villette

This tour will take you past legacies of early-20th-century industrialized Paris—its tree-lined piers, iron footbridges, old factories, and warehouses—relics that evoke the days when Edith Piaf lifted the spirits of the nation with her soulful "La Vie en Rose" (1946). Today, this area, both scruffy and cosmopolitan, is one of the city's most happening districts. Its bohemian vibe and new canal-side galleries and cafes make it a fun place to stroll. In summer, the Parc de la Villette—with its science and music museums, concert halls, and open-air film festival—is a hip place to hang out.
START: **Métro to République.**

An iron footbridge on the Canal Saint-Martin.

❶ ★ **Canal Saint-Martin.** Walk across Place de la République to Rue Beaurepaire, lined with trendy shops and cafes. At the end of the street, you're on Quai de Valmy. The Canal Saint-Martin, built between 1805 and 1825, begins at Bastille but hides underground until it gets to Boulevard Richard Lenoir. This is the prettiest stretch, lined with chestnut trees and iron foot-bridges that beg to be photographed. If you remember the cult 2001 film *Amélie,* you might recognize the canal from the stone-skimming scene.

Opposite Rue Beaurepaire, cross the footbridge onto Quai de Jemmapes.

❷ **L'Hôtel du Nord.** Director Marcel Carné's 1938 film Hôtel du Nord made this building (which still has its original facade) famous. Today, it's a bistro serving hearty French cuisine with a typical 1930s interior—a fine choice for coffee or lunch. *102 Quai de Jemmapes, 10th.* www.hoteldunord.org. ☎ 01-40-40-78-78. $$.

Cross back over the Canal onto Quai de Valmy.

❸ ★★ **Quai de Valmy Shops.** New boutiques keep appearing along this stretch of the canal (and its adjacent streets). The best ones are **Artazart,** on Quai de Valmy

Along the Quai de Valmy.

(no. 83; www.artazart.com; ☎ 01-40-40-24-00), a cutting-edge bookshop stocking glossy art and design publications. Farther up, at no. 95, you'll find kitsch clothes and collectables by **Antoine & Lili** (www.antoineetlili.com; ☎ 01-40-37-41-55). On Rue de Marseille (no. 2), don't miss **Centre Commercial** (www.centrecommercial.cc; ☎ 01-42-02-26-08), a concept store that stocks funky clothes and accessories by up-and-coming French designers.

❹ **Bassin de la Villette.** At the top of the Canal Saint-Martin, you reach the circular Barrière de la Villette, one of the few remaining 18th-century tollhouses designed by Nicolas Ledoux (now a hip cafe and restaurant). The modernist fountains in front channel your view up the Canal de l'Ourcq past the twin MK2 cinema complex. If you're a film buff, spend a few moments in the MK2's specialized bookshop (Quai de la Loire, 19th). If you fancy a film in English, look out for VO *(version originale)* written next to the title (providing it's an English-language film, of course!).

Cross the Passerelle de la Moselle footbridge to the Quai de la Seine and head right, before making a left down Rue Riquet and a right into Rue Curial.

❺ **kids** ★★ **Le Centquatre.** This lively multidisciplinary arts center epitomizes the city's urban renewal. Set in the former municipal morgue, it's now the place to go for edgy art exhibitions, concerts, and a spot of vintage shopping. *See p 45.*

Retrace your steps, cross back over the footbridge, then head north along Quai de la Loire.

6 **Bar Ourcq.** Cheap drinks make this a popular bar with residents, especially on a hot day, when boules can be hired at the bar for a game of pétanque on the sand in front of the door. Be daring and challenge a local to a game (opens 3pm). *68 Quai de la Loire, 19th.* ☎ *01-42-40-12-26. $.*

Walk northward along the Canal de l'Ourcq.

7 **Canal de l'Ourcq.** Created in 1813 by Napoleon to provide drinking water and an additional route for transporting goods, this stretch is now characterized by 1960s and '70s tower blocks. An unusual 1885 hydraulic lifting bridge separates it from the Bassin de la Villette.

8 **kids** ★★★ **Parc de la Villette.** The city's former abattoir

district is now a vast retro-futurist park with wide-open lawns and play areas for children. On-site is also the excellent **Cité des Sciences** museum (www.cite-sciences.fr; ☎ 01-40-05-70-00), with a section entirely dedicated to kids (Cité des Enfants); the **Philharmonie de Paris** music museums and concert hall (www.philharmoniedeparis.fr; ☎ 01-44-84-44-84; p 146); the **Zenith** concert hall (www.le-zenith. com), where international bands play; and the brand new **Boom Boom Villette** entertainment center (https://villup.com), filled with movie theaters, an escape game, and food stalls. In August, the park becomes an outdoor cinema *(cinéma en plein-air)* with Europe's biggest inflatable screen. *Av. Corentin-Cariou, 19th. www.villette. com.* ☎ *01-40-03-75-75. Métro: Porte de la Villette or Porte de Pantin.*

The Géode in the Parc de la Villette is a 3D IMAX theater.

Montparnasse

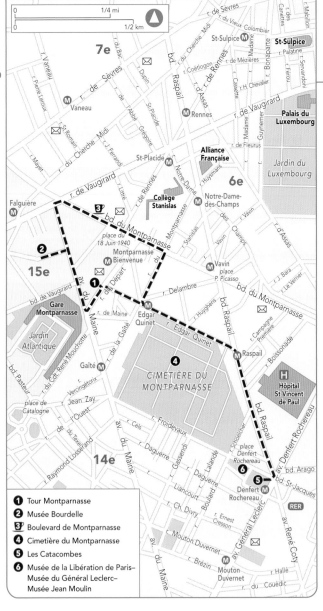

1 Tour Montparnasse
2 Musée Bourdelle
3 Boulevard de Montparnasse
4 Cimetière du Montparnasse
5 Les Catacombes
6 Musée de la Libération de Paris–
  Musée du Général Leclerc–
  Musée Jean Moulin

When Montmartre artists did their jobs so well that the neighborhood became popular and rents went up, they all moved to Montparnasse. Before long, Picasso, Léger, and Chagall had joined Man Ray, Henry Miller, and Gertrude Stein on its somewhat forbidding streets. In terms of beauty, the two areas don't compare—concrete is abundant in Montparnasse, but it offers plenty of sights to keep you busy. Reserve ahead if you want to visit Tour Montparnasse and the Catacombes. START: **Métro to Montparnasse-Bienvenüe.**

The view from the 56th floor of the Tour Montparnasse.

❶ kids ★★ Tour Montparnasse. Completed in 1973 and rising 210m (689 ft.) above the skyline, Paris's most famous inner-city skyscraper was denounced by some as "bringing Manhattan to Paris." The city soon outlawed any further structures of this size in the heart of the city. Today, it is frequented for its panoramic viewing platform on the 56th floor. Take in the skyline before splurging on a cocktail or dinner in the Ciel de Paris restaurant (www.cieldeparis.com; ☎ 01-40-64-77-64), famed for its views. *33 av. de Maine, 15th. www.tourmontparnasse 56.com. ☎ 01-45-38-52-56. Admission 18€ adults, 13.50€ ages 12–17 & students, 9.50€ ages 4–11, free for children 3 & under (prices rise by 1€ weekends & in summer). Apr–Sept daily 9:30am–11:30pm; Oct–Mar Sun–Thurs 9:30am–10:30pm, Fri–Sat & eve of public holidays 9:30am–11pm. Last lift 30 min. before closing. Métro: Montparnasse-Bienvenüe.*

❷ ★★★ Musée Bourdelle. Surrounded by pretty gardens, this museum is where French sculptor Antoine Bourdelle (1861–1929) worked. It was here that he pioneered 20th-century monumental sculpture, and you can't help but feel dwarfed by the sheer size of his masterpieces, which—as you walk through his atmospheric old atelier and gardens—each tell their own mythical story. Bourdelle is buried in the Cimetière de Montparnasse, stop ❹ of this tour. ⓘ *1 hr. 18 rue Antoine-Bourdelle, 15th. www.bourdelle.paris.fr. ☎ 01-49-54-73-73. Free admission to the permanent collection. Tues–Sun 10am–6pm. Métro: Montparnasse-Bienvenüe.*

❸ Boulevard du Montparnasse. Just a block from the train station, this well-traveled street gets busiest at night, when its brasseries and cinemas are aglow, but at any time of day the enticing aromas may lure you to one of its many creperies or brasseries. Succumb to a full meal at no. 108, Le Dôme, now a seafood restaurant ($$–$$$, www.restaurant-ledome.com); or at no. 102, La Coupole, a fabulous Art Deco brasserie

The Tour Montparnasse inspired a law preventing additional skyscrapers in the center of Paris.

($$–$$$, www.lacoupole-paris.com). A bit farther along, at no. 171, La Closerie des Lilas includes among its former fans an unlikely combination of Picasso, Trotsky, Lenin, and Hemingway ($$$, www.closeriedeslilas.fr).

④ ★★ Cimetière du Montparnasse. A short walk down Boulevard Edgar-Quinet, past its many attractive cafes, takes you to this well-known burial ground. For literary and philosophical types, it's a must-see, with the graves of Samuel Beckett, Charles Baudelaire, and Man Ray, as well as the shared grave of Simone de Beauvoir and Jean-Paul Sartre, usually covered in tiny notes of intellectual affection from fans. *3 bd. Edgar-Quinet, 14th. www.paris.fr/lieux/cimetiere-du-montparnasse-4082.* ☎ *01-44-10-86-50. A map is posted to the left of the main gate. Free admission. Mon–Fri 8am–6pm, Sat 8:30am–6pm, Sun 9am–6pm. Métro: Edgar Quinet.*

⑤ ★★★ kids Les Catacombes. Just before the Revolution, Paris's cemeteries were bursting at the seams, spreading disease. To solve the problem, millions of bones were transferred underground into the quarried tunnels that sprawl beneath

the Denfert-Rochereau district. These catacombs, 18m (60 ft.) underground, can be visited today. It feels incredibly strange seeing miles of neatly stacked bones and skulls, and it's surprisingly rather moving. Older kids will love it; younger ones will probably have nightmares. ① *1 hr. 1 avenue du Colonel Henri Roi-Tanguy, 14th. www.catacombes.paris.fr.* ☎ *01-43-22-47-63. Admission 18€–29€ adults, 16€ ages 18–26, free for children 17 & under. Tues–Sun 9:45am–8:30pm (last entry 7:30pm). Métro/RER B: Denfert-Rochereau.*

⑥ ★★★ Le Musée de la Libération de Paris—Musée du Général Leclerc–Musée Jean Moulin. The museum with the longest name in Paris fills you in on World War II France and the French Resistance. It leads you through wartime events, with displays of around 300 items, including official documents and rare films. Part of the visit takes you through the underground bunker where Colonel Rol-Tanguy planned the Liberation of Paris. ① *2 hr. pl. Denfert-Rochereau, 14th. www.museeliberation-leclerc-moulin.paris.fr.* ☎ *01-71-28-34-70. Free admission except to temporary exhibitions. Tues–Sun 10am–6pm. Métro/RER: Denfert-Rochereau.* ●

Six million skeletons stretch 910m (2,986 ft.) through underground tunnels in Les Catacombes beneath Paris.

Shopping Best Bets

Best **Department Store**
★ Le Bon Marché, *22–24 rue de Sèvres, 7th (p 91)*

Best **Flea Market**
Marché aux Puces de St-Ouen, *Rue des Rosiers, 94300 Saint-Ouen (p 88)*

Best **Contemporary Art**
★ Art Generation, *67 rue de la Verrerie, 4th (p 89)*

Best **Working Art Atelier**
★ 59 Rivoli, *59 rue de Rivoli, 1st (p 88)*

Best **Children's Clothing**
★★ Milk on the Rocks, *7 rue Mezières, 6th (p 90)*

Best **Toy Store**
★★ Au Nain Bleu, *14 rue Saint-Roch, 1st (p 90)*

Best **Place to Buy a Picnic Lunch**
★★★ Maison Plisson, *93 bd. Beaumarchais, 3rd (p 94)*

Best **Place to Buy Photography**
★★ Paris Est une Photo, *55 passage Jouffroy, 9th (p 96)*

Best **Kitchenware**
E. Dehillerin, *18 rue Coquillière, 2nd (p 96)*

Best **Vintages Wines**
★★★ Ryst Dupeyron, *79 rue du Bac, 7th (p 94)*

Best **Place for English-Language Books & Magazines**
Smith & Son, *248 rue de Rivoli, 1st (p 89)*

Best **Place for Gifts**
★★★ Deyrolle, *45 rue du Bac, 7th (p 95)*

Best **Porcelain**
★★★ Astier de Villatte, *173 rue St-Honoré, 1st (p 90)*

Best **Place for a Hipster**
Kiliwatch, *64 rue Tiquetonne, 2nd (p 92)*

Best **Place for Perfume**
★★★ Serge Lutens, *142 Galerie de Valois, 1st (p 96)*

Shopping in the narrow streets of Montmartre.

Right Bank (8th & 16th–17th)

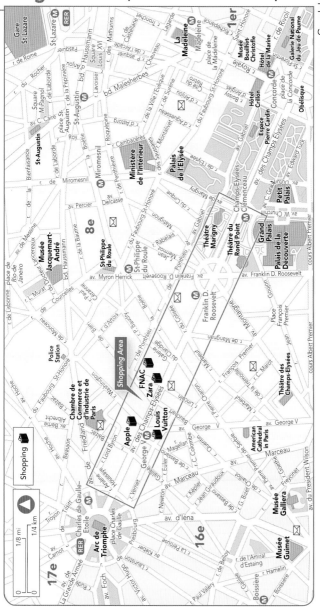

Shopping

0 — 1/8 mi
0 — 1/4 km

17e

16e

8e

1er

Gare St-Lazare

La Madeleine

Musée Jacquemart-André

Ministère de l'Intérieur

Palais de l'Élysée

Hôtel Crillon

Espace Pierre Cardin

Obélisque

Musée Bouilhet Christofle

Galerie National du Jeu de Paume

St-Augustin

St-Philippe du Roule

Théâtre Marigny

Théâtre du Rond Point

Grand Palais

Palais de la Découverte

Petit Palais

Police Station

Chambre de Commerce et d'Industrie de Paris

Shopping Area

FNAC

Zara

Apple

Louis Vuitton

Théâtre des Champs-Élysées

American Cathedral in Paris

Franklin D. Roosevelt

Arc de Triomphe

Musée Galliera

Musée Guimet

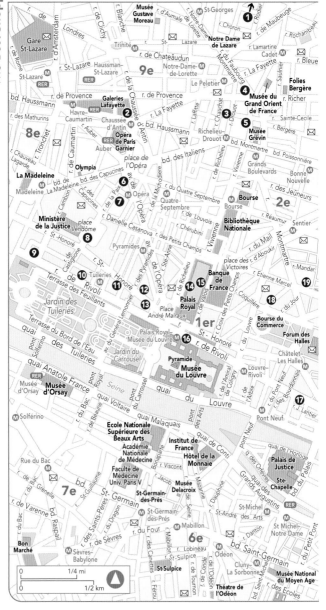

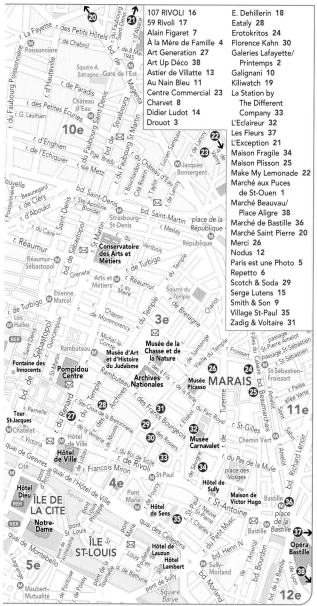

107 RIVOLI 16
59 Rivoli 17
Alain Figaret 7
À la Mère de Famille 4
Art Generation 27
Art Up Déco 38
Astier de Villatte 13
Au Nain Bleu 11
Centre Commercial 23
Charvet 8
Didier Ludot 14
Drouot 3

E. Dehillerin 18
Eataly 28
Erotokritos 24
Florence Kahn 30
Galeries Lafayette/
   Printemps 2
Galignani 10
Kiliwatch 19
La Station by
   The Different
   Company 33
L'Eclaireur 32
Les Fleurs 37
L'Exception 21
Maison Fragile 34
Maison Plisson 25
Make My Lemonade 22
Marché aux Puces
   de St-Ouen 1
Marché Beauvau/
   Place Aligre 38
Marché de Bastille 36
Marché Saint Pierre 20
Merci 26
Nodus 12
Paris est une Photo 5
Repetto 6
Scotch & Soda 29
Serge Lutens 15
Smith & Son 9
Village St-Paul 35
Zadig & Voltaire 31

Left Bank (5th–6th)

Bonpoint **9**
Deyrolle **1**
La Maison Ivre **7**
Le Bon Marché **3**
Librairie Galerie Louis Rozen **11**
Marché Biologique **6**
Milk on the Rocks **5**
Poilâne **4**
Ryst Dupeyron **2**
Shakespeare & Company **10**
Vanessa Bruno **8**

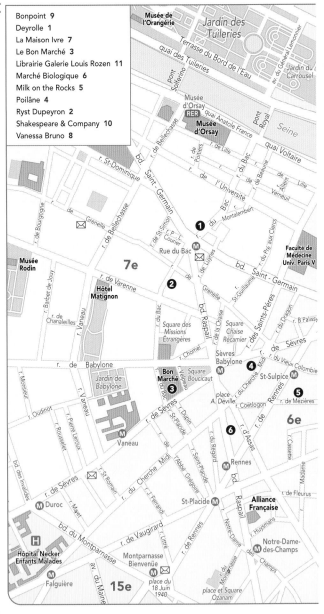

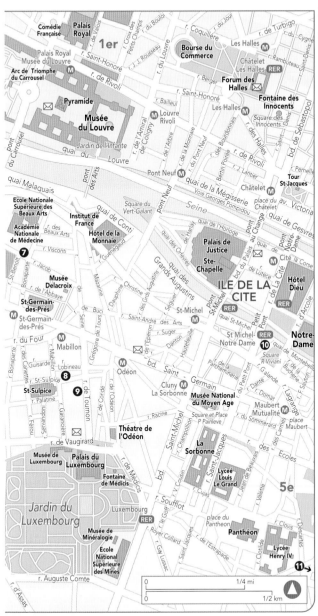

Shopping A to Z

Shopping for antiques at Marché aux Puces de St-Ouen.

Antiques & Collectibles

Drouot GRANDS BOULEVARDS
This venerable auction house is just the place to find fine art, collectibles, and a surprisingly large number of bargains. Come the day before the sale (11am–6pm) or between 11am and noon on auction day (auction usually start at 2pm) to peruse the items. During the sale, a simple hand gesture is enough to bid. But even if you don't buy, it's a fun show. *9 rue Drouot, 9th. www.drouot.com.* ☎ *01-48-00-20-20. Métro: Richelieu-Drouot. Map p 84.*

Marché aux Puces de St-Ouen
NORTH OF MONTMARTRE This massive, permanent site, one of the largest flea markets in Europe, contains many 18th- and 19th-century treasures, but you'll have to haggle for them. Beware of pickpockets. *All around Rue des Rosiers in St-Ouen 94300. From the Métro, walk north along av. de la Porte de Clignancourt (18th), then av. Michelet and turn right. www.pucesdeparissaintouen.com.* ☎ *01-40-11-77-36. Some stalls are cash only. Métro: Porte de Clignancourt. Map p 84.*

Village St-Paul MARAIS This quiet cluster of antiques and art dealers spreads across four interlocking courtyards and sells quality early-20th-century furniture, bric-a-brac, and art. *23–27 rue St-Paul, 4th. www.levillagesaintpaul.com. No phone. Some boutiques are cash only. Métro: St-Paul. Map p 84.*

Art

★ **59 Rivoli** CHÂTELET This former art squat is now a fanciful, innovative residence for artists who open their ateliers to show off works in progress as well as

The studios at 59 Rivoli offer an opportunity to interact with the resident artists.

finished pieces. It's one of the few places that lets buyers deal directly with creators. *59 rue de Rivoli, 1st. www.59rivoli.org.* ☎ *01-44-61-08-31. Most artists accept cash only. Métro: Châtelet. Map p 84.*

★ **Art Generation** MARAIS   Prices here range from 60€ to 2,500€ for original, cutting-edge photographs, paintings, sculpture, video, and drawings. Who knows—the pieces you buy might be worth much more one day. *67 rue de la Verrerie, 4th.* ☎ *01-53-01-83-88. www.artgeneration.fr. Métro: Hôtel de Ville. Map p 84.*

★ **Art Up Déco** BASTILLE   Part of the fabulous Viaduc des Arts (boutiques and craft shops nestled beneath the arches of a converted 19th-century viaduct), this is the place to pick up affordable contemporary paintings, photos, and sculptures by France's up-and-coming artists. Prices start at around 60€ and rarely go over 3,000€. *39-41 av. Daumesnil, 12th. www.artup-deco. com.* ☎ *01-46-28-80-23. Métro: Gare de Lyon or Ledru Rollin. Map p 84.*

Books

Galignani TUILERIES   This wood-paneled bookstore, opened in 1801, sells a vast selection of books in French and English. *224 rue de Rivoli, 1st. www.galignani.com.* ☎ *01-42-60-76-07. Métro: Tuileries. Map p 84.*

★★ **Librairie Galerie Louis Rozen** LATIN QUARTER   This is the place to pick up literary curiosities, from 1930s editions of *Robin Hood* to '70s make-your-own paper airplane kits. There's a beautiful range of vintage photography books too. Mostly in French, but you'll find some English tomes. *8 rue Lacépède, 5th. www.librairiegalerie louisrozen.com.* ☎ *01-43-43-53-53. Métro: Place Monge. Map p 86.*

★★★ **Shakespeare & Company** LATIN QUARTER   The most famous bookstore in Paris is still a joyous, higgledy-piggledy labyrinth of tomes. It's an essential stop on our "Hemingway's Paris" tour, p 46. Expats gather here to swap books and catch readings in English. Expect to wait in line to get in. *37 rue de la Bûcherie, 5th. www.shakespeareand company.com.* ☎ *01-43-25-40-93. Métro: Maubert-Mutualité. Map p 86.*

★★★ **Smith & Son** CONCORDE   Come to this English-language bookshop for British and American bestsellers and classics. The upstairs kids' area is an Ali Baba's cavern of fairy stories, teen lit, and games. And you can load up on scones and cream in the tearoom. *248 rue de Rivoli, 1st. www.smithandson.com.* ☎ *01-44-77-88-99. Métro: Concorde. Map p 84.*

Shakespeare & Company has long been a hub for English-speaking expats.

Whimsical shopping for kids at Au Nain Bleu.

Children's Fashion & Toys

★★ Au Nain Bleu TUILERIES

The venerable "Bleu Dwarf" has been selling children's toys since 1836. You won't find anything plastic or electronic here—just hand-picked European (often handmade) cuddly teddies, dolls, pirate ships, trucks, costumes, and wooden puppets. *14 rue Saint-Roch, 1st. www.aunainbleu.com.* ☎ *09-75-89-28-43. Métro: Tuileries. Map p 84.*

★★ Bonpoint CONCORDE This

place borders on haute couture for kids, so the diminutive outfits—presented in a stately 18th-century mansion—are tailored, traditional, and (though gorgeous) expensive. *6 rue de Tournon, 6th. www.bonpoint.com.* ☎ *01-40-51-98-20. Métro: Odéon. Map p 86.*

★★ Milk on the Rocks ST-

GERMAIN-DES-PRÈS This is where you'll find eco-friendly clothes for the whole brood, from babies to early teens. Style tends to be relaxed, with fun touches, from animal print shorts to T-shirts with pockets embroidered to look like chip packets. *7 rue Mezières, 6th. www.milkontherocks.net.*

☎ *01-45-49-19-84. Métro: Saint-Sulpice. Map p 86.*

China & Porcelain

★★★ Astier de Villatte PALAIS

ROYAL This space once housed Napoleon's silversmith. Nowadays, it sells top-of-the-line handmade tableware and knickknacks inspired by 17th- and 18th-century designs. *173 rue St-Honoré, 1st. www.astierdevillatte.com.* ☎ *01-42-60-74-13. Métro: Palais-Royal. Map p 84.*

★★ La Maison Ivre ST-GERMAIN-

DE-PRES Handmade country-style pottery fills this adorable kitchenware shop. There's an emphasis on Provençal and artisanal ceramics. *38 rue Jacob, 6th. www.maison-ivre.com.* ☎ *01-42-60-01-85. Métro: St-Germain-des-Prés. Map p 86.*

★★★ Maison Fragile MARAIS

This is where those in the know come for beautiful, contemporary tableware from the French city of Limoges, the historic center for France's porcelain industry, still renowned today. Expect stunning geometric and floral patterns. *4 rue de Jarente, 4th. https://maisonfragile.com.*

Galeries Lafayette's stained-glass cupola is classified as a historic monument.

☎ 06-22-46-29-10. Métro: St-Paul. Map p 84.

Concept & Department Stores

Galeries Lafayette/Printemps

OPERA Although separate entities, these department stores with Art Nouveau cupolas stand like twin temples to shopping along the Boulevard Haussmann. Galeries Lafayette stocks more than 200 womenswear brands and has a sumptuous food gallery (Lafayette Le Gourmet). Printemps has a vast shoe department (more than 200 brands) and six floors of both mid-range and designer fashion. *Galeries Lafayette: 40 bd. Haussmann, 9th. www.galerieslafayette.com.* ☎ *09-69-39-75-75. Printemps: 64 bd. Haussmann, 9th. www.printemps. com.* ☎ *01-42-82-50-00. Métro for both: Opéra or Chaussée d'Antin Lafayette. RER: Auber. Map p 84.*

★ Le Bon Marché INVALIDES

Paris's oldest department store is jammed with luxury boutiques, such as Dior and Chanel, for both men and women. If you grow weary of the clothes, check out the dazzling Grande Épicerie food hall. *22–24 rue de Sèvres, 7th. www.lebon marche.com.* ☎ *01-44-39-80-00. Métro: Sèvres-Babylone. Map p 86.*

★★ L'Exception NORTH-EAST

This whopper of a store in a former fire station by Gare de l'Est is the sort you go to for cool, eco-responsible ready-to-wear French clothes and come away with a pineapple-shaped light and a scented candle. Over 400 labels grace the shelves, some of it second hand. There's a cafe too. *12 rue Philippe de Girard, 10th. www.lexception.com.* ☎ *01-76-44-01-44. Métro Stalingrad or Louis Blanc; Métro/RER: Gare de l'Est. Map p 84.*

★★★ Merci MARAIS/BASTILLE

This is Paris's first ever charity concept store. Items aren't always secondhand (some clothes, furniture lines, and other items have been created especially for the shop), and prices aren't always low, but there are bargains to be had. The money raised goes to humanitarian organizations. There are also two funky cafes. *111 bd. Beaumarchais, 3rd. www.merci-merci.com.* ☎ *01-42-77-01-90. Métro: St-Sébastien–Froissart. Map p 84.*

Fashion

★★ Alain Figaret OPERA One

of France's foremost designers of men's shirts offers a broad range of fabrics and elegant silk ties. *21 rue de la Paix, 2nd. www.figaret.com.* ☎ *01-42-65-04-99. Métro: Opéra. Map p 84.*

Shopping on the Champs-Élysées

High-street stores line the Champs-Élysées between Métros Champs-Élysées-Clémenceau and Charles de Gaulle-Étoile. It's here you'll find the big FNAC store (no. 74; p 96), Zara (no. 92) and Apple (no . 114); designer biggies include Louis Vuitton (no. 101). It's expensive, it's touristy, but it must be done at least once. With the Arc de Triomphe at one end and the Louvre in the distance at the other, few places on earth offer shopping opportunities against such an iconic backdrop.

★★★ Charvet OPERA Charvet

made shirts for fashionable Frenchmen for years before he was discovered by English royalty. (The company has made shirts for King Charles III.) Shop here for crisp men's and women's designs in lush fabrics. *28 place Vendôme, 1st. www.charvet.com.* ☎ *01-42-60-30-70. Métro: Opéra. Map p 84.*

★★★ Didier Ludot PALAIS-

ROYAL Recent and rare vintage

haute couture, and buyers with an eye for young talent (i.e., sussing out the vintage clothes of the future) make Didier Ludot an institution. *20–24 Galerie de Montpensier, Palais Royal, 1st.* ☎ *01-42-96-06-56. Métro: Palais Royal–Musée du Louvre. Map p 84.*

★★ **Erotokritos** BASTILLE/ MARAIS This small boutique offers trendy men's and women's fashions with a fun, eccentric edge: Think gingham skirts, schoolboy-style men's shorts, and customizable bags. *109 bd Beaumarchais, 3rd. www.erotokritos.com.* ☎ *01-42-78-14-04. Métro: St-Sébastien Froissart. Map p 84.*

★★★ **L'Eclaireur** MARAIS This futuristic-looking boutique stocks the likes of Jean Paul Gaultier and Maison Margiela, as well as exclusive one-offs by lesser-known designers. Its wild interior is worth seeing even if you don't buy. *40 rue de Sévigné, 3rd. www.leclaireur.com.* ☎ *01-48-87-10-22. Métro: St-Paul. Map p 84.*

★★★ **Marché Saint Pierre** MONTMARTRE DIY fashionistas flock to this fabric market and its surrounding shops to hunt for everything from Toile de Jouy prints to sleek velvets and see-through cottons. There are fabulous buttons and ribbons too. *2 rue Charles Nodier, 18th. www. marchesaintpierre.com.* ☎ *01-46-06-92-25. Métro: Anvers. Map p 84.*

★★ **Nodus** TUILERIES This men's shirt specialist has floor-to-ceiling displays of shirts in every color as well as a few accessories, including cuff links and ties. *274 rue St-Honoré, 1st. www.nodus.fr.* ☎ *01-42-60-35-13. Métro: Tuileries. Map p 84.*

Fashion: Parisian-Style Dressing
★★ **Centre Commercial** CANAL ST. MARTIN This hipster HQ is a fab place to pick up men's and women's clothes with an arty flair. Labels are hand-picked French, British, and Danish, so there's little chance you'll find the same items elsewhere in Paris. *2 rue de Marseille, 10th. www.centrecommercial. cc.* ☎ *01-42-02-26-08. Métro: Jacques Bonsergent. Map p 84.*

Kiliwatch ETIENNE MARCEL You'll score a mix of one-off vintage finds alongside funky, modern street wear, hoodies, leather, and even sunglasses at this trendsetting boutique. Start at the back, work your way forward, and enjoy the treasure hunt. *64 rue Tiquetonne, 2nd. https://kiliwatch-paris.com.* ☎ *01-42-21-17-37. Métro: Etienne Marcel. Map p 84.*

Repetto sells costumes for professional dancers and fashion inspired by the art.

Browsing for chocolates at A La Mère de Famille.

★★★ Make My Lemonade

CANAL ST. MARTIN This brightly colored boutique is where fashion-forward *Parisiennes* come for fun, affordable boho-chic garb, made in Europe, and with excellent cuts for all shapes and sizes. *61 Quai de Valmy, 10th. www.makemylemonade.com.* ☎ *09-67-42-23-97. Métro: Jacques Bonsergent. Map p 84.*

★★★ Repetto OPERA This

pretty boutique is about more than just the tutus and ballet shoes for professional dancers. It also sells gorgeous, rainbow-hued neo-Cinderella dance boots, shoes, and sneakers for the general public, so you can add a touch of theater to your street wear. *22 rue de la Paix, 2nd. www.repetto.fr.* ☎ *01-44-71-83-12. Métro: Opéra. Map p 84.*

Scotch & Soda MARAIS Hippie-chic ethnic-print jackets, pastel tie-dye T-shirts, and floaty floral-print dresses: This store sells women's daywear with just enough attitude to be carried into the evening. *42 rue Vieille du Temple, 4th. www.scotch-soda.com.* ☎ *01-42-71-02-67. Métro: St-Paul. Map p 84.*

Vanessa Bruno SAINT-GERMAIN-DES-PRES Bruno's unique clothes are deeply feminine without being frilly. Her years in Japan gave her an appreciation for sleek lines and simple, clean fabrics. Great bags, too. *25 rue St-Sulpice, 6th. www.vanessabruno.com.* ☎ *01-43-54-41-04. Métro: Odéon. Map p 86.*

Zadig & Voltaire MARAIS This is one of several Z&V branches in Paris. Shelves are stocked with hip clothes in classic styles for men and women. Cotton tops, cashmere sweaters, and faded jeans are big sellers. *42 rue des Francs-Bourgeois, 3rd. www.zadig-et-voltaire.com.* ☎ *01-44-54-00-60. Métro: St-Paul or Hôtel-de-Ville. Map p 84.*

Food & Drink

★★★ A la Mère de Famille

GRANDS BOULEVARDS Founded in 1761, this olde-worlde place is where you'll find classic chocolates as well as old-fashioned bonbons like *berlingots*, lemon drops, caramels, and jellied fruits. Twelve other locations are around the city. *35 rue du Faubourg Montmartre, 9th. www.lameredefamille.com.* ☎ *01-47-70-83-69. Métro: Grands Boulevards. Map p 84.*

★★★ Eataly MARAIS Food lov-

ers flock to this 3-story emporium of Italian food, where artisanal products made both in France and Italy line the shelves, alongside market counters of cheese and cold meats. The emporium also has multiple restaurants, where you can sample the food with a glass of Italian wine. *37 rue Sainte-Croix de la*

Bretonnerie, 4th. https://eataly.fr.
☎ 01-83-65-81-00. Métro: Hôtel-de-Ville. Map p 84.

★ **Florence Kahn** MARAIS This Jewish bakery, one of the best in the city, has all the heavy cakes, poppy seeds, apples, and cream cheese you could want. *24 rue des Ecouffes, 4th. www.florence-kahn.fr.* ☎ 01-48-87-92-85. Métro: St-Paul. Map p 84.

★★★ **Maison Plisson** MARAIS This store is a picnicker's dream, selling farm-fresh vegetables, award-winning charcuterie, and rows of hand-picked wines in the basement. Their neo-canteen next door sports a fabulous bakery and serves top-notch, wholesome food at meal-times. *93 bd. Beaumarchais, 3rd. www.lamaisonplisson.com.* ☎ 01-71-18-19-09. Métro: Chemin Vert or Saint-Sébastien-Froissart. Map p 84.

★★★ **Poilâne** ST-GERMAIN-DES-PRES One of the city's best-loved bakeries, with irresistible apple tarts, butter cookies, and crusty croissants. Get in line. *8 rue du Cherche-Midi, 6th. www.poilane.com.* ☎ 01-45-48-42-59. Métro: St-Sulpice. Map p 86.

★★★ **Ryst Dupeyron** ST-GERMAIN-DES-PRES Fill up on vintage wines and specialty

whiskies in this family-run gem of a liquor store founded in 1905. Gourmet treats (such as foie gras and prunes in brandy) and friendly service complete the experience. *79 rue du Bac, 7th. www.maisonryst dupeyron.com.* ☎ 01-45-48-80-93, Métro: Rue du Bac. Map p 86.

Food & Drink: Markets
Marché Beauvau/Place Aligre LEDRU ROLLIN The Marché d'Aligre is one of Paris's cheapest fruit, vegetable, and flower markets—and one of the best (Mon–Fri 7am–1:30pm, Sat–Sun 7am–2:30pm). The more expensive, covered Marché Beauvau offers uncompromisingly good meat, fish, and cheese. *Place d'Aligre, 12th. Some stalls are cash only. Métro: Ledru-Rollin. Map p 84.*

Marché Biologique SAINT-GERMAIN Along Boulevard Raspail, this organic market (Sun 9am–3pm) sells top-notch produce, often locally sourced, plus hot soups, crêpes, and oysters to go. *Bd. Raspail (btw. rue du Cherche-Midi and Rue de Rennes), 6th. Some stalls are cash only. Métro: Rennes. Map p 86.*

★★ **Marché de Bastille** BASTILLE This huge market (Thurs 7:30am–1:30pm; Sun 7am–2:30pm) is an excellent source for local

Foodies will swoon over the vast selection of cheeses in Paris's markets and gourmet shops.

All the produce is organic at Marché Biologique in Saint-Germain.

cheese, meat, and fresh fish. Street performers usually liven up the experience. *Bd. Richard Lenoir, 11th. Some stalls are cash only. Métro: Bastille. Map p 84.*

Gifts & Jewelry

107 RIVOLI LOUVRE You don't need a ticket to enter the Arts Décoratifs' museum shop—the best place in central Paris to find innovative, design-themed jewelry, tableware, fashion accessories, and beautiful coffee-table books. It's not cheap, but it's well worth a browse. *107 rue de Rivoli, 1st. https://madparis.fr. ☎ 01-42-60-64-94. Métro: Palais Royal-Musée du Louvre. Map p 84.*

★★★ **Deyrolle** SAINT-GERMAIN This taxidermy/curiosity shop is filled with stuffed wildlife. The chances of you leaving with a tiger in your bag are slim, but there are oodles of nature books, garden gadgets, and jewelry. The butterfly cabinets upstairs are particularly dazzling. *45 rue du Bac, 7th. www. deyrolle.com. ☎ 01-42-22-32-31. Métro: Rue du Bac. Map p 86.*

★★ **Les Fleurs** BASTILLE Hidden down a tiny passageway, this understatedly trendy boutique's jewelry and bags became so popular that they had to open a second store (a 5-min. walk away). Both boutiques are worth checking out; the first for its trinkets, the second for its hand-picked range of household items. *6 passage Josset & 5 rue Trousseau, 11th. www.boutiqueles fleurs.com. ☎ 01-43-55-12-94, Métro: Ledru Rollin. Map p 84.*

Photography prints from Paris Est une Photo.

Established in 1820, E. Dehillerin is a magnet for professional chefs.

★★ Paris Est une Photo

GRANDS BOULEVARDS   Tucked in a delightful covered passage, this hybrid gallery-boutique is the place to come for stunning Paris-themed photos. Some of them are old black and white; others are quirky and contemporary. Everything would look good on a wall at home. *55 passage Jouffroy, 9th. https://photo. paris.* ☎ *01-56-92-04-47. Métro: Grands Boulevards. Map p 84.*

Kitchen

E. Dehillerin LES HALLES   This shop has outfitted great chefs for nearly 2 centuries. Nothing here comes cheap, but a Dehillerin sauté pan is forever. Unlike elsewhere in Paris, prices are displayed without VAT, which is added when you pay. *18 rue Coquillière, 1st. www.e dehillerin.fr.* ☎ *01-42-36-53-13. Métro: Les Halles. Map p 84.*

Music & Tickets

FNAC CHAMPS-ÉLYSÉES   This supermarket of culture (with various branches) is where you can pick up CDs and vinyl (cool again, now they're vintage items) of French and international artists, DVDs (another obsolete comeback), video games, and electronics. It's also a convenient place to buy tickets for concerts, plays, sports events, and museums, both inside the stores and online at www.fnac.com. The branch on the Champs-Élysées stays open until 10:30pm (Sun until 8:45pm). *74 av. des Champs-Élysées, 8th. www.fnac.com.* ☎ *08-25-02-00-02. Métro: George V. Map p 83.*

Perfume & Makeup

★★ La Station by The Different Company

MARAIS   Indeed, something *is* different about this perfume company. This independent operation, founded in 2000, makes its own unique fragrances with mostly natural materials. Signature scents include Osmanthus, Sel de Vétiver, and Rose Poivrée. *10 rue Ferdinand Duval, 4th. https:// lastationdc.fr.* ☎ *01-42-78-19-34. Métro: St-Paul. Map p 84.*

★★★ Serge Lutens

PALAIS ROYAL   This purple Belle Epoque boutique is so beautiful it's worth seeing even if you don't buy any fragrances or makeup. This is one of a handful of boutiques to sell Lutens's "exclusives" perfume range. *142 Galerie de Valois, 1st. www.serge lutens.com.* ☎ *01-49-27-09-09. Métro: Palais Royal. Map p 84.* ●

Jardin des Tuileries

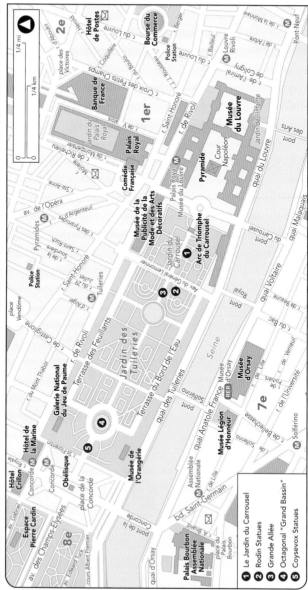

1 Le Jardin du Carrousel
2 Rodin Statues
3 Grande Allée
4 Octagonal "Grand Bassin"
5 Coysevox Statues

Previous Page: The Roue de Paris is a transportable Ferris Wheel open seasonally in summer and winter.

More a statue garden than, as its name implies, a "garden of tiles" (the clay earth here was once used to make roof tiles), the Tuileries stretches from the Louvre all the way down to the Place de la Concorde. Under lacy chestnut trees, paths branch and curl off the dusty main allée, and each seems to hold something to charm you—statues, ice-cream stands, and ponds surrounded by chairs in which you can read or simply relax and contemplate the beauty around you. It's open daily from 7am to 11pm in summer and from 7:30am to 7:30pm in winter. START: **Métro to Tuileries or Concorde.**

❶ Le Jardin du Carrousel. Start by the Louvre's glass pyramid and walk past the Arc de Triomphe du Carrousel—an elaborate arch ordered by Napoleon in 1806 and copied from Rome's Septimus Severus Arch—into the Jardin du Carrousel. (Just so you know, the last word refers to equestrian exhibitions—there's no merry-go-round here.) The gold-tipped obelisk you see gleaming at the end (the Luxor Obelisk, a gift from Egypt) marks the Place de la Concorde. As you walk into the garden, you'll find beautiful boxwood hedges, among which 20 graceful statues by Aristide Maillol seemingly play hide and seek.

❷ Rodin Statues. Extricate yourself from the crowds and keep walking until you cross Avenue du Général-Lemonnier. Four typically graceful statues by Auguste Rodin (*The Kiss* [the original is in the Musée Rodin, p 39], *Eve*, *Meditation*, and *The Shadow*) flank the paths. The glimmering golden statue in the distance at Place des Pyramides is *Joan of Arc*; she assembled her army against the British from a spot not far from here, on Avenue de l'Opéra.

❸ Grande Allée. Off to the sides of the Grande Allée, several modern statues peek at you from the greenery—Henry Moore's *Figure Couchée* lounges leisurely, and Alberto Giacometti's *Grande Femme II* sits near Jean Dubuffet's dazzling *Le Bel Costume.*

❹ Octagonal "Grand Bassin." The statues surrounding this pond date from the days when this was a royal park fronting the ill-fated Palais Tuileries, which burned to the ground during a battle in 1871. But the area's layout has changed little since André Le Nôtre, Louis XIV's landscape architect, first designed it in the 17th century. The statues are all allegories—of the seasons, French rivers, the Nile, and the Tiber.

❺ Coysevox Statues. At the end of the garden, at the gates facing the Place de la Concorde, are copies of a set of elaborate statues originally created by Charles-Antoine Coysevox (1640–1720), one of Louis XIV's sculptors. They depict the gods Mercury and Fame riding winged horses.

The Grand Bassin in the Jardin des Tuileries.

Cimetière du Père-Lachaise

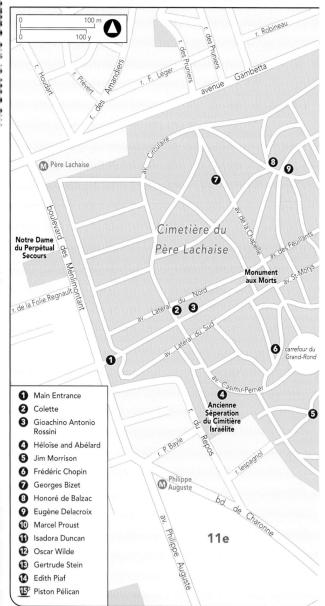

1. Main Entrance
2. Colette
3. Gioachino Antonio Rossini
4. Héloïse and Abélard
5. Jim Morrison
6. Frédéric Chopin
7. Georges Bizet
8. Honoré de Balzac
9. Eugène Delacroix
10. Marcel Proust
11. Isadora Duncan
12. Oscar Wilde
13. Gertrude Stein
14. Edith Piaf
15. Piston Pélican

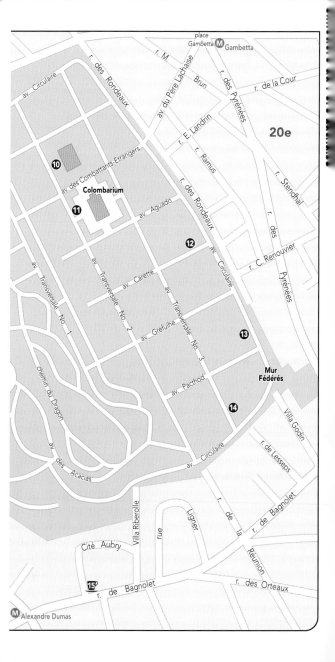

Père-Lachaise became one of the world's most famous cemeteries when Jim Morrison died (or didn't die, as some fans believe), in 1971. Almost immediately, Morrison's grave became a site of pilgrimage and the place filled with tourists, most of whom you can avoid if you stay away from Morrison's grave. Aside from its VIP RIPs, Père Lachaise is a peaceful place to get away from the hub-bub of city life. It's also a magnet for lovers of sculpture, who can admire some of Europe's most intricate and beautiful 19th-century tombstones. START: **Métro to Philippe-Auguste or Père Lachaise.**

❶ Main Entrance. Before you go, download a map from www.paris.fr/pages/cimetieres-117. *8 bd. de Ménilmontant.* ☎ *01-55-25-82-10. Free admission. Daily 8am (Sat 8:30am, Sun & public holidays 9am) to 6pm (winter until 5:30pm). Métro: Philippe-Auguste or Père-Lachaise.*

❷ Colette. French writer Sidonie-Gabrielle Colette published 50 novels. Her most famous story, *Gigi*, became a successful Broadway play and film. When she died in 1954, she was given a state funeral but was refused Roman Catholic rites because of her naughty lifestyle. *Section 4.*

❸ Gioachino Antonio Rossini. The Italian composer is best known for the operas *The Barber of Seville* and *William Tell,* the overture of which is one of the most famous in the world. His dramatic style led to his nickname among other composers—"Monsieur Crescendo." *Section 4.*

❹ Héloïse & Abelard. If you turn right down Avenue du Puits, near Colette's grave, you'll soon come to the oldest inhabitants of the cemetery. These star-crossed medieval lovers were kept apart their entire lives by Héloïse's family. Their passionate love letters to one another were published and have survived the ages. Abelard died first. Local lore maintains that when Héloïse died, a romantic abbess opened Abelard's grave to put Héloïse's body inside, and his corpse opened its arms to embrace his long-lost love. *Section 7.*

❺ Jim Morrison. If you must visit Morrison's grave, follow the crowds. The bust that once stood at the head of the tomb was stolen years ago by one of his "fans." The cigarette butts stubbed out on the grave are also courtesy of his "fans." As are the graffiti and the stench of old beer. What a mess. *Section 6.*

❻ Frédéric Chopin. Retrace your steps across Avenue Casimir-Périer to section 11, where you'll

Famed pianist Frédéric Chopin's tomb.

find the elaborate grave of the piano maestro marked with a statue of Erato, the muse of music. *Section 11.*

❼ Georges Bizet. The 19th-century composer of the impossibly infectious opera *Carmen* died 3 months after the premiere of his most famous work, convinced it was a failure. *Section 68.*

❽ Honoré de Balzac. The passionate French novelist wrote for up to 15 hours a day, drinking prodigious quantities of coffee to keep him going. His writing was often sloppy and uninspired, but it makes an excellent record of 19th-century Parisian life. *Section 48.*

❾ Eugène Delacroix. This dramatic and intensely romantic painter's *Liberty Leading the People* is a lesson in topless inspiration. In stark contrast, his tomb is sobriety incarnate: just a dark stone sculpture shaped like a coffin and decorated with a single row of white-centered flowers. *Section 49.*

❿ Marcel Proust. The wistful 19th-century novelist died before he could finish editing his famous series of books, *A la Recherche du Temps Perdu (In Search of Lost Time)*, yet he's considered one of the world's great writers. *Section 85.*

⓫ Isadora Duncan. The tragic death of this marvelous modern dancer is legendary—she favored long, dramatic scarves and convertibles, and one day one of those wrapped around the other and that was the end of Isadora. *Section 87.*

⓬ Oscar Wilde. The bluntly named Avenue des Étrangers Morts pour la France (Avenue of Dead Foreigners, basically) leads to the fantastical tomb of this gay 19th-century wit and writer. The size of the male genitals with which the statue atop the grave was

The dramatic tomb of Oscar Wilde.

equipped was quite the buzz in Paris until a vengeful woman knocked them off in the early 1960s. *Section 89.*

⓭ Gertrude Stein. The early-20th-century writer, art collector, and unlikely muse shares a simple double-sided tomb with her longtime companion, Alice B. Toklas. *Section 94.*

⓮ Edith Piaf. Just one more stop before you collapse—the resting place of famed French songbird Edith Piaf, beloved by broken-hearted lovers and gay men everywhere. *Section 97.*

⓯ Exit. If possible, leave the cemetery at Rue de la Réunion (this exit sometimes closes early), and from there head right down Rue de Bagnolet to the Alexandre Dumas Métro station. On the way, shabby-chic bar Le Piston Pélican is perfect for a glass of wine alongside arty crowds. *15 rue de Bagnolet, 20th. www.lepistonpelican.com. ☎ 01-43-71-15-76. Open noon–2:30pm, then from 6pm (closed Sun).*

Exploring the **Bois de Boulogne**

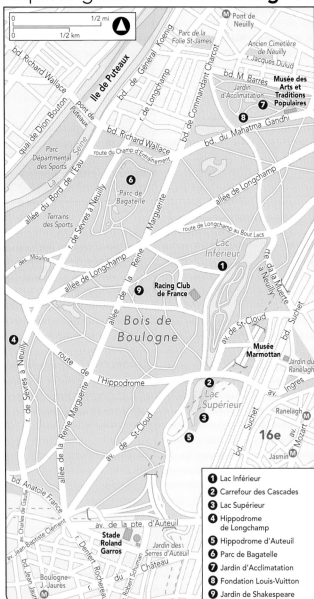

1. Lac Inférieur
2. Carrefour des Cascades
3. Lac Supérieur
4. Hippodrome de Longchamp
5. Hippodrome d'Auteuil
6. Parc de Bagatelle
7. Jardin d'Acclimatation
8. Fondation Louis-Vuitton
9. Jardin de Shakespeare

This former forest, once used for royal hunts, has two per-sonalities. By day, it's a family park where children gambol and ride ponies, while walkers and cyclists take in the beauty of its lakes and waterfalls. By night, it's one of the city's busiest prostitution districts and a hub for other nefarious activities, so make sure you get out before sundown. While you're there, however, you're in for a bucolic day amid birds, woodlands, and 19th-century tropical greenhouses. Between June and September, you can even take in music and theater (sometimes in English) among the sweet-scented roses of the Jardin de Shakespeare. START: **RER to Avenue Foch.**

❶ Lac Inférieur. Most easily accessed by way of Avenue Foch, this unfairly named lake (it's the larger of the two) has two pictur-esque islands connected by fanciful footbridges. You can rent a boat and paddle across to the islands' cafes and restaurants. On a hot summer day, it's also a perfect spot for a picnic.

❷ Carrefour des Cascades. The scenic walkway between the upper and lower lakes is an attraction in itself, with willows dipping their branches languorously in the water, and a handsome, fabricated waterfall creating a gorgeous backdrop. You can even walk under the waterfall.

❸ Lac Supérieur. The smaller of the two lakes has more of everything you find on the larger lake, with lots of boats to paddle and several res-taurants and cafes dotted about.

❹ Hippodrome de Longchamp. If your euros are burning a hole in your pocket, head to the southern end of the park, where two horse-racing courses—the excellent Hip-podrome de Longchamp and the smaller Hippodrome d'Auteuil (see next stop)—offer galloping action. The Qatar Prix de l'Arc de Triomphe held at Longchamp in September/ October is a major derby that draws people from all over the world. *Route des Tribunes, 16th. www. france-galop.com.* ☎ *01-44-30-75-00. Métro: Porte Maillot then bus 244 and get off at Carrefour de Longchamp.*

❺ Hippodrome d'Auteuil. This racetrack, the smaller of the two in Bois de Boulogne, is known for its heart-pounding steeplechases and obstacle courses. *Route d'Auteuil aux Lacs, 16th. www.france-galop. com.* ☎ *01-40-71-47-47. Métro: Porte d'Auteuil-Hippodrome.*

Paddling in the Bois de Boulogne, known as the green lung of the French capital.

Bois de Boulogne: Practical Matters

Bois de Boulogne is open daily from dawn to dusk. Because it's such a large park, it has several entrances and several public transportation options. Nearby Métro stops include Les Sablons (north, on av. Charles de Gaulle), Porte Maillot (northeast, on av. de la Grande Armée), Porte Dauphine (northeast, on av. Foch), or Porte d'Auteuil (southeast, on av. de la Porte d'Auteuil). Take the RER to Avenue Foch or Avenue Henri Martin. In the park are numerous cafes and restaurants. A miniature train runs to the Jardin d'Acclimatation from Porte Maillot—a fun touch for kids. You won't be able to do the whole of the Bois in one day, but to see a maximum of sites, do as Parisians do, and grab a self-service Vélib' bike for the day (1-day passes 5€–10€; see p 183). A handy bike station is near the park's entrance at Porte Maillot: no. 16003 at 2 bis boulevard André-Maurois.

⑥ Parc de Bagatelle. In the shadow of a bijou château built for Marie-Antoinette, this romantic 18th-century park-within-a-park in the northwest of Bois de Boulogne is a riot of colorful tulips in spring, and the rose garden blooms spectacularly by late May. A sequence of little bridges, grottoes, and water features also make it one of Paris's most popular spots for a tryst. *www.paris.fr/lieux/parc-de-bagatelle-1808.* ☎ *01-40-67-97-00. Métro: Porte d'Auteuil or Jasmin.*

⑦ ★★ kids Jardin d'Acclimatation. Those with small children may want to head straight to this amusement park on the north end of Bois de Boulogne, which boasts colorful rides, a small zoo, and a kid-size train. *See p 31,* ⑥.

⑧ ★ Fondation Louis-Vuitton. Architect Frank Gehry is the brain behind this slick creation—all futuristic glass and metal sails. It's stunningly incongruous when seen emerging through the Bois de Boulogne's tree-lined paths. Inside, expect innovative art exhibitions by a plethora of international names,

Riding the rockets at Jardin d'Acclimatation.

and contemporary classical music concerts. *See p 45,* ⑤.

⑨ ★★ Jardin de Shakespeare. This must be one of the most beautiful open-air theaters in the world— a lawn encircled by bright, buzzing flowerbeds and draping trees. Every summer, it becomes the idyllic stage for music and theater productions. *In the Jardin Pré-Catelan. www.paris.fr/lieux/pre-catelan-et-jardin-shakespeare-2780. Métro: Porte de la Muette.* ●

Dining Best Bets

Best for Steak Frites
★★ Le Relais de l'Entrecôte $$
101 bd du Montparnasse, 6th (p 121)

Best for High Tea
★★ Angélina $$ *226 rue de Rivoli,
1st (p 114)*

Best for Kids
★ Schwartz's $–$$ *16 rue des
Ecouffes, 4th (p 122)*

Best Cheap Meal in Belle Epoque Surroundings
★★ Bouillon Julien $ *16 rue du
Faubourg St Denis, 10th (p 115)*

Best Cutting-edge Cuisine
★★★ Le Grand Restaurant $$$$$
7 rue d'Aguesseau, 8th (p 120)

Best Vegetarian
★★ Le Potager du Marais $$ *26
rue St-Paul, 4th (p 121)*

Best Seafood
★★★ Restaurant Auguste $$$$
54 rue de Bourgogne, 7th (p 121)

Best for a Michelin-Starred Feast
★★★ La Dame de Pic $$$$$ *20
rue du Louvre, 1st (p 118)*

Best Big Portions
★★ Chez Gladines $ *44 bd Saint-
Germain, 5th (p 116)*

Best for Food Critics
★★★ Restaurant Eels $$ *27 rue
d'Hauteville, 10th (p 121)*

Best Meal on a Boat
★★★ Don Juan II $$$$$ *5 Port
Debilly, 16th (p 117)*

Best for Contemporary French Cuisine
★★ Septime $$$$ *80 rue de Charonne, 11th (p 122)*

Best Cheap Lunch
Higuma $ *32 bis rue Ste-Anne, 1st
(p 118)*

Best Romantic Summer Splurge
★★ Lasserre $$$$ *17 av. Franklin
Roosevelt, 8th (p 119)*

Best Grandiose Setting
★★★ Le Jules Verne $$$$$ *Eiffel
Tower, 7th (p 120)*

Best Local's Haunt
★★★ Au Petit Panisse $$ *35 rue
de Montreuil, 11th (p 114)*

Best Food in a Tourist Spot
★ Le Fumoir $$ *6 rue de l'Amiral de
Coligny, 1st (p 119)*

Previous page: At Le Jules Verne, your table has a view from the Eiffel Tower.

Right Bank (8th & 16th–17th)

Don Juan II 1
Lasserre 2
Le Coq & Fils 4
Le Grand Restaurant 3

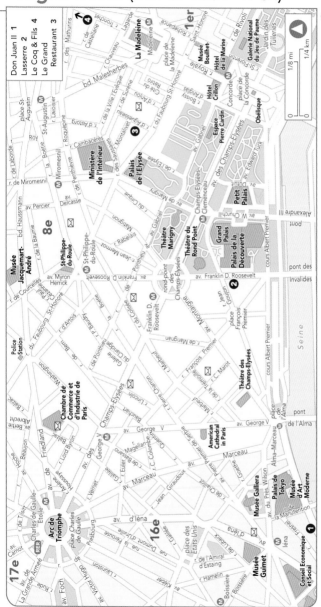

Right Bank (1st–4th & 9th–11th)

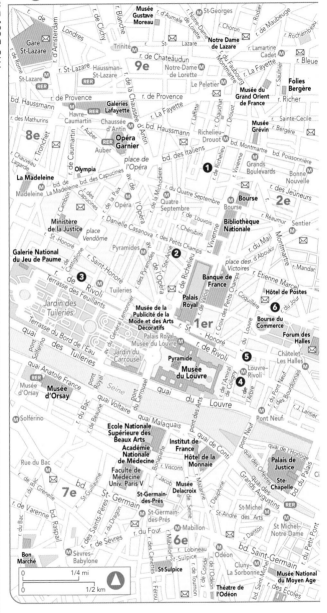

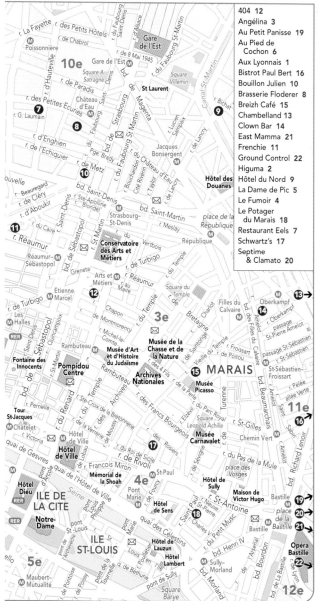

404 **12**
Angélina **3**
Au Petit Panisse **19**
Au Pied de Cochon **6**
Aux Lyonnais **1**
Bistrot Paul Bert **16**
Bouillon Julien **10**
Brasserie Floderer **8**
Breizh Café **15**
Chambelland **13**
Clown Bar **14**
East Mamma **21**
Frenchie **11**
Ground Control **22**
Higuma **2**
Hôtel du Nord **9**
La Dame de Pic **5**
Le Fumoir **4**
Le Potager du Marais **18**
Restaurant Eels **7**
Schwartz's **17**
Septime & Clamato **20**

Left Bank (5th–7th, 14th)

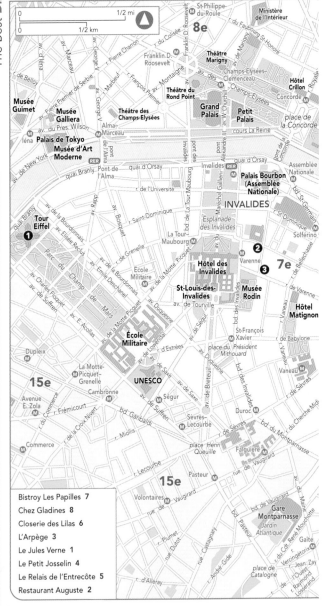

Bistroy Les Papilles **7**

Chez Gladines **8**

Closerie des Lilas **6**

L'Arpège **3**

Le Jules Verne **1**

Le Petit Josselin **4**

Le Relais de l'Entrecôte **5**

Restaurant Auguste **2**

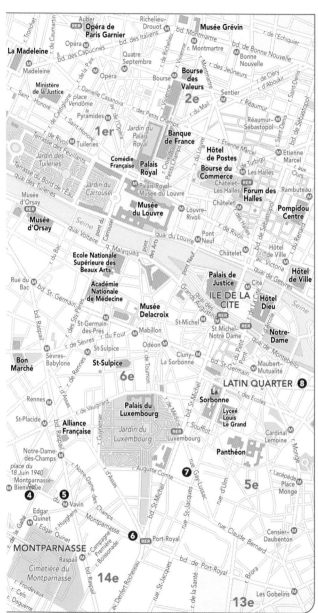

Restaurants A to Z

Diners under the vaulted arcades of the Marais district.

★★ **404** MARAIS *NORTH AFRICAN* Step through this restaurant's 16th-century doorway and you're in another world—a supercool Berber world of poufs, North African carpets, and mouthwatering Moroccan dishes. Feeling hungry? The harira soup starter (chickpeas, lamb, and lentils) is almost a meal on its own. Follow it with the 404 Couscous (with lamb skewers and hot merguez sausages) and you'll be wishing you wore your stretchy pants.

A selection of pastries at Angélina.

But do save room for dessert: The pastries and Berber pancakes with honey are delectable. *69 rue des Gravilliers, 3rd. www.404-resto.com.* ☎ *01-42-74-57-81. Prix-fixe lunch from 19€, entrees 20€–34€. Lunch & dinner daily, brunch Sat & Sun. Métro: Arts et Métiers. Map p 110.*

★★ **Angélina** TUILERIES *TEA SHOP* This traditional salon de thé serves its high-society patrons tea, pastries, and sandwiches on silver platters. If you have a sweet tooth, try the Mont Blanc, a gooey meringue, cream, and chestnut cake. The hot chocolate is some of the best in Paris too. It's popular, so be prepared to wait in line. *226 rue de Rivoli, 1st. www.angelina-paris.fr.* ☎ *01-42-60-82-00. Fixed-price breakfast 22€–32€, brunch 42€, entrees 17€–31€, tea 9€–20€. Breakfast, lunch & tea daily. Métro: Tuileries or Concorde. Map p 110.*

★★★ **Au Petit Panisse** FAIDHERBE *FRENCH* This retro-style café, with its bric-a-brac furniture, is where freelancing parents on the post-school run go for coffee and end up staying for lunch. The reason? The aromas floating from the kitchen around 10am are

Au Pied de Cochon serves fresh seafood around the clock.

so delicious it's hard to walk away. People stay (laptop in tow) for the 18€ fixed-price lunch menu, which might include dishes like sea snails with caper mayo, or duck tartare. At night, the a la carte dinner is just as wonderful. *35 rue de Montreuil, 11th.* ☎ *01-43-71-37-90. Fixed-price lunch 18€. Entrees 19€–25€. Breakfast, lunch & dinner daily. Métro: Faidherbe-Chaligny or Rue des Boulets. Map p 110.*

★★ Au Pied de Cochon LES
HALLES *FRENCH* Where else in Paris can you get such a good meal at 3am? Specialties include onion soup, grilled pigs' feet with béarnaise sauce, and *andouillettes* (sausages). On the street outside, the restaurant sells some of the freshest oysters in town. *6 rue Coquillière, 1st. www.pieddecochon.com.* ☎ *01-40-13-77-00. Entrees 17€–48€. Breakfast 6.50€–13€. Daily 8am–5am. Métro: Les Halles or Louvre Rivoli. Map p 110.*

★★ Aux Lyonnais GRANDS
BOULEVARDS *LYONNAIS* Famed chef Alain Ducasse, the best in Paris at Lyonnais cuisine, creates such dishes as calf's liver with parsley, pike dumplings, skate meunière, and peppery coq au vin in a restaurant designed to look like a 19th-century bistro. *32 rue St-Marc, 2nd. www.auxlyonnais.com.* ☎ *01-42-96-65-04. Reservations required. Prix-fixe menu 55€ (lunch), entrees 36€. Lunch & dinner Wed–Sat, lunch*

Sun. Métro: Grands Boulevards. Map p 110.

★★★ kids Bistrot Paul Bert
FAIDHERBE *FRENCH* This locals' haunt has old tile floors and a real zinc bar—just as a Parisian bistro should be. The food is just as authentic, and also delicious: crispy duck confit with garlicky potatoes, homemade pâtés, and possibly the best île flottante (whisked egg whites in a vanilla sauce) in town. *11 rue Paul Bert, 12th. https://bistrotpaulbert.fr.* ☎ *01-43-72-24-01. Entrees 20€–44€. 3-course lunch menu 24€. Lunch & dinner Tues–Sat. Métro: Faidherbe-Chaligny. Map p 110.*

★★ Bistroy Les Papilles LATIN
QUARTER *BISTRO/WINE BAR* Lined with shelves upon shelves of delectable bottles, this bustling wine shop/bistro/gourmet grocery matches simple but excellent fare with terrific samples of the fruit of the vine. At lunchtime, the fixed-price menu offers great value—four courses for 40€—but no choices. If you don't want the menu, try the *marmite du marché*, the stew of the day served in a cast-iron pot (around 20€). *30 rue Gay-Lussac, 5th. www.lespapillesparis.fr.* ☎ *01-43-25-20-79. Entrees 24€–32€; fixed-price lunch 40€. Tues–Sat lunch & dinner. RER: Luxembourg. Map p 112.*

★★ kids Bouillon Julien
NORTH EAST *TRADITIONAL FRENCH* This unpretentious,

affordable fin-de-siècle restaurant has glorious Art Nouveau decor and the sort of dishes Parisians have been eating for decades—try the beef bourguignon (in red-wine sauce), the sausage in mustard sauce, or the fish sauerkraut. Look for the mahogany bar: It's an Art Nouveau original by Louis Majorelle—a pure work of art. Reserve in advance, or wait in a long line. *16 rue du Faubourg Saint-Denis, 10th. www.bouillon-julien.com.* ☎ *01-47-70-12-06. Entrees 8.90€– 14€. Lunch & dinner daily. Métro: Strasbourg Saint-Denis. Map p 110.*

★★ Brasserie Floderer
NORTHEAST PARIS *TRADITIONAL FRENCH* This Alsatian restaurant is a bit hard to find, down a discreet cobbled passage, but you'll be glad you tracked it down when you try the onion soup, sole meunière, or the steak, flambéed at your table. *7 cour des Petites-Ecuries, 10th. www.floderer-paris.com.* ☎ *01-47-70-13-59. Reservations recommended. Entrees 20€–45€, prix-fixe lunch & dinner 28€–36€. Lunch & dinner daily. Métro: Château d'Eau or Strasbourg-St-Denis. Map p 110.*

★★ kids Breizh Café
MARAIS *CRÊPERIE* You could be in Brittany at this upbeat modern creperie (as one of eight in Paris intra muros), which uses top-notch, mostly organic produce in its unusual and delicious fillings: Think potato and smoked herring, or 70% cocoa solids in the chocolate dessert crêpes. You can wash it all down with one of 15 artisanal ciders. *109 rue Vieille-du-Temple, 3rd. www.breizhcafe.com.* ☎ *01-42-72-13-77. Crêpes 7.50€–18€. Lunch & dinner daily. Métro: Filles du Calvaire. Map p 110.*

★★ kids Chamfelland
OBERKAMPF *ORGANIC GLUTEN-FREE* Every single product in this fabulous bakery and cafe is gluten-free. But don't be fooled: So utterly

Putting the finishing touches on some gluten-free pastries at Chambelland.

delicious are the items (think door-stop sandwiches made with bread baked in the cellar, and sweet chestnut muffins) that most of the clientele don't have gluten allergies. Come for breakfast, lunch, or an early-evening snack (closing is at 7:30pm, 6pm on Sun); and on a sunny day, sit outside and watch the locals stroll to and fro across the tranquil square. *14 rue Ternaux, 11th. http://chambelland.com.* ☎ *01-43-55-07-30. Sandwiches 8€. Breakfast & lunch Tues–Sun. Métro: Parmentier or Oberkampf. Map p 110.*

★★ kids Chez Gladines
SAINT-GERMAIN-DES-PRÈS *SOUTH-WESTERN* Hungry? Come here for enormous and tasty portions of rib-sticking southwestern French specialties. That means crispy duck confit with sautéed potatoes; Basque-style chicken (with tomatoes and bell peppers); *and* gargantuan salads, filled with goodies like bacon, goat cheese, smoked ham, and foie gras, the lot topped with fried potatoes. *44 bd Saint-Germain, 5th. www.gladines.com.* ☎ *01-46-33-93-88. Entrees 10€–15€. Lunch & dinner daily. Métro: Maubert Mutualité. Map p 112.*

★★★ Closerie des Lilas

MONTPARNASSE *TRADITIONAL FRENCH* This restaurant and brasserie was a favorite of Gertrude Stein, Hemingway, and Picasso (not to mention Lenin and Trotsky—a revolution marches on its stomach, apparently). Have a champagne julep before stuffing yourself with filet of beef in Bourbon sauce (Hemingway's favorite), prepared at your table. *171 bd. du Montparnasse, 6th. www.closeriedeslilas.fr. ☎ 01-40-51-34-50. Reservations far in advance for the restaurant, not needed for the brasserie. Restaurant entrees 32€–60€; brasserie entrees 23€–33€. Lunch & dinner daily. Métro: Port Royal or Vavin. Map p 112.*

★★★ Clown Bar

BASTILLE/MARAIS *MODERN FRENCH* This charming restaurant is the lair of food-savvy locals who squeeze into its jam-packed dining room to sample innovative takes on French classics, such as panko-fried snails and hearty duck pie. If the menu doesn't convince you, the setting should: Adorned in clown-themed Belle Epoque tiles, it's one of the prettiest dining rooms in town. Rumor has it that Toulouse Lautrec used to prop himself up at the zinc bar. *114 rue Amelot, 3rd. www.clown-bar-paris.fr. ☎ 01-43-55-87-35. Entrees 28€–31€. Lunch & dinner Mon–Fri. Métro: Filles du Calvaire or Oberkampf. Map p 110.*

★★★ Don Juan II

TROCADERO *FRENCH* Imagine yourself floating down the Seine on an Art Deco boat, tucking into Michelin-starred cuisine as the city's sparkling monuments flit past your window like moving postcards. Chef Frédéric Anton's 190-minute dinner cruise offers just this, and it's the stuff travel dreams are made of. The single, five-course dinner menu costs 240€, but it includes memorable dishes like fennel cream with caviar, langoustine ravioli, and pan-fried lamb with nutmeg, the lot topped off with the best chocolate soufflé in town. Reservations required. *Yacht de Paris, 5 Port de Debilly (opposite the Eiffel Tower), 16th. ☎ 01-83-77-44-40. Fixed-price dinner 240€. Dinner Tues–Sat. Métro: Iéna. Map p 109.*

★★ kids East Mamma

BASTILLE *ITALIAN/PIZZA* This place regularly has a line out the door. The reason? Quite simply some of the tastiest, freshest pizzas, pastas, and cocktails in town, served in a beautiful rustico-1970s dining room with an open kitchen; shelves of Parmesan cheese; and shiny, metal barrels of olive oil. To avoid the evening lines, arrive before 6:50pm or after 9pm. Throughout Paris, six other locations serve everything from pizza to steak (check the website for details). *133 rue du Faubourg St-Antoine, 11th. www.bigmamma.fr. ☎ 01-43-41-32-15. Pizzas from 12€. Lunch & dinner daily. Métro: Ledru Rollin. Map p 110.*

★ Frenchie

SENTIER *MODERN FRENCH* In the gentrifying Sentier

The stunning view from Don Juan II.

garment district, this teeny restaurant is one of the buzziest eateries in town. Book at least 1 month in advance for the 7pm sitting (3 months for 9:30pm). Get in, and you'll rejoice over a 140€ prix-fixe menu with dishes like red tuna with preserved lemon, and chicken in gooseberry and mustard sauce. If it's full, turn up anyway (at 6:30pm): you can leave your name with the staff, then hit their wine bar over the road. If there's a no-show they'll call you; if not, you can still fill up on great finger food and atmosphere. *5 rue du Nil, 2nd. www.frenchie-ruedunil.com.* ☎ *01-40-39-96-19. Tasting menu 140€. Dinner Mon–Fri. Métro: Sentier or Bonne Nouvelle. Map p 110.*

★★ 🧒 **Ground Control** GARE DE LYON *STREET FOOD* There's an underground feel to this sprawling venue near Gare de Lyon, a vast multidisciplinary arts center with its own radio station, exhibition spaces, and a food hall set in disused SNCF hangars. The food court is the place to get delicious Chinese, Mexican, and Central African Republic dishes, plus coffee and cake for dessert. Outside, converted buses hawk everything from British fish and chips, to ham and cheese crepes, to fresh oysters, with seating at vintage benches and tables. Just make sure you get your drink before you order food. None of the stalls sell beverages, and it's annoying to have to wait in line while your food is hot. *81 rue du Charolais, 12th. No phone. www.ground controlparis.com. Main courses 8€–16€. Lunch & dinner daily. Métro/RER: Gare de Lyon. Map p 110.*

Higuma OPERA *JAPANESE* This no-frills Japanese canteen is always full, so get here early (before noon for lunch and before 6:30pm for dinner) if you don't want to queue in the street at mealtimes. The reasons behind its popularity are the quirky open kitchen, which fills the air with delicious-smelling steam, and the low prices—around 9€ for a giant bowl of soup, rice, or noodles, piled high with meat, seafood, or stir-fried vegetables. *32 bis rue Ste-Anne, 1st. www.higuma.fr.* ☎ *01-47-03-38-59. Prix-fixe menu from 13€, entrees 9€–12€. Lunch & dinner daily. Métro: Pyramides. Map p 110.*

★ **Hôtel du Nord** CANAL SAINT MARTIN *FRENCH* With 1930s-inspired decor and oodles of history (it gave its name to Marcel Carné's 1938 classic movie, *Hôtel du Nord*), this lowkey canal-side eatery is perfect for an inexpensive meal with atmosphere. My favorites are the beef carpaccio with *frites*, and, for dessert, the crème-brûlée. Simple, but satisfying! *102 Quai de Jemmapes, 10th. www.hoteldunord.org.* ☎ *01-40-40-78-78. Entrees 18€–35€, prix-fixe lunch 17€. Breakfast, lunch & dinner daily. Métro: République or Jacques Bonsergent. Map p 110.*

★★★ **La Dame de Pic** LOUVRE *CONTEMPORARY FRENCH* Run by Michelin-starred chef Anne-Sophie Pic, this restaurant exudes

Higuma features an open kitchen, tasty soups, and low prices.

savoir-faire. Choose your menu using your sense of smell: The waiters offer perfumed cards that correspond to ingredients used in the dishes. Then tuck into veal with bacon and saffron, or pigeon with rhubarb, and such desserts as strawberry and mint baba—all as photogenic as they are delicious. *20 rue du Louvre, 1st. www.ladamedepic.fr.* ☎ *01-42-60-40-40. Prix-fixe lunch 90€, prix-fixe dinner 120€–195€. Lunch & dinner Wed–Sun. Métro: Louvre-Rivoli. Map p 110.*

★★ **L'Arpège** INVALIDES *FRENCH* Supplies for this exclusive eatery come from chef Alain Passard's own farms in the Sarthe, Eure, and Mont-Saint-Michel regions, where horses replace polluting machinery, and pesticides (when necessary) are vegetable-based. Expect such Michelin-starred dishes as roasted Brittany turbot with smoked potatoes and blue lobster in honey. *84 rue de Varenne, 7th. www.alain-passard.com.* ☎ *01-47-05-09-06. Entrees 152€–240€. Prix-fixe lunch 185€, prix-fixe dinner 520€. Lunch & dinner Mon–Fri. Métro: Varenne. Map p 112.*

★★ **Lasserre** CHAMPS-ÉLYSÉES *HAUTE FRENCH* Eating here, with fine cutlery and elegant porcelain, waiters plying to your every whim, and Michelin-starred food on your plate, is a treat available to only a lucky few (celebrity guests have included Salvador Dalí, Audrey Hepburn, and Robert De Niro). If you can afford it, do it, especially in summer, when the restaurant roof opens to let in the dwindling light and the warm breeze. It's desperately romantic. *17 av. Franklin Roosevelt, 8th. www.restaurant-lasserre. com.* ☎ *01-43-59-02-13. Reservations required. Prix-fixe dinner 170€–310€, entrees 85€–180€. Dinner Thurs–Sat. Métro: Champs-Élysées Clémenceau. Map p 109.*

The elegant dining room at La Dame de Pic.

★★ **Le Coq & Fils** MONTMARTRE *ROTISSERIE* Bohemian-bourgeois foodies climb up Montmartre's Butte for a table at this "bistro of beautiful birds." And rightly so: The pedigreed roast chicken is succulent every time and comes with lip-smacking gravy and crunch-perfect *frites*. Add to that the humongous *mille-feuilles au chocolat* (layers of pastry and chocolate cream), and the open kitchen, and you're in rotisserie heaven. *98 rue Lepic, 18th. https://lecoq-fils. com.* ☎ *01-42-59-82-89. Entrees 18€–52€, whole chickens for 4 people 132€–150€. Lunch & dinner daily. Métro: Blanche. Map p 109.*

★ **Le Fumoir** LOUVRE *BISTRO* This handy spot near the Louvre and Arts Décoratifs museums has a faithful following from Paris's literary and media crowds. Sink into a Chesterfield armchair and order a refreshing cocktail or fill up on Franco-Scandinavian dishes like herrings with cucumber cream or rump steak with bone marrow. *6 rue de l'Amiral de Coligny, 1st. www.lefumoir.com.* ☎ *01-42-92-00-24. Entrees average 20€; lunch from 30€; prix-fixe dinner*

from 40€. Lunch & dinner daily.
Métro: Louvre-Rivoli. Map p 110.

★★★ Le Grand Restaurant
CHAMPS-ÉLYSÉES *CONTEMPO-
RARY HAUTE CUISINE* Not far
from the Palais de l'Élysée (the
French President's home and work-
place), this sleek restaurant not only
looks good (all steely greys and
geometric diamond-shapes, including a futuristic glass ceiling), it's
also the city's most exciting place
for a meal-splurge. Genius chef
Jean-François Piège delights with
such dreamy dishes as air-blown
potato with caviar, a spaghetti
tower with belly pork and truffles,
and venison served on sugared
chestnuts. *7 rue Aguesseau, 8th.
www.jeanfrancoispiege.com.
☎ 01-53-05-00-00. Reservations
required. Prix-fixe lunch & dinner
146€ & 246€, prix-fixe dinner on Tues
590€ (with wine). Lunch Thurs–Fri,
dinner Mon–Fri. Métro: Madeleine or
Franklin D. Roosevelt. Map p 109.*

★★★ Le Jules Verne EIFFEL
TOWER *MODERN FRENCH*
Sometimes Paris is about embracing the clichés, and dining on the
2nd floor of the Eiffel Tower is

definitely a cliché worth embracing.
Not only are the views magnificent,
with the city's iconic rooftops
undulating in graceful higgledy-
piggledydom, but award-winning
chef Frédéric Anton's food is also
worth writing home about. Try won-
ders like langoustine ravioli in tarra-
gon sauce, vanilla-salted pigeon,
and a bitter chocolate soufflé. Then
look out the window and sigh. Reservations required at least 2 months
in advance. *2nd floor of Eiffel Tower,
av. Gustave Eiffel, 7th. www.
restaurants-toureiffel.com. ☎ 01-83-
77-34-34. Prix-fixe lunch 140€ (Mon–
Fri only), prix-fixe tasting menu lunch
& dinner 215€ & 255€. Daily lunch &
dinner. Métro: Bir-Hakeim or Troca-
déro/RER Champs de Mars Tour
Eiffel. Map p 112.*

★★ Le Petit Josselin MONT-
PARNASSE *CRÊPERIE* Of the dozens of crêperies concentrated near
the Montparnasse train station, this
tiny dining room is one of the best.
The *galettes* and crepes are perfectly cooked with lacy, crispy
edges, and include fillings like
bacon and egg, smoked salmon,
and the can-do-no-wrong classic
ham and cheese. Try to save room

Crepes at Le Petit Josselin.

for a sweet crepe after—the salted caramel butter crepe is a wonder. Tradition demands that this meal be accompanied by a bowl of "brut" cider (low alcohol content, for adults only). *59 rue du Montparnasse, 14th. www.creperielepetit josselin.fr.* ☎ *01-43-22-91-81. Entrees 6€–15€. Mon–Sat lunch & dinner. Métro: Edgar Quinet. Map p 112.*

★★ Le Potager du Marais

MARAIS *VEGETARIAN*   Vegetarians and vegans flock to this organic offering, arguably the best of its kind in Paris. Dishes are so tasty that meat eaters won't complain. The welcome is warm, and many items are gluten-free. *26 rue St. Paul, 4th. www.lepotagerdumarais.fr.* ☎ *01-57-40-98-57. Entrees 14€–18€. Lunch & dinner Wed–Sun. Métro: Saint-Paul. Map p 110.*

★★ kids Le Relais de l'Entrecôte

MONTPARNASSE *FRENCH*   When you're hankering after a decent *steak-frites* (steak and fries), this is the place to come. The only real choice on the menu is for dessert (think chocolate profiteroles or lemon sorbet); for the rest it's the cut of the day, skinny fries, and the restaurant's secret sauce. Wine starts at a reasonable 20€/bottle. Other branches can be found at 20 rue Saint-Benoît, 6th, and 14 rue Marbeuf, 8th. *101 bd du Montparnasse, 6th. www.relais entrecote.fr.* ☎ *01-46-33-82-82. Entrees 28€. Lunch & dinner daily. Métro: Vavin. Map p 112.*

★★★ Restaurant Auguste

INVALIDES *SEAFOOD*   One of the city's best seafood restaurants draws crowds with such dishes as scallops with foie gras and enoki mushrooms or lacquered monkfish with lobster oil and nutmeg, and just plain oysters. Chef Gael Orieux's love of the sea has led him to become spokesperson for an

The elegant seafood at Restaurant Eels.

association dedicated to protecting the oceans, so what you see on your plate is not only delicious, but also ecologically correct. *54 rue de Bourgogne, 7th. www.restaurant auguste.fr.* ☎ *01-45-51-61-09. Entrees 49€–66€, lunch menus from 44€, dinner prix-fixe 95€. Lunch & dinner Mon–Fri. Métro: Varenne p 112.*

★★★ Restaurant Eels

NORTH EAST *CONTEMPORARY FRENCH*   Foodies have been flocking to this fabulous seafood-oriented bistro ever since it opened in 2017. And once you've tasted the namesake starter of smoked eels with apple, you'll understand why. Every single dish is a taste explosion—from the grilled sea trout with confit of fennel to the veal haunch with caper leaves, and the chocolate crisp with cardamom and pomegranate cream. At 39€, the three-course lunch menu is a steal. If you're up for an all-gourmet experience, the 79€ five-course tasting menu is a special experience. *27 rue d'Hauteville, 10th. www.restaurant-eels.com.* ☎ *01-42-28-80-20. Entrees 25€–34€. Lunch &*

Sometimes, even in Paris, you need a burger.

dinner Tues–Sat. Métro: Bonne Nouvelle or Poisonnière. Map p 110.

★ kids **Schwartz's** MARAIS JEWISH   This New York–style Jewish deli bustles throughout the day with hungry folk looking to fill up on smoked herring, pastrami, chunky bagels, burgers, and hot dogs. The cheesecake is a treat. *16 rue des Ecouffes, 4th. www.schwartzs deli.fr.* ☎ *01-48-87-31-29. Entrees 12.50€–20€. Lunch & dinner daily. Métro: St-Paul. Map p 110.*

★★ **Septime & Clamato** CHARONNE *CONTEMPORARY FRENCH*   With reservations made at least a month in advance, people cross the city for this rustic-chic eatery near Bastille. The hype? Such dishes as succulent pork with caramelized rutabaga, smoked duck with leek and ricotta, mackerel with asparagus, and roasted apple with cream—all flawless. Next door is the seafood tapas bar Clamato, which makes you feel as though you've been transported to the seaside; at the tiny wine bar across the street, Septime La Cave, you can enjoy an aperitif before heading over for your meal. *80 rue de Charonne, 11th. www.septime-charonne.fr.* ☎ *01-43-67-38-29. Prix-fixe lunch 65€, dinner 105€. Lunch & dinner Mon–Fri. (Clamato Mon–Fri lunch & dinner, Sat–Sun lunch.) Métro: Charonne. Map p 110.* ●

You can get modern French comfort food at Septime, or tapas next door at Clamato.

Nightlife Best Bets

Best Bohemian Bar
★★ Chez Prune, 36 rue Beaurepaire, 10th (p 133)

Best Chic Cocktails
★★★ Experimental Cocktail Club, 37 rue St-Sauveur, 2nd (p 133)

Best Place to Steal a Kiss
★★ La Palette, 43 rue de Seine, 6th (p 134)

Best Wine Bar
★★ Le Baron Rouge, 1 rue Théophile-Roussel, 12th (p 136)

Best for Paris-Brewed Beer
★★ Paname Brewing Company, 41 bis Quai de la Loire, 19th (p 135)

Best for Ping-Pong Fans
★★ Gossima, 4 rue Victor Gelez, 11th (p 133)

Best for Fans of Papa
★★★ Harry's Bar, 5 rue Daunou, 2nd (p 134)

Best for Swing & Jazz
★★ Caveau de la Huchette, 5 rue de la Huchette, 5th (p 130)

Best Outdoor Partying
★★ Rosa Bonheur, 2 allée de la Cascade, Parc des Buttes Chaumont, 19th (p 135)

Best Hip Club
★★ Bonnie, 10 rue Agrippa d'Aubigné, 4th (p 130)

Best Speakeasy
★★★ Candelaria, 52 rue Saintonge, 3rd (p 133)

Best Rooftop Drinks
★★★ Le Perchoir, 14 rue Crespin du Gast, 11th (p 134)

Best Cutting-Edge Club
★★ Sacré, 142 rue de Montmartre, 2nd (p 131)

Best for the Latest Electro Sounds
★★ Rex Club, 5 bd. Poissonnière, 2nd (p 131)

Best Gay Bars
★★★ Café Cox, 15 rue des Archives, 4th (p 131)

Best Lesbian Club
★★ Chez Moune, 54 rue Jean-Baptiste Pigalle, 9th (p 132)

Best Boudoir
★★★ Wilde's Lounge at L'Hôtel, 13 rue des Beaux-Arts, 6th (p 135)

Previous page: Start a night out in Paris with a view of the sparkling Eiffel Tour.

Montmartre & Pigalle (9th & 18th)

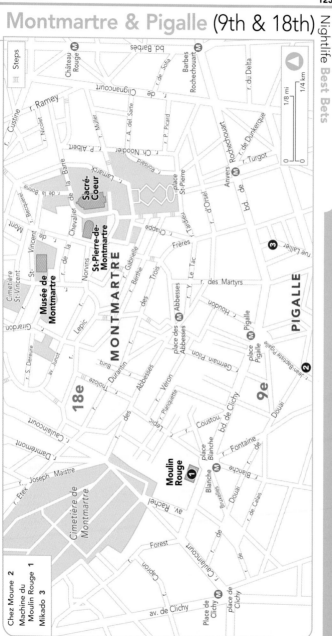

Chez Moune 2
Machine du
Moulin Rouge 1
Mikado 3

Right Bank (1st–4th & 9th–11th)

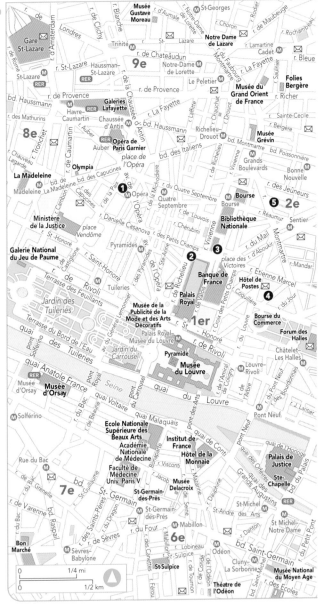

BAPBAP 10
Bonnie 20
Café Cox 16
Candelaria 14
Caves Legrand 3
Chez Prune 9
Experimental
  Cocktail Club 18
Favela Chic 7
Frenchie Bar à Vin 11
Gossima Ping Pong Bar 10
Harry's Bar 1
Juveniles 2
La Belle Hortense 17
La Cave à Michel 9
La Vache dans les Vignes 19
Le Baron Rouge 19
Le Perchoir 12
Le Tango 13
Moonshiner 4
Mutinerie 15
Paname Brewing Company 8
Rex Club 6
Rosa Bonheur 9
Sacré 5

Left Bank (5th–7th, 13th)

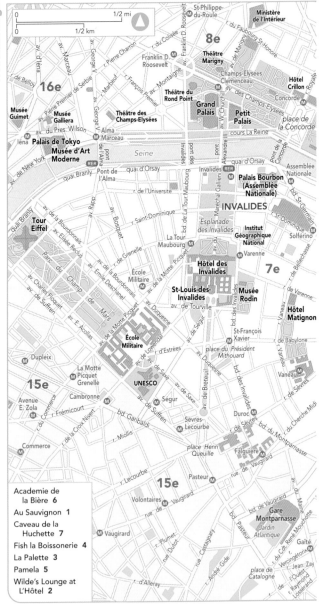

Academie de la Bière 6
Au Sauvignon 1
Caveau de la Huchette 7
Fish la Boissonerie 4
La Palette 3
Pamela 5
Wilde's Lounge at L'Hôtel 2

Dancing at Caveau de la Huchette.

Dance Clubs

★★ Bonnie SULLY MORLAND
On the 16th floor of the chic SO/
PARIS hotel, with floor-to-ceiling
windows over the Seine, the
Islands, and even, in the distance,
the Eiffel Tower, this exclusive
retro-chic club is a fashion-week
favorite, packing in the young and
energetic for dancing and cocktails
to the sound of '60s and '70s music.
It's hard to get in, so dress up, or
reserve a table and champagne in
advance. *10 rue Agrippa d'Aubigné,
4th. https://bonnie-restaurant.com.*
☎ *01-78-90-74-74. No cover. Métro:
Sully Morland. Map p 126.*

★★ Caveau de la Huchette
LATIN QUARTER   This rocking
club has an emphasis on good
times and loud funk, jazz, and classic swing; the crowd tends to be in
their 30s and above. *5 rue de la
Huchette, 5th. www.caveaudela
huchette.fr.* ☎ *01-43-26-65-05.
Cover 10€–15€. Métro: St-Michel.
Map p 128.*

★★ Favela Chic RÉPUBLIQUE
This Brazilian hot spot is where
patrons dance to bossa jazz, samba
rap, and tropical electro into the
wee hours of the night. Sip cocktails in the 1930s-inspired speakeasy beforehand, and come early
for dinner in the restaurant, which
whips up big plates of Franco-
Brazilian delights (service is sometimes slow). *18 rue du Faubourg du
Temple, 11th. www.favelachic.com.*
☎ *01-40-21-38-14. No cover. Métro:
République. Map p 126.*

**★★ Machine du Moulin
Rouge** MONTMARTRE   Set in the
nightclub adjoining Paris's most
famous cabaret, this is the latest
hot spot for electronic music lovers.
Expect DJ sets by famous names, a
big dance floor, and youthful club
kids soaking up the vibes. *90 bd. de
Clichy, 18th. www.lamachinedumoulin
rouge.com. No phone. Cover free to
30€. Métro: Blanche. Map p 125.*

★★ Mikado PIGALLE   Dressed
up like an Art Deco speakeasy, this

not-so-late-night club (it closes at 2am) sits beneath the Hôtel Rochechouart and woos with the promise of cool electro music, the occasional live band, and excellent cocktails. Try the namesake Mikado, made with gin, verbena, apple juice, dry curaçao, and egg white (14€). *55 bd de Rochechouart, 9th. www.hotelrochechouart.com/mikado dancing. ☎ 01-42-81-91-00. Cover free. Métro: Pigalle. Map p 125.*

★★ **Pamela** ST-GERMAIN-DES-PRÈS It was in Pamela's toilets (when in was called the Rock 'n' Roll Circus) that some say Jim Morrison overdosed on heroin in 1971. The mystery around his death pervades, adding to the aura of this labyrinthine underground nightspot, where hip crowds come to sip drinks under its vaulted ceiling and boogie to the DJ's disco house music. *62 rue Mazarine, 6th. www. facebook.com/pamelaclubparis. ☎ 06-84-08-44-53. No cover. Métro: Mabillon. Map p 128.*

★★ **Rex Club** GRANDS BOULE-VARDS This place is known for its cutting-edge electronic music, with top DJs playing weekly and frequent free nights. Check local listings to see who's at the helm. *5 bd. Poissonnière, 2nd. https://rexclub. com. ☎ 01-42-36-10-96. Cover free to 25€. Métro: Bonne Nouvelle. Map p 126.*

★★ **Sacré** BOURSE It was here in 1898 that Emile Zola's famous open letter, "J'Accuse," was printed in the newspaper *Aurore.* The printers are long gone, replaced today by this funky club, where serious lovers of disco, house, techno, and hip hop dance until the wee hours. Hungry? Arrive at 7pm at the discobar for food and natural wines. Club nights start at midnight. Check the website for special events with guest DJs and bands (tickets usually 20€). *142 rue de Montmartre, 2nd. www.sacre. paris. No phone. Cover free to 20€. Métro: Bourse or Grands Boulevards. Map p 126.*

Gay & Lesbian Bars & Clubs

★★★ **Café Cox** MARAIS This gay men's bar can't be missed. A giant sausage sticks out from the wall outside, while inside, sausages

Nightlife Basics

Over the last few years (the pandemic aside), Paris's night scene has exploded, from exclusive clubs headed by international DJs to intimate speakeasies and inventive mixology cocktail bars. Many of the city's bars and cafes chip in, too, by staying open until 1 or 2am. If you plan to hit a trendy nightclub, you should know that most are open 11pm to 6am, and that Parisian bouncers—*physionomistes* (literally "face-checkers")—are extremely picky and often rude. Dress up, smile, and hope they let you in; or ensure entry the expensive way by reserving a table with bottle service, where you pay around 150€ for a bottle of champagne or a spirit.

The legal drinking age in France is 18. Expect to pay around 6€ for a glass of wine or 4€ for beer in a bar or cafe, and 13€ to 20€ for a cocktail. Drinks in nightclubs usually start at 15€. Clubbing nights are usually Wednesday or Thursday to Saturday.

BAPBAP brews its own beer.

are hung from all the walls and ceiling. You get the idea. It's a place with a sense of humor and it's where you'll find the most mixed gay crowd in Paris. *15 rue des Archives, 4th. www.cox.fr.* ☎ *01-42-72-08-00. Métro: Hôtel-de-Ville. Map p 126.*

★★ **Chez Moune** SOUTH PIGALLE   This fun lesbian club is open to everybody, and is always jam-packed largely thanks to its eclectic music, which covers everything from cheesy disco to classic hip-hop and house. The decor is very "boudoir": all red velvet and leopard print. Men are welcome. *54 rue Jean-Baptiste Pigalle, 9th. www. instagram.com/chezmouneparis. No phone. Métro: Pigalle. Map p 125.*

★★ **Le Tango (aka La Boîte à Frissons)** REPUBLIQUE   Open on weekends, this wacky, hetero-friendly gay and lesbian dance hall plays cheesy Madonna songs and accordion music alike. Couples practice dancing the foxtrot and tango early on, and then a DJ takes over and plays everything except techno. *13 rue au Maire, 2nd. www. facebook.com/letangoparis.*

☎ *01-48-87-25-71 Cover varies. Métro: Arts et Métiers. Map p 126.*

★★ **Mutinerie** MARAIS   More than just a party spot, this shabby LGBT bar acts as a local cafe, library, concert venue, and even a yoga center. DJs spin everything from ragga and pop to cool electro and rock. *176-178 rue St. Martin, 3rd. www.lamutinerie.eu.* ☎ *01-42-72-70-59. No cover. Métro: Rambuteau or Etienne Marcel; RER Châtelet-les-Halles. Map p 126.*

Pubs & Bars

★★ **Académie de la Bière** LATIN QUARTER   This rustic-looking "academy of beer" can get downright raucous. Most of the beers on tap come from Belgium. Soak it up with delicious *moules-frites*. *88 bd. de Port-Royal, 5th. www. academie-biere.com.* ☎ *01-43-54-66-65. RER: Port Royal. Map p 128.*

★★ **BAPBAP** OBERKAMPF   Not many visitors know that Paris makes its own beers. And this boutique-slash-brewery is a relaxed place to try some of the best: craft brews like Canopée (an organic IPA with a grapefruit tang) and the signature Originale, a pale ale with notes of caramel. If you want to see where your drink was made, book one of the brewery tours (25€). *79 rue St-Maur, 11th. www.bapbap. paris.* ☎ *01-77-17-52-97. Métro: Rue St-Maur. Map p 126.*

★★★ Candelaria MARAIS
What this tiny taqueria lacks in space it makes up for in trendiness—especially at night, when a young, hip crowd makes a beeline for the speakeasy-style cocktail bar hidden behind the taco counter. Try—if you dare—the spicy *Guêpe Verte* (Green Wasp), made from Ocho Blanco tequila infused with hot pepper, coriander, cucumber, and lime. *52 rue de Saintonge, 3rd. www.candelaria-paris.com.* ☎ *09-50-84-19-67. Métro: Filles du Calvaire. Map p 126.*

★★ Chez Prune CANAL SAINT-MARTIN
This casual spot serves excellent, well-priced food, including some vegetarian dishes (from 14€), plus coffee, beer, and wine to local arty types and cool idlers taking in the canal-side view. *36 rue Beaurepaire, 10th. www.instagram. com/chez_prune_bistrot_canal.* ☎ *01-42-41-30-47. Métro: République. Map p 126.*

★★★ Experimental Cocktail Club SENTIER
This cozy place, with its wooden beams and exposed stone, is known for its gourmet cocktails and speakeasy vibe. Live DJs play on weekends, though the music is never cranked up to a wild party level. Things stay cool and refined as you sip the splendid house creations. *37 rue St-Sauveur, 2nd. www.experimental group.com.* ☎ *01-45-08-88-09. Métro: Sentier. Map p 126.*

★★ Gossima Ping-Pong Bar PÈRE LACHAISE
Set in a converted garage, this quirky, vintage-style bar is the only place in Paris you can drink cocktails and play Ping-Pong at the same time. With two floors of tables, a thrashing sound system, and an all-round jovial atmosphere, it's a top spot for a night out with friends. *4 rue Victor Gelez, 11th.*

The Candelaria speakeasy.

Hemingway fans and expats flock to Harry's Bar, birthplace of the Sidecar.

http://gossima.fr. 📞 *01-48-07-43-35. Métro: Père Lachaise or Rue Saint-Maur. Map p 126.*

★★★ Harry's Bar OPERA

This place is sacred to Hemingway disciples as the place where he and the rest of the ambulance corps drank themselves silly during the Spanish Civil War. This bar is responsible for the White Lady and the Sidecar, along with numerous damaged livers. A pianist plays in the cellar; the area upstairs is somewhat less sophisticated. Filled with expats, this place is more fun than you might think. *5 rue Daunou, 2nd. www.harrysbar.fr.* 📞 *01-42-61-71-14. Métro: Opéra or Pyramides. Map p 126.*

★★ La Palette ST-GERMAIN-DES-PRES

This is a favorite rendezvous for students from the nearby fine-arts school. It's also rather romantic (especially the fresco-painted back room). A drink here means following in the steps of Ernest Hemingway and Jim Morrison. A handy base for exploring Saint-Germain's art galleries. *43 rue de Seine, 6th. www.lapalette-paris.com.* 📞 *01-43-26-68-15. Métro: Odéon. Map p 128.*

★★★ Le Perchoir

MENILMONTANT   Take in amazing views of eastern Paris from this rooftop bar, one of multiple other high-altitude Perchoirs all over town (check website for locations). Sip a cocktail on an outdoor sofa and gaze at Sacré-Coeur, or cozy up to the snack bar. The restaurant just below showcases visiting chefs. It's popular, so reserve at least a week ahead. *14 rue Crespin du Gast, 11th. https://leperchoir.fr.* 📞 *01-48-06-18-48. Métro: Ménilmontant. Map p 126.*

★★★ Moonshiner BASTILLE

This speakeasy-style joint is hidden at the back of a small, red-fronted pizzeria (Pizza da Vito). Nibble on pies laden with salmon or spicy sausage, then step through the

The stunning views from Le Perchoir.

The historic L'Hôtel.

fridge door into an Art Deco boudoir where vintage jazz plays as you sip wonderful cocktails. *5 rue Sedaine, 11th. https://moonshiner-bar.fr.* ☎ *09-50-73-12-99. Métro: Bréguet-Sabin. Map p 126.*

★★ Paname Brewing Company
CANAL SAINT-MARTIN   This hip waterside joint is the latest spot for Paris-made craft beers and street food. Five beers are brewed on-site, in a converted 19th-century warehouse. Choices range from the refreshing, amber-hued *Barge du Canal* to the *Bête Noire* (aka Black Beast), a delicious dark ale with a licorice/caramel finish. *41 bis Quai de la Loire, 19th. www.paname brewingcompany.com.* ☎ *01-40-36-43-55. Métro: Laumière or Ourcq. Map p 126.*

★★ Rosa Bonheur NORTHEAST
Smack bang in the un-touristy Parc des Buttes Chaumont (a beautiful urban park set in former quarries), this is where those-in-the-know come for after-hours drinking and partying. It's magical looking out

across the moonlit park, drink in hand, with nothing but the rustling of trees (and like-minded Parisians) for company. *2 allée de la Cascade, 19th; after dark enter at 7 rue Botzaris, opposite no. 74. www.rosa bonheur.fr.* ☎ *01-42-00-00-45. Métro: Botzaris or Jourdain. Map p 126.*

★★★ Wilde's Lounge at L'Hôtel ST-GERMAIN-DES-PRES
This wee hotel bar is appropriately theatrical (a Victorian color scheme, baroque touches) when you consider that its regulars tend to be in the film industry—or want to be. This was the hotel where Oscar Wilde died, impoverished and alone (hence the bar's name); it's a lovely historic place for a drink and a ponder, and there are free jazz nights on Thursdays. *13 rue des Beaux-Arts, 6th. www.l-hotel.com.* ☎ *01-44-41-99-00. Métro: St-Germain-des-Prés. Map p 128.*

Wine Bars
★ Au Sauvignon ST-GERMAIN-DES-PRES   This tiny bar has tables overflowing onto the terrace, where

a cheerful crowd downs wines ranging from cheap Beaujolais to the pricey Grand Crus. *80 rue des St-Pères, 7th.* ☎ *01-45-48-49-02. Métro: Sèvres-Babylone. Map p 128.*

★ Caves Legrand

BOURSE   Nestled in the chocolate-box Passage Vivienne (a covered passage), this old-world wine shop doubles as a bar, a delicatessen, and a bookshop. Sidle up to a tasting counter and let serendipity guide you, or enlist help from the sommelier. Excellent seasonal menus for food and wine pairings complete the offering. *1 rue de la Banque, 2nd. www.caves-legrand. com.* ☎ *01-42-60-07-12. Métro: Bourse. Map p 126.*

★★ Fish la Boissonerie SAINT-GERMAIN   International, after-work crowds pile into this playful wine bar restaurant for a glass of something tasty and an excellent fish-focused menu. Snag a spot at the bar or opt for a sit-down dinner—either way, you're in for a treat. *69 rue de Seine, 6th. www.fish laboissonnerie.com.* ☎ *01-43-54-34-69. Métro: Saint Germain des Prés. Map p 128.*

★★ Frenchie Bar à Vin SENTIER

Off the beaten tourist track north of Les Halles, this adorable wine bar belongs to **Frenchie,** the acclaimed restaurant across the street (p 117). Fans come for French wine for every budget and delicious small tasting menus. Get here early if you don't want to queue; no reservations. *6 rue du Nil, 2nd. www. frenchie-bav.com.* ☎ *01-40-39-96-19. Métro: Sentier or Réamur Sebastopol. Map p 126.*

★ Juveniles BOURSE   This sleek place with a trendy crowd prides

itself on its enormous wine cellar with labels from around the world. *47 rue des Richelieu, 1st. www. juvenileswinebar.com.* ☎ *01-42-97-46-49. Métro: Palais Royal. Map p 126.*

La Belle Hortense MARAIS   The fact that this quirky bar has a bookshop within its walls makes it a perpetual favorite for bookish wine lovers. *31 vielle du Temple, 4th. www.cafeine.com.* ☎ *01-48-04-71-60. Métro: Hôtel-de-Ville. Map p 126.*

★★ La Cave à Michel

NORTHEAST   It's standing-only at this long narrow bar—which is part of the fun as you slurp the impressive collection of natural wines, accompanied by delicious plates like marinated sea bass ceviche. *36 rue Ste-Marthe, 10th. www.lacave amichel.fr.* ☎ *01-42-45-94-47. Métro: Belleville. Map p 126.*

★★★ La Vache dans les Vignes CANAL SAINT-MARTIN

That magical duo—cheese and wine—come into their own at this hip neighborhood spot. Just choose your wine, then sit back and let the staff pair it with one of their in-house matured cheeses. *46 Quai de Jemmapes, 10th. www.facebook. com/lavachedanslesvignes.* ☎ *01-77-10-88-36. Métro: République or Goncourt. Map p 126.*

★★ Le Baron Rouge BASTILLE

Be prepared to fight for elbow room at this popular locals' haunt (opposite the Aligre market), where excellent wine is sold by the glass and drunk on wine barrels posing as tables. Grab a plate of charcuterie or oysters (when in season). *1 rue Théophile-Roussel, 12th. http:// lebaronrouge.net.* ☎ *01-43-43-14-32. Métro: St-Paul. Map p 126.* ●

Arts & Entertainment Best Bets

Best Theater for Musicals
★★★ Théâtre du Châtelet, *1 place du Châtelet, 1st (p 147)*

Best Place to Walk in the Phantom's Footsteps
★★★ Opéra Garnier, *Place de l'Opéra, 9th (p 146)*

Best Place to Hear Classical Music
★★★ Philharmonie de Paris, *221 av. Jean-Jaurès, 19th (p 146)*

Best Theater
★ Comédie Française, *Place Colette, 1st (p 147)*

Best Drag Show
★★★ Cabaret Michou, *80 rue des Martyrs, 18th (p 142)*

Best Place to Hear Modern French Chanson
★ Les Trois Baudets, *64 bd. de Clichy, 18th (p 144)*

Best Place to See Dance
★★ Théâtre National de Chaillot, *1 place du Trocadéro, 16th (p 147)*

Best Cabaret
★★★ Paradis Latin, *28 rue du Cardinal Lemoine, 5th (p 142)*

Best Place for 20-Somethings
★★ Supersonic, *9 rue Biscornett, 12th (p 145)*

Best Place to See a Movie
★★★ Studio 28, *10 rue Tholozé, 18th (p 148)*

Best Overall Jazz Club
★★★ Duc des Lombards, *42 rue des Lombards, 1st (p 143)*

Best Nouvelle Orleans Jazz
★★★ Le Sunset/Le Sunside, *60 rue des Lombards, 1st (p 144)*

Best Live Music with Your Meal
★★ La Bellevilloise, *19–21 rue Boyer, 20th (p 144)*

Best Indie Rock Concerts
★★ La Boule Noire, *120 bd. de Rochechouart, 18th (p 144)*

Previous page: The ornate ceiling of the Opéra Garnier. Above: The Opéra Bastille was inaugurated in 1989 for the Revolution's bicentennial.

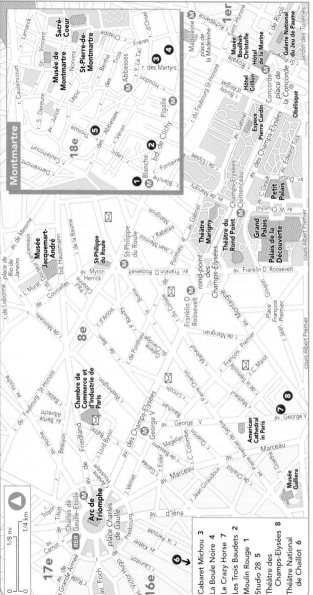

Cabaret Michou 3
La Boule Noire 4
Le Crazy Horse 7
Les Trois Baudets 2
Moulin Rouge 1
Studio 28 5
Théâtre des
  Champs-Élysées 8
Théâtre National
  de Chaillot 6

Right Bank (1st–4th & 9th–11th)

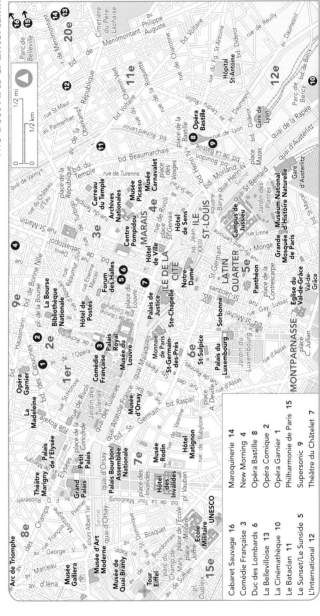

Left Bank (5th–6th)

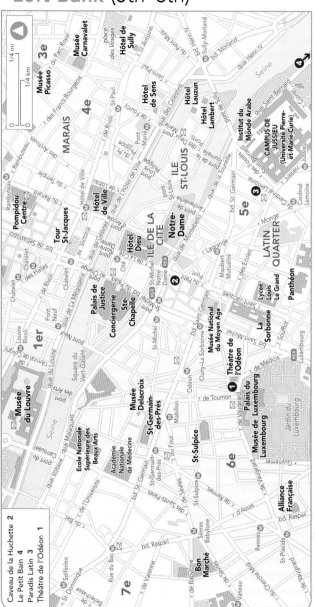

Caveau de la Huchette **2**
Le Petit Bain **4**
Paradis Latin **3**
Théâtre de l'Odéon **1**

Arts & Entertainment A to Z

Cabarets

★★★ Cabaret Michou

PIGALLE   This fun, eccentric place is where 20 cross-dressing belles lip-sync to Céline Dion and Lady Gaga while wearing bright costumes. And they look remarkably similar to their real counterparts. If you don't have dinner, you must stand at the bar (from 55€ including one drink). *80 rue des Martyrs, 18th. www.michou.com.* ☎ *01-46-06-16-04. Cover including dinner, half bottle champagne & show 120€–160€. Métro: Pigalle. Map p 139.*

★★ Le Crazy Horse CHAMPS-

ÉLYSÉES   This sophisticated joint's nude revue thrives on genuinely good choreography and the beauty of the women, who dance dressed in little more than light. Far from sleazy, the show is actually quite mesmerizing. *12 av. George-V, 8th. www.lecrazyhorseparis.com.* ☎ *01-47-23-32-32. Reservations* recommended. Cover dinner & show (w/drinks) 200€–360€, dinner & show (no drinks) 180€. Métro: George-V or Alma-Marceau. Map p 139.*

★★ Moulin Rouge

MONTMARTRE   Toulouse-Lautrec immortalized this windmill-topped building and its scantily clad can-can dancers (this is where the risqué dance was invented). Today, it's true to its original theme and very cheesy, but the dancing is perfectly synchronized. *Place Blanche, 18th. www.moulinrouge.fr.* ☎ *01-53-09-82-82. Show only from 77€, show & half bottle champagne from 210€, dinner & show 190€–420€. Métro: Blanche. Map p 139.*

★★★ Paradis Latin LATIN

QUARTER   This cabaret boasts architecture designed by Gustave Eiffel, and though it may be a bit less glitzy than the others, it makes more of an attempt to harken back

The windmill atop the Moulin Rouge is a landmark in Montmartre.

The circus-themed Cabaret Sauvage.

to the cabarets of yesteryear, which featured live and sometimes renowned performers. The current show, L'Oiseau Paradis (Bird of Paradise) includes plenty of daring numbers with topless beauties in sparkly costumes, and a rollicking cancan. *28 rue du Cardinal Lemoine, 5th. www.paradislatin.com.* ☎ *01-43-25-28-28. Show only 80€; 140€ lunch and show; 85€ cakes and show; 175€–200€ dinner and show. Métro: Cardinal Lemoine. Map p 141.*

Jazz, Rock & More
★★ **Cabaret Sauvage** VILLETTE Is it a cool club or a circus tent? The answer is not clear at this unusual space where you are just as likely to encounter Brazilian samba, electro funk, or trapeze artists. Blues bands from the Balkans and Vietnamese jazz musicians share the calendar with avant-garde circus acts and Algerian acrobats. *Parc de la Villette, entrance at 59 bd. MacDonald, 19th. www.cabaret sauvage.com.* ☎ *01-42-09-03-09.*

Cover varies. Métro: Porte de la Villette. Map p 140.

★★ **Caveau de la Huchette** LATIN QUARTER This celebrated jazz and swing cave draws a young crowd, mostly university students, who dance to the music of well-known jazz combos. Robespierre hung out here in his time, so you can tell everyone you're here for the history. *5 rue de la Huchette, 5th. www.caveaudelahuchette.fr.* ☎ *01-43-26-65-05. Cover 14€–16€. Métro: St-Michel. RER: St-Michel-Notre-Dame. Map p 141.*

★★★ **Duc des Lombards** CHATELET This thriving jazz club has seen all the greats of Paris's jazz era pass through its doors. Today, it features performances nightly that range from free jazz to hard bop. Tables can be reserved, and meals (prepared with mostly fair-trade produce) are served. *42 rue des Lombards, 1st. www.ducdes lombards.com.* ☎ *01-42-33-22-88. Cover free to 41€. Métro: Châtelet. Map p 140.*

★★ La Bellevilloise

MENILMONTANT   This multidisci-plinary venue (set inside France's first cooperative building) has several bars, two restaurants, a night-club, an exhibition space, and a concert hall where some of Paris's most exciting bands have launched themselves to fame. It's a place to relax, soak up the atmosphere, and spend the whole evening. *19–21 rue Boyer, 20th. www.labellevilloise. com.* 01-46-36-07-07. *Cover varies. Métro: Gambetta, or Ménilmontant. Map p 140.*

★★ La Boule Noire PIGALLE

The Black Ball is one of those intimate, divey Parisian haunts that attract such biggies as the Dandy Warhols, Metallica, Cat Power, Franz Ferdinand, and Jamie Cullum. Despite the star-studded lineup, the cover tends to hover around the 20€ mark, making this one of the cheapest venues around. *120 bd. Rochechouart, 18th. www.laboule-noire.fr.* 01-49-25-81-75. *Cover varies. Métro: Anvers or Pigalle. Map p 139.*

Le Bataclan REPUBLIQUE

Behind the brightly colored facade of this former music hall (established in 1864), the Bataclan is a flagship of Paris's music scene with top funk, rock, jazz, and hip-hop acts from across the globe. *50 bd. Voltaire, 11th. www.bataclan.fr.* 01-43-14-00-30. *Cover varies. Métro: Oberkampf. Map p 140.*

★ Le Petit Bain BIBLIOTHEQUE

This wooden and chartreuse rect-angle, floating on the Seine, is one of the city's best concert venues, with a stream of up-and-coming bands and a handful of well-known French musicians. Dine in the res-taurant beforehand or sip a cool *bière* on the upper terrace. Then watch Paris's lights reflect like diamonds on the water. *7 port de la Gare, 13th. www.petitbain.org.* 01-43-49-68-92. *Cover varies. Métro: Quai de la Gare. Map p 141.*

★ Les Trois Baudets PIGALLE

Between 1947 and 1966, this small theater launched more musical careers than anywhere else (Gains-bourg, Brel, and Henri Salvador all started here). Nowadays it's Paris's main francophone music theater, with a jam-packed program of rock, electro, folk, *chanson,* and slam poetry. *64 bd. de Clichy, 18th. www. lestroisbaudets.com.* 01-42-62-33-33. *Cover varies. Métro: Pigalle. Map p 139.*

★★★ Le Sunset/Le Sunside

CHÂTELET   This staple of the Pari-sian jazz circuit is two bars in one, with separate jazz shows going on simultaneously. The look is mini-malist, and artists are both Euro-pean and U.S.-based. Le Sunside favors classic jazz, and Le Sunset goes for electric jazz and world music. Take your pick. *60 rue des Lombards, 1st. www.sunset-sunside. com.* 01-40-26-46-60. *Cover var-ies. Métro: Châtelet. Map p 140.*

L'International OBERKAMPF

Arty types flock to this grungy bar for its winning formula of cheap beer and free live music. A stream of on-the-up bands play here, mak-ing it a great joint in which to spot the talent of the future and get familiar with Paris's electro-rock scene. *5–7 rue Moret, 11th. www. linternational.fr.* 01-49-29-76-45. *No cover. Métro: Ménilmontant. Map p 140.*

Maroquinerie BELLEVILLE

Up-and-coming rock acts take center stage at this hip concert venue, which doubles as a restaurant, bar, and literary cafe. You can easily spend the whole night here. *23 rue Boyer, 20th. www.lamaroquinerie.fr.*

☎ 01-40-33-35-05. *Cover varies. Métro: Ménilmontant or Gambetta. Map p 140.*

★ **New Morning** EASTERN PARIS   Jazz fanatics pack this respected club to drink, talk, and dance, not to mention check each other out—this is one of the city's "it" places to see and be seen. The club is popular with African and European musicians. *7–9 rue des Petites-Ecuries, 10th. www.new morning.com.* ☎ *01-45-23-51-41. Cover varies. Métro: Château d'Eau. Map p 140.*

★★ **Supersonic** BASTILLE   In a cool industrial building at Bastille, this temple to the independent spirit is free and promotes unknown stars of tomorrow. Live bands play anything from garage and electro to post-punk and psych, and there's a specialist indie music record shop open on Wednesday to Saturday from 3 to

8:30pm. *9 rue Biscornet, 12th. www. supersonic-club.fr.* ☎ *01-46-28-12-90. Cover free. Métro: Bastille. Map p 140.*

Opera, Dance & Classical

★★★ **Opéra Bastille** BASTILLE This huge, contemporary building hosts outstanding opera performances, such as Mozart's *Marriage of Figaro* and Tchaikovsky's *Queen of Spades,* in its three concert halls. Symphony and dance performances are held here occasionally as well. *2 place de la Bastille, 4th. www. operadeparis.fr.* ☎ *08-92-89-90-90. Tickets 15€–240€. Métro: Bastille. Map p 140.*

★★ **Opéra Comique** BOURSE Come to this charming venue, built in the 1880s, for light opera on a smaller scale than at the city's major opera houses. It's a lovely place to see *Carmen, Don Giovanni,* or *Tosca. 5 rue Favart, 2nd. www.opera-comique.com.*

Indie musicians are the main draw at Supersonic.

Shows in English

English-language theater performances are rare (Théâtre du Châtelet (p 147) sometimes hosts English productions), but a few comedy nights are worth a detour. One of the best stand-up performers is **Sebastien Marx** (https://sebmarx.com/en), who presents the **"New York Comedy Night,"** every Saturday at 10pm at the Petit Palais des Glaces (www.palaisdesglaces.com), where multiple local English-speaking comics perform, along with the occasional international star. Another good show is **"How to Become a Parisian in One Hour"** (at Théâtre des Nouveautés; reservations at www.oliviergiraud.com), a one-person show written by Olivier Giraud, a Frenchman who spent several years in the U.S. And look out for Irish-British **Paul Taylor** (https://paultaylorcomedy.com), who has taken his stand-up show to big theaters like the Zénith (https://le-zenith.com). For open-mic nights, check the **Comedy in Paris** website (www.comedyinparis.com). And if you're looking for "theater" proper (so to speak), an excellent English-language box-office service is **Theatre in Paris** (www.theatreinparis.com), with tickets to multiple shows offering English supertitles.

☎ 01-70-23-01-31. Tickets 6€–165€. Métro: Richelieu-Drouot. Map p 140.

Theater Tip

Many theaters are closed over the summer, so check beforehand to avoid disappointment. Also, where possible, make advance reservations: Parisians are enthusiastic theatergoers, and tickets can go like hotcakes.

★★★ Opéra Garnier OPERA
The Phantom did his fictional haunting here. Now the opera house is home to the city's ballet scene, although it still hosts opera from time to time. Charles Garnier's 1875 building is a rococo wonder with a ceiling painted by Chagall. The roof is home to several beehives, which produce the Opéra honey for sale in the shop. Place de l'Opéra, 9th. www.operade paris.fr. ☎ 08-92-89-90-90. Tickets 15€–240€. Métro: Opéra, RER: Auber. Map p 140.

★★★ Philharmonie de Paris
VILLETTE This multimillion-euro structure houses a state-of-the-art concert hall, libraries, and two museums: one on musical instruments across the ages; the other for kids' ages 4 to 10 (p 31). It has an eclectic program, ranging from baroque quartets to symphonic orchestras, opera recitals, and jazz ensembles—all big names. 221 av. Jean-Jaurès, 19th. www.philharmonie deparis.fr. ☎ 01-44-84-44-84. Tickets 10€–196€. Métro: Porte de Pantin. Map p 140.

★★ Théâtre des Champs-Élysées CHAMPS-ÉLYSÉES
National and international orchestras (such as the Vienna Philharmonic) perform at this Art Deco

theater, to the delight of its well-dressed audiences. *15 av. Montaigne, 8th. www.theatrechampselysees.fr.* ☎ *01-49-52-50-50. Tickets 15€–125€. Métro: Alma–Marceau. Map p 139.*

★★ Théâtre National de Chaillot TROCADERO

In the sumptuous, Art Deco Palais de Chaillot, this contemporary dance theater offers a consistently excellent, avant-garde program of contemporary dance and theater. It also provides some of the city's most breathtaking Eiffel Tower views from its bar and restaurant, where you can eat before the show. **Note:** Closed for renovations until 2024. *1 place du Trocadéro, 16th. www.theatre-chaillot.fr.* ☎ *01-53-65-31-00. Tickets 35€–70€. Métro: Trocadéro. Map p 139.*

Theater & Musicals

★ Comédie Française PALAIS ROYAL

Those with even a modest understanding of French will enjoy a sparkling production at this national theater, where the main goal is to keep the classics alive while promoting contemporary authors. *Place Colette, 1st. www.comedie-francaise.fr.* ☎ *01-44-58-15-15. Tickets 15€–70€. Métro: Palais Royal–Musée du Louvre. Map p 140.*

★ Théâtre de l'Odéon ODEON

More than just a theater, the Odéon hosts debates on literature, philosophy, and European politics. The stage hosts quality plays in different European languages, including (occasionally) English. *Place de l'Odéon, 6th. www.theatre-odeon.fr.* ☎ *01-44-85-40-40. Tickets 20€–50€. Métro: Odéon. Map p 141.*

★★★ Théâtre du Châtelet CHÂTELET

This Belle Epoque masterpiece is the only place in Paris to show Broadway standard musicals in English with full orchestras and parts sung by some of the world's best artists. Previous triumphs have included *Sweeney Todd* and *The Sound of Music.* Top-notch classical concerts, opera, and dance round out the program. *1 place du Châtelet, 1st. www.chatelet.com.* ☎ *01-40-28-28-40. Tickets 35€–150€. Métro/RER: Châtelet. Map p 140.*

Film

★★★ La Cinémathèque BERCY

In a quirky, cruise ship–inspired building designed by Frank Gehry, you can retrace the history of cinema in the museum named after George Méliès, father of special effects, and then take in a movie. The center is known for holding fabulous retrospectives on master filmmakers. *51 rue de Bercy, 12th. www.cinematheque.fr.* ☎ *01-71-19-33-33. Tickets museum 10€, movie 7€. Métro: Bercy. Map p 140.*

Théâtre du Châtelet.

★★★ **Studio 28** MONTMARTRE This quaint art house movie theater is scandalous! It was here where Luis Buñuel's polemical 1930 movie, *L'Age d'Or,* was censored after only two showings. Today it's a glorious spot with a bar, a little garden, and—in the movie theater—light fittings by none other than Jean Cocteau. *10 rue Tholozé, 18th. www.cinema-studio28.fr.* ☎ *01-46-06-36-07. Tickets 10€. Métro: Blanche or Abbesses. Map p 139.* ●

Buying Tickets

The easiest way to get tickets nowadays is online, in advance, from the venue's website. If you're staying in a first-class hotel, your concierge can probably arrange your tickets, too. A service fee may be added, but you won't waste precious sightseeing hours securing hard-to-get tickets.

Cheaper tickets, with discounts of up to 50%, can be found at the **Kiosque Théâtre** (www.kiosqueculture.com). One is in front of the Montparnasse train station (place Raoul Dautry; Tues–Sat 12:30–2:30pm and 3–7:30pm), another on the west side of the Madeleine (facing 15 pl. de la Madeleine, exit rue Tronchet from the Madeleine Métro stop; Tues–Sat 12:30–2:30pm and 3–7:30pm, Sun 12:30–3:45pm), and a third in Paris's main tourist office (Office de Tourisme et des Congrès de Paris; 29 rue de Rivoli, 4th; Tues–Sat 12:30–5:30pm, Sun 12:30–3:45pm). Plenty of ticket discounts can also be had at **BilletRéduc,** www.billetreduc.com (in French).

Another good place to try is any branch of the **FNAC** media store (or www.fnac.com; you can usually download your tickets straight from the site). It handles tickets for most museums, concerts, and shows across France. The Champs-Élysées branch is open until 10:30pm (p 96).

Lodging **Best Bets**

Best **Budget Sleep**
★ Le Vert Galant $ *43 rue Croulebarbe, 13th (p 162)*

Best **for Swimming**
★★ Molitor by Mgallery $$$$ *3 rue Nungesser et Coli, 16th (p 162)*

Best **Boutique Hotel**
★★★ L'Hôtel $$$$$ *13 rue des Beaux-Arts, 6th (p 162)*

Best **Kid-Friendly Hotel**
★★ Hôtel de la Porte Dorée $$ *273 av. Daumesnil, 12th (p 158)*

Coolest **Hostel**
★ Generator Hostel $ *9-11 place du Colonel Fabien, 10th (p 156)*

Best **Quirky Hotel**
★★★ OFF Paris Seine $$$ *20-22 Port d'Austerlitz, 13th (p 163)*

Best **Boudoirlike Luxury**
★★★ Monsieur George $$$$$ *17 rue Washington, 8th (p 163)*

Best **Hip Hotel**
★★ Mama Shelter $$ *107 rue de Bagnolet, 20th (p 162)*

Best **Eco-Friendly Hotel**
★★★ Solar Hôtel $ *22 rue Boulard, 14th (p 164)*

Best **Family-Run Hotel**
★★★ Hôtel Louison $$$ *105 rue de Vaugirard, 6th (p 160)*

Best **"Only in Paris" Hideaway**
★★★ Eden Lodge $$$ *175 rue de Charonne, 11th (p 156)*

Best **Seine Views**
★★ Cheval Blanc Paris $$$$$ *8 Quai du Louvre, 1st (p 156)*

Best **for Foodies**
★★ Grand Pigalle Hotel $$$ *29 rue Victor Massé, 9th (p 156)*

Best **Friendly B&B**
52 Clichy $ *52 rue de Clichy, 9th (p 164)*

Lodging Tip

From world-class palaces to tiny B&Bs, Paris has it all—except huge rooms (unless you fork over the money for a suite). Many hotels are in historic buildings that cannot be changed structurally, so rooms are generally "cozy." Price-wise, always look for Internet discounts on the hotels' own websites. Discount travel sites, such as www.booking.com and www.expedia.com also offer deals on select hotels. Prices vary with the season. August (low season) is usually cheapest; the rest of the year fluctuates, peaking during trade fairs and fashion week (check dates at www.fashionweek-dates.com). When choosing your hotel, here's a brief guide to the arrondissements (districts): Postcodes are from 75001 to 75020. Areas 1 (75001) to 8 (75008) are very central; 9 to 11 and 17 to 20 are the city's up-and-coming, trendy areas; and 12 to 16 are largely residential but have plenty of atmosphere. Arrondissement 13 contains the city's main Chinese neighborhood.

Previous page: Spectacular views from Cheval Blanc.

Right Bank (8th & 16th–18th)

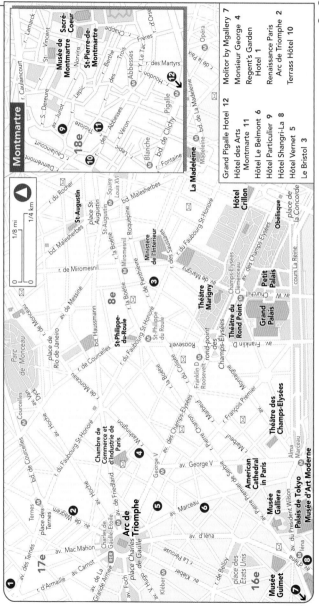

Grand Pigalle Hotel 12
Hôtel des Arts Montmartre 11
Hôtel Le Belmont 6
Hôtel Particulier 9
Hôtel Shangri-La 8
Hôtel Vernet 5
Le Bristol 3

Molitor by Mgallery 7
Monsieur George 4
Regent's Garden Hotel 1
Renaissance Paris Arc de Triomphe 2
Terrass Hôtel 10

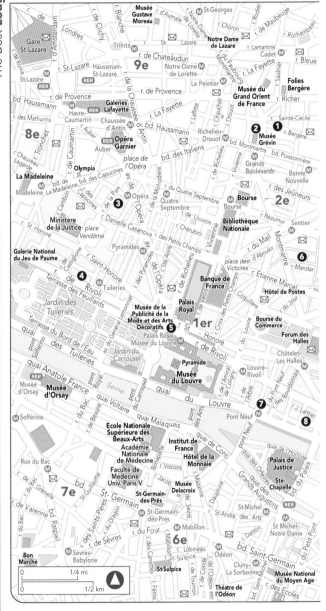

Gare St-Lazare

St-Lazare

Musée Gustave Moreau

St-Georges

Notre Dame de Lazare

9e

Trinité

Notre-Dame de Lorette

Le Peletier

Haussman-St-Lazare

Folies Bergère

Musée du Grand Orient de France

Galeries Lafayette

Havre-Caumartin

Chaussée d'Antin

8e

Olympia

Opéra Garnier

place de l'Opéra

La Madeleine

2 Musée Grévin

1

Grands Boulevards

Bonne Nouvelle

Bourse
Bourse

2e

Sentier

Ministère de la Justice

place Vendôme

Quatre Septembre

Bibliothèque Nationale

Galerie National du Jeu de Paume

Pyramides

place des Victoires

6

r-Mandar

4 Tuileries

Jardin des Tuileries

Terrasse des Feuillants

Banque de France

Hôtel de Postes

Terrasse du Bord de l'Eau

quai des Tuileries

Musée de la Publicité de la Mode et des Arts Décoratifs **5**

Palais Royal

Bourse du Commerce

Forum des Halles

1er

Pyramide

Musée du Louvre

Châtelet-Les Halles

quai Anatole France

Musée d'Orsay

Musée d'Orsay

Solférino

Jardin du Carrousel

Louvre-Rivoli

Pont Neuf

7

8

Ecole Nationale Supérieure des Beaux-Arts

Académie Nationale de Médecine

Institut de France

Hôtel de la Monnaie

Palais de Justice

Rue du Bac

Faculté de Médecine Univ. Paris V

Musée Delacroix

Ste-Chapelle

7e

St-Germain-des-Prés

St-Germain-des-Prés

St-Michel

St Michel-Notre Dame

Bon Marché

Sèvres-Babylone

Mabillon

6e

Odéon

Musée National du Moyen Age

Cluny-La Sorbonne

St-Sulpice

St-Sulpice

Théâtre de l'Odéon

0 ___ 1/4 mi
0 ___ 1/2 km

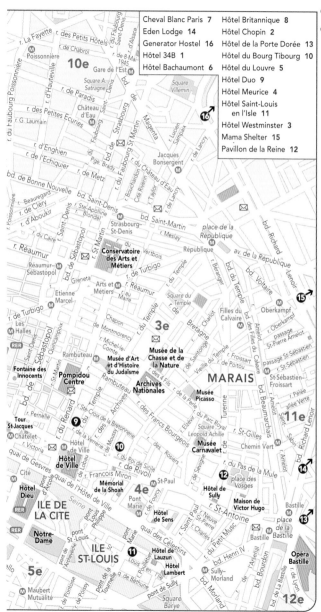

The Best Lodging

Left Bank (5th–7th, 13th)

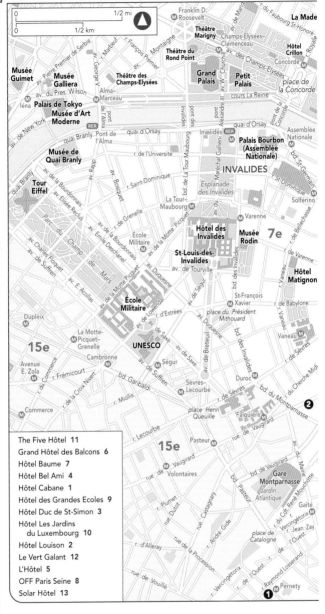

The Five Hôtel **11**

Grand Hôtel des Balcons **6**

Hôtel Baume **7**

Hôtel Bel Ami **4**

Hôtel Cabane **1**

Hôtel des Grandes Ecoles **9**

Hôtel Duc de St-Simon **3**

Hôtel Les Jardins
   du Luxembourg **10**

Hôtel Louison **2**

Le Vert Galant **12**

L'Hôtel **5**

OFF Paris Seine **8**

Solar Hôtel **13**

Hotels A to Z

★★ Cheval Blanc Paris

CHÂTELET Set within the iconic Samaritaine Paris department store (www.dfs.com/en/samaritaine), this ultra-refined spot is one of the only hotels in Paris to overlook the Seine—and not just any stretch of the river: the historic part, where the water flows gracefully around the islands, past Notre-Dame and the city's glorious tree-lined quays. If that's not romantic enough for you, romance oozes inside the hotel's Dior spa (home to a 30m/98-ft. pool and a hammam) and in the chic rooftop brasserie, which morphs into an all-day cocktail bar with 360° skyline views—perfect for a panoramic tête-à-tête. Even if you can't afford a night, stop by for the rooftop. *8 Quai du Louvre, 1st. www.cheval blanc.com.* ☎ *01-40-28-00-00. 72 units. Double 1,350€ and up. Métro: Louvre-Rivoli or Châtelet. Map p 152.*

★★★ Eden Lodge Paris

NORTH-EAST Hidden from the street in a beautiful garden, this modern wooden structure combines environmental awareness with extremely comfortable lodgings. Quality insulation, LED lighting, solar panels, and zero-carbon output give these lodgings their ecological cred, as well as self-cleaning tiles that absorb air pollution. Rooms are chic, warm, and minimalist, with high-tech Japanese toilets. Bicycles are on hand. *175 rue de Charonne, 11th. www.eden lodgeparis.net.* ☎ *01-43-56-73-24. 5 units. Double 235€–365€. Métro: Alexandre Dumas. Map p 152.*

★★ The Five Hôtel LATIN

QUARTER The fun rooms here are small but impressive, with Chinese lacquer, velvet fabrics, fiber-optic lighting that makes you feel as though you're sleeping under a starry sky, and your own room fragrance. In all, it's a fine design hotel and convenient base for exploring the Left Bank. *3 rue Flatters, 5th. www.thefivehotel.com.* ☎ *01-43-31-74-21. 24 units. Double 150€–290€. Métro: Les Gobelins. RER: Port Royal. Map p 154.*

★ Generator Hostel COLONEL

FABIEN Set in a revamped office block, this funky, next-generation hostel offers vintage-chic dorms and private rooms with their own rooftop-view terraces. The other draws are the cafe (overlooking a garden; it's a great spot for breakfast), and the rooftop bar, which serves snacks, plays music, and offers uninterrupted views over the city. You're a 15-minute walk from the Gare du Nord Eurostar terminal, too. *9-11 place du Colonel Fabien, 10th. https://staygenerator. com/hostels/paris.* ☎ *01-70-98-84-00. 198 units. Shared rooms from 29€, private rooms from 78€. Métro: Colonel Fabien. Map p 152.*

★★ Grand Hôtel des Balcons

ST-GERMAIN-DES-PRÈS For the neighborhood, the rooms in this simple hotel are remarkably spacious. Most have small balconies, and if you look up the street you'll see the columns of the 18th-century Odéon theater. The roomy triples and quads are a good bet for families, and a wheelchair-accessible room is on the ground floor. The lobby has an Art Nouveau feel, and the well-kept rooms are impeccably clean, if not particularly stylish. *3 rue Casimir Delavigne, 6th. www. balcons.com.* ☎ *01-46-34-78-50. 49 units. Double 140€–200€. Métro: Odéon. Map p 154.*

★★ Grand Pigalle Hotel

PIGALLE This cool hangout just

got even cooler thanks to chef Gregory Marchand, of Frenchie fame (p 117). In his new restaurant here, you can tuck into innovative tapas like bacon scones and cheese pastry puffs (gougères, 8€), and mains like lamb with stuffed onion (32€), then sleep it off in artful, vintage-style rooms with bold wallpaper and granny-chic headboards. Corner rooms look up at Montmartre (ask when you book). You couldn't ask for a better spot for exploring both trendy SoPi (South Pigalle) and Montmartre's cobbled streets. *29 rue Victor Massé, 9th. www.grandpigalle.com. ☎ 01-85-73-12-00. 37 units. Double 248€–315€. Métro: Pigalle. Map p 151.*

★★ Hôtel 34B GRANDS BOULEVARDS

This quirky, France-themed hotel offers comfortable lodgings at great prices. Rooms have modern decor, with cool headboards made to look like stripy French t-shirts or clusters of berets. Wallpaper is a bold recreation of the French flag (blue, white, and red stripes), a design mirrored on the facades overlooking the lobby atrium (which doubles as the breakfast room). There's also a fitness room and sauna. *34 rue Bergère, 9th. https://en.astotel.com/hotel/34b-en/overview. ☎ 01-47-70-34-34. 128 units. 120€–160€. Métro: Grands Boulevards. Map p 152.*

★★ Hôtel Bachaumont

MONTORGEUIL Both travelers and Parisians come here, thanks to its excellent brasserie and hip cocktails. Sit below the beautiful glass ceiling and tuck into delights like juicy steak in wine-rich Bordelaise sauce, and langoustines with sage potatoes. Then sleep it off in sleek, blue-toned rooms set with dark-wood retro furnishings. If you're a light sleeper, ask for a courtyard room overlooking the brasserie's atrium. *18 rue Bachaumont, 2nd.*

www.hotelbachaumont.com. ☎ 01-81-66-47-00. 49 units. Double 194€–300€. Métro: Sentier or Etienne-Marcel. Map p 152.

★★★ Hôtel Baume ODEON

Set on a tranquil street near the neo-classical Théâtre de l'Odéon (and a 5-min. walk from the Luxembourg gardens), this chic neo-'30s-style hotel offers exquisite rooms (all pinks, blues, or terracottas) that follow themes such as jewelry, fashion, design, and film. Some have private terraces, and some suites are so big you feel as though you're in an apartment. There's a quaint little walled breakfast terrace to boot. *7 rue Casimir Delavigne, 6th. www.baume-hotel-paris.com. ☎ 01-53-10-28-50. 35 units. Double 269€–390€. Métro: Odéon. Map p 154.*

★★ Hôtel Bel Ami LATIN QUARTER

Recently restored, this sleek, art-conscious hotel has a refined, vintage-chic look with a clean design aesthetic. Earth-tone guest rooms have a Zen-like air. Check the website for deals. *7–11 rue St-Benoit, 6th. www.hotel-bel-ami.com. ☎ 01-49-27-09-33. 115 units. Double 295€–480€. Métro: St-Germain-des-Prés. Map p 154.*

The facade of Hôtel Bachaumont.

★★ **Hôtel Britannique** HOTEL DE VILLE   Plush, in an old-school kind of way, this lovely place has cultivated a kind of English graciousness. Guest rooms are small but nicely appointed and soundproof. The location is so central, you can walk almost anywhere. *20 av. Victoria, 1st. www.hotelbritannique.com.* ☎ *01-42-33-74-59. 39 units. Double 138€–500€. Métro: Châtelet. Map p 152.*

★★ **kids Hôtel Cabane** MONTPARNASSE   A great deal, especially for families (perks include reduced-rate breakfast for children ages 4–12; baby cribs, bottle warmers, and highchairs available). Understatedly elegant rooms have either garden views or vistas over the typically Parisian street below. Romance? Book the hidden wooden cabin with its two-person light-therapy shower, and its own garden terrace. *76 rue Raymond Losserand, 14th. www.hotelcabane.com.* ☎ *01-40-52-12-40. 43 units. Double 128€–154€; from 225€ for La Cabane. Métro: Pernety. Map p 154.*

★★ **Hôtel Chopin** GRANDS BOULEVARDS   This intimate hotel

The Hôtel Chopin is hidden down a covered passageway.

is hidden inside a curious 19th-century covered passage. The Victorian lobby has elegant woodwork, rooms are comfortably furnished, and the staff is friendly. *10 bd Montmartre, 9th. www.hotelchopin-paris-opera.com.* ☎ *01-47-70-58-10. 36 units. Double 118€–150€. Métro: Grands Boulevards. Map p 152.*

★★ **kids Hôtel de la Porte Dorée** BOIS DE VINCENNES   True, it's on the edge of town, but these lovely lodgings are well worth the Métro fare into the city center (about 15 min.). Soothing neutral tones, antique headboards, high ceilings, wood floors, and original curlicue moldings are all part of the package at this hotel, which goes the extra mile for both the environment (ecologically correct policies) and babies (toys, playpens, and even potty seats available). What's more, it is right next to the verdant **Bois de Vincennes,** where you can rent bikes, picnic, or visit the Paris zoo (www.parczoologiquedeparis. fr). *273 av. Daumesnil, 12th. www.hoteldelaportedoree.com.* ☎ *01-43-07-56-97. 43 units. Double 104€–155€. Métro: Porte Dorée. Map p 152.*

★★★ **Hôtel des Arts Montmartre** MONTMARTRE   On a narrow street just off lively rue des Abbesses, this unassuming hotel once hosted artists and sculptors and even a few dancers from the Moulin Rouge. It's currently run by the third generation of the Lameyre family. Rooms are small yet spotless, with funky decor, reminiscent of the '80s. A few have distant views of the Eiffel Tower over Parisian rooftops. *5 rue Tholozé, 18th. www.arts-hotel-paris.com.* ☎ *01-46-06-30-52. 50 units. Double 200€–280€. Métro: Blanche or Abbesses. Map p 151.*

★★★ **Hôtel des Grandes Ecoles** LATIN QUARTER   This country house—with its

The Hôtel des Grandes Ecoles seems to transport you to the French countryside.

old-fashioned floral wallpaper, chintz, and lace—is a welcome break from the city hubbub. The bucolic feel continues in the flower-filled garden, where noisy traffic dissolves into the twittering of birds—the perfect place for a lazy breakfast. Rooms are spotlessly clean and the welcome is friendly. *75 rue Cardinal Lemoine, 5th. https://hoteldes grandesecoles.com.* ☎ *01-43-26-79-23. 51 units. Double 185€–260€. Métro: Cardinal Lemoine. Map p 154.*

★★ Hôtel du Bourg Tibourg

MARAIS   Hotels with far less style can cost twice as much as this well-located place. Rooms are small but comfortable, with romantic modern decor and lush fabrics in everything from leopard print to stripes. There's even a tiny courtyard garden, where you can enjoy a glass of wine. *19 rue du Bourg-Tibourg, 4th. www. bourgtibourg.com.* ☎ *01-42-78-47-39. 30 units. Double 320€–450€. Métro: Hôtel-de-Ville. Map p 152.*

★★★ Hôtel Duc de St-Simon

INVALIDES   A sweet courtyard welcomes you into this hopelessly romantic hotel that has seduced the likes of Lauren Bacall. Rooms are filled with antiques, objets d'art, and lush fabrics. Some have terraces overlooking a garden. *14 rue de St-Simon, 7th. www.hotelducde saintsimon.com.* ☎ *01-44-39-20-20. 34 units. Double 315€–440€. Métro: Rue du Bac. Map p 154.*

★★★ Hôtel du Louvre LOUVRE

This former home of painter Camille Pissarro is now a beautiful Belle Epoque luxury hotel, resplendent with a mix of period and contemporary design features. Guest rooms are plush and airy, with warm tones and heavy fabrics. The hotel's chic brasserie is an ode to the late world-famous chef Paul Bocuse, serving many of his iconic recipes. *Place André Malraux, 1st. www.hyatt. com.* ☎ *01-44-58-38-38. 177 units. Double 450€–700€. Métro: Palais Royal or Louvre Rivoli. Map p 152.*

★★ Hôtel Duo MARAIS   One of

the city's trendiest hotels, with a location right in the heart of the Marais. Decor has an old-meets-new-world charm thanks to sleek rooms all dressed up in cool browns, creams, and bold-print wallpaper. It's also one of the only hotels in the area to have its own sauna. *11 rue du Temple, 4th. www.duo-paris. com.* ☎ *01-42-72-72-22. 45 units. Double 280€–490€. Métro: Hôtel-de-Ville. Map p 152.*

★★ Hôtel Le Belmont CHAMPS-

ÉLYSÉES   Luxurious, beautiful, and kitted out with a spa, this gem of a hotel throws you back to the Napoleon III era, with opulent furnishings and deep wood paneling. Rooms are theatrical (quite literally when it comes to the stage-curtain head-boards) and the black marble in the bathrooms sparkles like onyx. For an extra treat, book a massage in the spa or check out the Turkish bath and gym. *30 rue de Bassano, 16th. www.belmont-paris-hotel.com.* ☎ *01-53-57-75-00. 74 units. Double 295€–475€. Métro: Kléber or Georges V. Map p 151.*

★★ Hôtel Les Jardins du Luxembourg
LUXEMBOURG These intimate lodgings, tucked away on a quiet cul-de-sac, are where Sigmund Freud stayed on his first visit to Paris. Today it exudes elegance, from the nature-themed wallpaper behind the beds to the glossy white tiles in the bathrooms. Some rooms have small balconies. *5 impasse Royer-Collard, 5th. www.hoteljardins luxembourg.com.* ☎ *01-40-46-08-88. 26 units. 189€–274€ double; 380€ suite. Métro: Cluny–La Sorbonne. RER: Luxembourg. Map p 154.*

★★★ kids Hôtel Louison
MONTPARNASSE/SAINT-GERMAIN Rooms in this family-run hotel are lushly decorated in thick, patterned fabrics and parquet floors. The hearty breakfasts are served in a bistro-style room that feels like a Left Bank institution. Families are welcome here, but the atmosphere is nonetheless romantic, too. *105 rue Vaugirard, 6th. www.louison-hotel. com.* ☎ *01-53-63-25-50. 42 units. Double 180€–385€. Métro: Montparnasse or St-Placide. Map p 154.*

★★★ Hôtel Meurice
CONCORDE Salvador Dalí once made this hotel his headquarters. It's gorgeous, with perfectly preserved mosaic floors, hand-carved moldings, and an Art Nouveau glass roof. Rooms are sumptuous and individually decorated, all with plush antiques. Restaurant le Meurice Alain Ducasse has dramatic decor inspired by Versailles. *228 rue de Rivoli, 1st. www.dorchester collection.com/en/paris/le-meurice.* ☎ *01-44-58-10-10. 160 units. Double 1,750€ and up. Métro: Tuileries or Concorde. Map p 152.*

★★★ Hôtel Particulier
MONTMARTRE You'll be hard-pressed to find somewhere more romantic or stylish than this hidden gem, nestled down a leafy passage by a rock called Rocher de la Sorcière (Witch's Rock). Avant-garde artists have given each room a special touch. The hotel's a favorite local haunt too, thanks to its excellent brunches and cocktails. *23 av Junot, 18th. www.hotelparticulier.com.* ☎ *01-53-41-81-40. 5 units. Double 790€–890€. Métro: Lamarck-Caulincourt. Map p 151.*

★ Hôtel Saint-Louis en l'Isle
ÎLE ST-LOUIS A charming family atmosphere reigns at this classic hotel in a 17th-century town house. The rooms are small but well

Even the bathrooms at the Hôtel Meurice have their own elegance.

Hôtel Particulier.

decorated, there are lots of lovely touches, and the location is excellent. Great value for the price. *75 rue St-Louis-en-l'Île, 4th. www.hotel saintlouis.com.* ☎ *01-46-34-04-80. 19 units. Double 205€–295€. Métro: Pont Marie or St-Michel-Notre-Dame. Map p 152.*

★★★ Hôtel Shangri-La

CHAILLOT Set inside the 19th-century palace Napoleon built for his great-nephew Prince Roland Bonaparte, this hotel drips with fine furniture, chandeliers, and antiques. But there's a modern edge, too, in the classy rooms, lounge, and two superlative eateries: **Shang Palace,** the only Michelin-starred Chinese restaurant in France, and **La Bauhinia** brasserie, which mixes Asian and French flavors. The spa has one of the city's loveliest pools. *10 av. d'Iéna, 16th. www.shangri-la. com.* ☎ *01-53-67-19-98. 81 units. Double 1,800€ and up. Métro: Iéna. Map p 151.*

★★ Hôtel Vernet ETOILE In

Paris's Golden Triangle (a luxe shopping district), this oasis of charm attracts guests drawn by the nearby designer shops on avenues Georges V and Montaigne. Contemporary styling throughout contrasts nicely with the Haussmann-era building—especially its restaurant, which sports a stunning Belle Époque glass cupola (with ironwork

by Eiffel himself). *25 rue Vernet, 8th. www.hotelvernet-paris.fr.* ☎ *01-44-31-98-00. 50 units. Double 450€–620€. Métro: Kléber or George V. Map p 151.*

★★★ Hôtel Westminster

OPERA This gorgeous hotel is favored by shoppers who prowl Place Vendôme, Rue du Faubourg Saint-Honoré, and the department stores around Opéra Garnier for chic attire. The decor is resolutely stylish: classic marbles, deep woods, and plush fabrics. The restaurant, Céladon, is a popular spot for lunch thanks to its 35€ menu. *13 rue de la Paix, 2nd. www.warwick hotels.com/hotel-westminster.* ☎ *01-42-61-57-46. 102 units. Double 345€–680€. Métro: Opéra. RER: Auber. Map p 152.*

★★★ kids Le Bristol CHAMPS-

ÉLYSÉES Paris's most discreet palace hotel is a favorite with celebrities, politicians, and royalty. Guest rooms are lavish, large, and luxurious. The swimming pool has views over the whole city. In the summer, the three-Michelin-starred restaurant, Epicure, opens onto Paris's biggest palace garden (1,500 sq. m/16,000 sq. ft.), and its one-starred 114 Faubourg brasserie is well worth crossing Paris for. If you can't afford a room, observe the glitterati over a cocktail in the bar. You might even meet Socrate, the resident cat—a hit with kids. *112 rue du Faubourg St-Honoré, 8th. www.oetkercollection.com/hotels/le-bristol-paris.* ☎ *01-53-43-43-00. 170 units. Double 1,190€ and up. Métro: Franklin-D.-Roosevelt. Map p 151.*

★ **Le Vert Galant** GOBELINS Set around a serene garden and attached to an excellent Basque restaurant, it isn't hard to see why this is one of the city's best budget hotels. Some rooms even have kitchenettes so you can save money by cooking. Pull up a chair at a table in the garden after a long day's sightseeing. It's a wonderful spot for winding down, drink in hand. *43 rue Croulebarbe, 13th. www.vertgalant.com.* ☎ *01-44-08-83-50. 17 units. Double 82€–180€. Métro: Gobelins. Map p 154.*

★★★ **L'Hôtel** ST-GERMAIN-DES-PRES The hotel where Oscar Wilde died is now one of the Left Bank's most distinctive boutique hotels. Each guest room is different, some with fireplaces, some with fabric-covered walls. There's a swimming pool in the cellar, and the cocktail bar has free live jazz concerts every Thursday (from 7:30pm). *13 rue des Beaux-Arts, 6th. www.l-hotel.com.* ☎ *01-44-41-99-00. 20 units. Double 430€–515€. Métro: St-Germain-des-Prés. Map p 154.*

★★ **Mama Shelter** PERE-LACHAISE Rooms in this starkly modern design hotel, set in a converted car park, are full of fun touches, such as lights made of superhero Halloween masks and 24" wall-mounted iMacs with TV, radio, and web access. Downstairs, a bar, pizza parlor, and restaurant draw a crowd of international trendies. It's still the place to see and be seen. *107 rue de Bagnolet, 20th. www.mamashelter.com.* ☎ *01-43-48-48-48. 170 units. Double 100€–400€. Métro: Alexandre Dumas or Porte de Bagnolet. Map p 152.*

★★ **Molitor by Mgallery** BOIS DE BOULOGNE Once an Art Deco swimming pool, inaugurated in 1929 by Johnny Weissmuller (the Olympic gold medal winner who went on to play Tarzan), this stunning, art-themed hotel—from its rooftop bar down to its basement Clarins spa—feels like a secret. It's an excellent spot for sports fans: The Roland Garros tennis grounds are across the road, and it's near both the Parc des Princes stadium and the Auteuil racetrack in the Bois de Boulogne (p 105). The cool, retro-inspired rooms are understatedly chic; the two huge pools are a godsend in summer. *3 rue Nung-esser et Coli, 16th. www.mgallery.com.* ☎ *01-56-07-08-50. 124 units.*

One of the stylish rooms at L'Hôtel.

The young and stylish flock to Mama Shelter, in the 20th arrondissement.

Double 350€–560€. Métro: Michel-Ange Molitor. Map p 151.

★★★ Monsieur George

CHAMPS-ÉLYSÉES Named after George Washington, this hotel is as refined as its surroundings. Chic boudoir-style rooms in blacks, grays, and blues have a distinct Art Deco feel that continues in the bathrooms, where the marble sinks and gold taps wouldn't look amiss on a luxury 1920s ocean liner. A few rooms overlook the Sacré-Coeur or the Eiffel Tower. Guests have access to the hotel's spa and fitness space, set under vaulted ceilings. There's also a hip bar and two gourmet restaurants. *17 rue Washington, 8th. www.monsieurgeorge.com.* ☎ *01-87-89-48-48. 46 units. Double 385€–650€. Métro: Georges V. Map p 151.*

★★★ OFF Paris Seine

AUSTERLITZ For a Seine-side sleep, try this quirky floating hotel, docked on the riverbanks at the foot of the Gare d'Austerlitz. Once inside, you'll feel like you're on a trendy ocean liner, especially as the music blasts when you are having a drink on one of the decks. On warm days, you can swim in a narrow outdoor pool. The chic, cabin-like rooms are small but well thought out; it's worth paying for a riverside room so you can gaze at the lights that reflect on the water at night. If you're a light sleeper, bring ear plugs; you can sometimes hear the Métro passing on the nearby bridge. *20–22 Port d'Austerlitz, 13th. www.offparisseine.com.* ☎ *01-44-06-62-65. 58 units. 215€–304€ double; Métro: Gare d'Austerlitz or Gare de Lyon. Map p 154.*

★★★ Pavillon de la Reine

MARAIS You pass through an arcade into a small formal garden to enter this elegant mansion, which is set back from the hustle and bustle of the Place des Vosges. The decor is a suave and subtle combination of modern and antique history. Guests have access to a full spa, offering sauna and fitness room. There's also a chic French restaurant, **Anne,** with a 49€ lunch menu and 150€ tasting menu that are worth staying in for. *28 pl. des Vosges, 3rd. www.pavillon-de-la-reine.com.*

Built on a floating river barge, OFF Paris Seine makes creative use of a small space.

Bed & Breakfasts in Paris

For a special, intimate Parisian experience, consider booking a B&B. Here are some reliable places to try: **Bed & Breakfast France** (www.bedbreak.com), which is promoted by City Hall and has a long, trustworthy selection; and **Alastair Sawday's** (www.sawdays.co.uk), which lists a few special B&Bs and apartments to rent. To live like a local in trendy SoPi (south Pigalle, below Montmartre), try **52 Clichy,** 52 rue de Clichy, 9th (www.52clichy.com; ☎ 06-66-01-75-44; from 125€), a fabulous B&B for two, with a separate flat that sleeps up to four people. Breakfast is copious; the balcony views over Paris's steely rooftops picturesque; and the welcome, by expat owner Rosemary, perfect. She can even give you a makeover (prices on request), as she's an image consultant by trade.

☎ 01-40-29-19-19. 56 units. Double 400€–755€. Métro: Bastille. Map p 152.

★★★ kids Regent's Garden Hotel CHAMPS-ÉLYSÉES   A

goodnight's sleep is guaranteed in this stately hotel, thanks to its setting away from the noise of the street, and quaint, flower-filled courtyard—perfect for a quiet breakfast alfresco. Rooms are elegant, in bold stripes and patterns. *6 rue Pierre Demours, 8th. www.hotel-regents-paris.com.* ☎ *01-45-74-07-30. 40 units. Double 240€–390€. Métro: Ternes or Charles de Gaulle–Etoile. Map p 151.*

★★ Renaissance Paris Arc de Triomphe CHAMPS-ÉLYSÉES

Book a Paris Sky View Room and watch the Eiffel Tower twinkle from your balcony in this trendy five-star hotel. It has elegantly modern architecture, and if you fancy Mediterranean cuisine, the Solis restaurant serves scrumptious mezze and cocktails. The fitness room is open 24/7, which is handy. *39 av de Wagram, 17th. www.marriott.com.* ☎ *01-55-37-55-37. 118 units. Double from 450€–577€. Métro: Ternes. Map p 151.*

★★★ Solar Hôtel DENFERT-

ROCHEREAU   Paris's first low-budget, environmentally friendly hotel has a fabulous concept: Modern rooms without frills but with A/C, TV, and phones; a pretty garden where you can eat the free organic breakfast and hire bikes; static prices year-round; and a genuine low-carbon charter. *22 rue Boulard, 14th. www.solarhotel.fr.* ☎ *01-43-21-08-20. 34 units. Double 99€. Métro/RER: Denfert-Rochereau. Map p 154.*

★ Terrass Hôtel MONTMARTRE

Most upper-floor rooms in this trendy hotel (once frequented by Dalí and Renoir) afford amazing cityscapes, some onto the filigreed silhouette of the Eiffel Tower. Head to the rooftop bar-restaurant to continue gazing over cocktails and delicious Mediterranean-fusion dishes. Or, after a busy day sightseeing, wind down in the hotel's Nuxe spa, with its massage rooms, hammam, sauna, and a rain shower. The fitness center offers weekend yoga or Pilates. *12 rue Joseph de Maistre, 18th. www.terrass-hotel.com.* ☎ *01-46-06-72-85. 100 units. Double 160€–450€. Métro: Place de Clichy or Blanche. Map p 151.* ●

10 The Best Day Trips & Excursions

Decadent Versailles

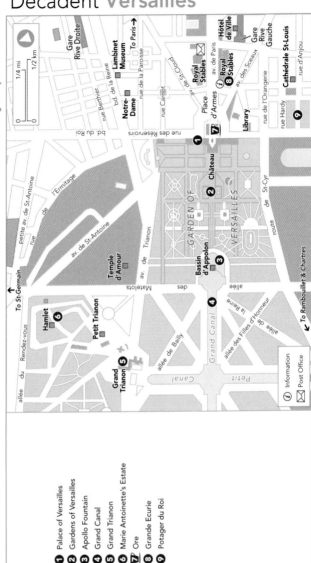

1 Palace of Versailles
2 Gardens of Versailles
3 Apollo Fountain
4 Grand Canal
5 Grand Trianon
6 Marie Antoinette's Estate
7 Ore
8 Grande Ecurie
9 Potager du Roi

Previous page: The Fountain of Apollo at Versailles.

Yes, it's touristy, and yes, it will be crowded in the summer, but come anyway. Versailles must be seen to be believed, and it is well worth the 35-minute journey. It took 40,000 workers 50 years to convert Louis XIII's hunting lodge into this extravagant palace. The major work was started in 1678 by Jules Hardouin-Mansart under Louis XIV, and before it was finished, entire forests had been removed to make way for its extensive gardens. It was here in the 18th century that French royalty lived a life of such excess in a time of widespread poverty that it spurred a revolution.

The Sun King's Hall of Mirrors reflects natural light back into the garden at Versailles.

❶ ★★★ Palace of Versailles. One of the first things you'll notice when you arrive is that this vast palace of 2,300 rooms is dwarfed by the grounds, which stretch for miles. Inside the palace, it's all over-the-top, all the time. The king and his family lived in the Petits Appartements much of the time, where the king's apartment and the queen's bedchamber are exquisitely overdone. One room, the Cabinet of the Meridian, was where Marie Antoinette finally gave birth to an heir in 1781, after 11 years of marriage. The King's Grand Appartement is actually an enfilade of seven terrifically decked-out rooms—showpieces for visitors to the court. The largest is the Hercules Salon, where the ceiling is painted with the *Apotheosis of Hercules*. The elaborate Mercury Salon is where the body of Louis XIV lay in state after his death. But the apartments pale in comparison to the 71m-long (233-ft.) Hall of Mirrors designed by Mansart.

The Hall of Mirrors was designed to reflect sunlight back into the garden and remind people that the "Sun King" lived here. On June 28, 1919, the treaty ending World War I was signed in this hall. Elsewhere in the palace there's an impressive Clock Room, designed in 1753 by architect Ange-Jacques Gabriel, with a gilded-bronze astronomical clock that is supposed to keep perfect time until 9999. ⏱ *2 hr.*

❷ ★★★ Gardens of Versailles. These vast, varied, vainglorious gardens were created by the landscape architect André Le Nôtre, who used lakes, canals, geometric flower beds, long avenues, fountains, and statuary to devise a French Eden. Thousands of men moved tons of soil, trees, and rock for the plan. The result—beautifully maintained for hundreds of years— is simply breathtaking. ⏱ *2 hr.*

❸ Apollo Fountain. At one time, hundreds of fountains

burbled around the grounds. The most famous surviving example is the Apollo fountain (created in 1670 by Jean-Baptiste Tuby after a drawing by Charles Le Brun), which depicts Apollo's chariot.

④ Grand Canal. The 1.6km (1-mile) canal is surrounded by lush, planted forests crossed by straight paths. So precise was Le Nôtre's design that on St. Louis Day (Aug 25), the sun sets in perfect alignment with the Grand Canal.

⑤ ★★ Grand Trianon. The elegant Grand Trianon was designed in 1687 by Jules Hardouin-Mansart. It was later the home of Napoleon and his family. Then, in 1963, President Charles de Gaulle had it turned into a guesthouse for French presidents, and parts are still used today for presidential functions. ⏱ *30 min.*

Travel Tip

Both the Grand Trianon and Marie Antoinette's estate can be reached by the "Petit Train" from the Parterre Nord (www.train-versailles. com; ☎ 01-39-54-22-00; 8.50€ adults, 6.50€ ages 11–18, free for kids 10 and under). The round trip takes about 50 minutes, but you can hop on and hop off at each site.

⑥ Marie Antoinette's Estate. Louis XVI's young wife is famed for her desire to flee the pomp of the Versailles court. Her retreat was this estate—made up of the Queen's Gardens, the **Hameau de la Reine** (a lovely thatch-roofed hamlet of fanciful faux farmhouses), and the **Petit Trianon** (a perfectly scaled gem of a building that architecture buffs flip for; it was also a meeting place for Louis XV and Madame de Pompadour). ⏱ *30 min.*

⑦ Ore. Within the palace, stop for a bite of famed chef Alain Ducasse's modern French cuisine in Versailles's grand Pavillon Dufour, a 19th-century addition, overlooking the cours royale and d'honneur (courtyards). The prix-fixe menus, at 45€ and 55€, are excellent, and include dishes like foie gras with marinated rhubarb, and haddock with asparagus. Or pop by at tea-time for mille-feuille (vanilla cream & pastry layered cake) 12€. Delicious! *Pavillon Dufour, 1st floor. www.ducasse-chateauversailles.com.* ☎ *01-30-84-12-96. Closed Mon. $$.*

The Pomp of Versailles Gardens

Each weekend between April and the end of October (and Tues between early May and the end of June), the palace's fountains spurt to the rhythms of baroque music during the 60- to 90-minute **Grandes Eaux Musicales,** a wonderful exhibition (10am–7pm) that takes you back to the time of the Sun King (10.50€ unless included in your passport ticket). Every Saturday evening between mid-June and mid-September (and July 14 and Aug 15), the pomp increases to include dramatic firework displays, as the fountains light up and classical music fills the air during the **Grandes Eaux Nocturnes.** Tickets are sold separately for this at https://tickets.chateau versailles-spectacles.fr (31€). Gates open at 5:30pm.

Versailles: Practical Matters

Versailles (www.chateauversailles.fr; ☎ 01-30-83-78-00) is open Tuesday to Sunday from 9am to 5:30pm (Apr–Oct until 6:30pm). The gardens are open daily year-round from 8am to 6pm (Apr–Oct until 8:30pm). Tickets are available day of, but advance purchase is recommended as you will need a time-stamped ticket for the château. Admission to the château is 18€ to 19.50€. Admission to the Grand Trianon and Marie Antoinette's estate is 12€ Admission to the gardens is free (except during the Grandes Eaux, when it's 10.50€).

However, the best and easiest way to visit Versailles is to buy a *Passeport Versailles* (28.50€; free for children 17 and under and visitors 25 and under from the EU, except during the Grandes Eaux Nocturnes events—see box above), which allows quick access to all the sites.

The 2-day passport is a good value if you plan to stay overnight and includes the Grande Ecurie show. Buy tickets online (53€). Upon arrival, depending on your ticket, look for the signs guiding you to the correct entrance (usually doors A or B). For tickets to the Grand Trianon and Marie Antoinette's estate, head straight to that entrance in the gardens.

Versailles has two main train stations—Rive Gauche (the nearest one to the château) and Rive Droite. To get to the former, take RER C from central Paris to Versailles–Rive Gauche; or take a normal train from Gare St-Lazare to Versailles–Rive Droite and then walk 10 minutes. By car, take the A-13 from Paris to the Versailles-Château exit. Pay parking is available on the Place d'Armes. The trip to Versailles takes about 30 to 40 minutes by car or train.

❽ Grande Ecurie. The famous Versailles horses are kept in high style here and trained in a variety of equine performance arts (at the Académie Équestre de Versailles). You can take in a performance on weekends (Sat 6pm, Sun and some Wed 3pm; extra dates during French school holidays; buy tickets in conjunction with your château visit (39€). For times and tickets check the website or call in advance. ⏱ *1 hr. 15 min. Near the palace entrance on av. Rockefeller.* www.bartabas.fr. ☎ *01-39-02-62-70. Performances 22€.*

❾ Potager du Roi. This enclosure, made up of 5,000 fruit trees tapered into extravagant shapes, is where the Sun King's fruit and vegetable plot stood. The garden (built between 1678 and 1683) is now separate from the château and well worth visiting. You can even buy the fruit and veggies grown here in the boutique. ⏱ *30 min. Access via Rue du Maréchal Joffre (left main entrance).* www.potager-du-roi.fr. ☎ *01-39-24-63-24. Admission 5€ (3€ Nov–Mar), free for people under age 26. Jan–Mar Tues & Fri 10am–6pm; Apr–Oct Tues–Sun 10am–6pm; Nov–Dec Tues & Fri 10am–6pm, Sat 10am–1pm. Closed May 1 & during Christmas school holidays.*

Disneyland Paris

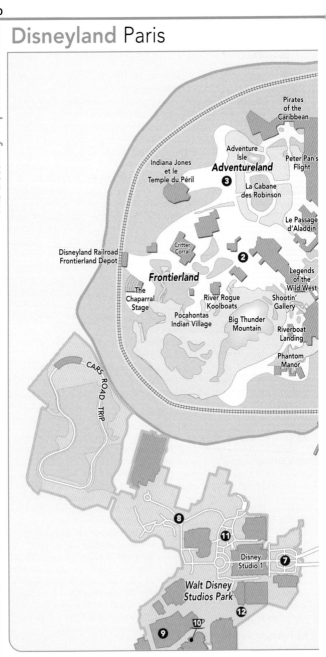

Pirates
of the
Caribbean

Adventure
Isle

Adventureland
❸

Indiana Jones
et le
Temple du Péril

Peter Pan's
Flight

La Cabane
des Robinson

Le Passage
d'Aladdin

Disneyland Railroad
Frontierland Depot

Critter
Corral

❷

Frontierland

Legends
of the
Wild West

The
Chaparral
Stage

River Rogue
Koolboats

Shootin'
Gallery

Pocahontas
Indian Village

Big Thunder
Mountain

Riverboat
Landing

Phantom
Manor

CARS ROAD TRIP

❽

⓫

Disney
Studio 1

❼

*Walt Disney
Studios Park*

⓬

❾

🔟

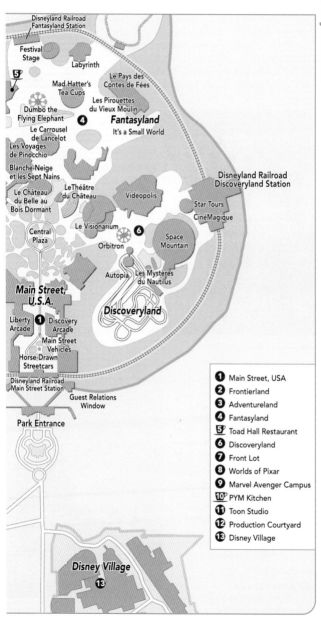

Disneyland Railroad
Fantasyland Station

Festival
Stage

Labyrinth

5

Mad Hatter's
Tea Cups

Le Pays des
Contes de Fées

Dumbo the
Flying Elephant

Les Pirouettes
du Vieux Moulin

Le Carrousel
de Lancelot

4 *Fantasyland*

It's a Small World

Les Voyages
de Pinocchio

Blanche-Neige
et les Sept Nains

Le Château
du Belle au
Bois Dormant

LeThéâtre
du Château

Vidéopolis

Disneyland Railroad
Discoveryland Station

Star Tours

CinéMagique

Central
Plaza

Le Visionarium

6

Orbitron

Space
Mountain

*Main Street,
U.S.A.*

Autopia

Les Mystères
du Nautilus

Discoveryland

Liberty
Arcade

1 Discovery
Arcade

Main Street
Vehicles

Horse-Drawn
Streetcars

Disneyland Railroad
Main Street Station

Guest Relations
Window

Park Entrance

1 Main Street, USA

2 Frontierland

3 Adventureland

4 Fantasyland

5 Toad Hall Restaurant

6 Discoveryland

7 Front Lot

8 Worlds of Pixar

9 Marvel Avenger Campus

10 PYM Kitchen

11 Toon Studio

12 Production Courtyard

13 Disney Village

Disney Village

13

Disneyland Paris is a blessing for travelers with kids who have wearied of the museums and churches and just want to go on the rides for a day, pleasepleaseplease! Overall, there's little difference between this amusement park and those in Florida and California, except here the cheeseburgers come with *pommes frîtes* instead of fries. There are two main parks: Disneyland Park, with its five lands, and Walt Disney Studios Park, split into five worlds, including the brand new, much-talked about Marvel Avengers Campus.

Shopping on Main Street, USA.

❶ Main Street, USA. Immediately after entering the park, you'll find yourself in an idealized American town, complete with horse-drawn carriages and street-corner barbershop quartets. This is also a good spot to catch the colorful parade floats.

❷ Frontierland. In this "pretend America," it's a conveniently short hop to the West, particularly if you board one of the steam-powered trains that takes you through a Grand Canyon diorama to get to it. Big Thunder Mountain, which hurtles you through a spooky gold mine, is the main draw here.

❸ Adventureland. Swashbuckling pirates battle near the Swiss Family Robinson's treehouse. Too

tame? Head for the Indiana Jones and the Temple of Peril ride, which travels backward at breakneck speed.

❹ Fantasyland. Young children will be charmed by Sleeping Beauty's Castle (*Le Château de la Belle au Bois Dormant*), complete with the obligatory fire-breathing dragon in its dungeon. From here, a flight with Peter Pan might just be necessary.

5 **Toad Hall Restaurant.** If you're looking for a quick stint in the English countryside, try this stately spot for a sit-down meal of traditional English fish and chips (fries). *Fantasyland. $$.*

Sleeping Beauty's Castle.

Disneyland Paris: Practical Matters

Drive 32km (20 miles) along the A4 east from Paris to exit 14; take the Disneyland Paris Express shuttle (from one of four stops in central Paris; www.disneylandparis.com/en-gb/tours/disneyland-paris-express); or take the RER A to the Marne-la-Vallée–Chessy stop (about 40 min.). The park is at Marne-la-Vallée, Paris (www.disneylandparis.com; ☎ 03448-008-898). Parking is 30€ per day. Admission varies depending on how many days you come for and the time of year. As a general guide, the price for 1 day (one park) hovers around 67€ for adults and kids over 12, 56€ ages 3–11, and free for children 2 and under; a 1-day hopper (both parks) is 92€ for adults and kids over 12, 81€ ages 3–11. Disneyland's opening times vary according to the season, so check the website for up-to-date information (www.disneylandparis.com/en-gb/faq/park-hours-schedules). The resort was designed as a total vacation destination, so within the enormous compound there are not only the two parks but also six hotels, campgrounds, the Village Disney entertainment center, a 27-hole golf course, and dozens of restaurants and shops.

6 Discoveryland. *Star Wars* fans rejoice. Here you can reach hyperspace on Star Wars Hyperspace Mountain, and board a Starspeeder in a 3D movie adventure.

7 Front Lot. Over in Walt Disney Studios Park, this area is done up like a movie studio lot. It's mostly shops, including Les Legendes d'Hollywood, where you can create your own Jedi lightsaber.

8 Worlds of Pixar. This is the place to shrink down to the size of Remy the Rat and try to escape from Gusteau's kitchen in the 4D ride, Ratatouille: The Adventure. Or think like Nemo and ride Crush's Coaster.

9 Marvel Avengers Campus. It's in this new high-tech zone that you can free your inner hero—on Spider-Man's interactive W.E.B. Adventure and the Avengers Assemble: Flight Force ride, where you join Iron Man to save the world.

10 PYM Kitchen. The fun theme here is Ant-Man's PYM particle changing technology, so the buffet-style food comes in all sizes—including "giant," which means some burgers are so huge they're served by the slice! *Marvel Avengers Campus.* $$.

11 Toon Studio. One for the little ones this, you'll find gentle Flying Carpets over Agrabah and meet 'n' greets with Olaf from Frozen.

12 Production Courtyard. Hollywood meets horror in this area, where the malevolent ghost of a girl causes the elevator to drop in the Twilight Zone Tower of Terror. There are musical shows too.

13 Disney Village. This haven for adults features endless entertainment options—dance clubs, snack bars, restaurants, shops, and bars. There's also a massive 3D IMAX cinema, where you can see all the latest blockbusters.

The Cathedral at Chartres

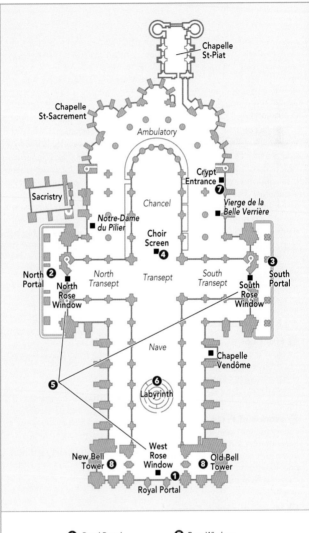

Chapelle St-Piat

Chapelle St-Sacrement

Ambulatory

Sacristy

Chancel

Crypt Entrance **7**

Vierge de la Belle Verrière

Notre-Dame du Pilier

Choir Screen **4**

North Portal **2**

North Rose Window

North Transept

Transept

South Transept

South Rose Window

South Portal **3**

Nave

Chapelle Vendôme

5

6 Labyrinth

West Rose Window

New Bell Tower **8**

Old Bell Tower **8**

1

Royal Portal

1 Royal Portal	**5** Rose Windows
2 North Portal	**6** Floor Labyrinth
3 South Portal	**7** Crypts
4 Choir Screen	**8** Towers

An hour from Paris, standing at the gateway to the Loire Valley, Chartres represents the highest architectural and theological aspirations of the Middle Ages in France. The cathedral was much the same in medieval times as it is now, which should give you a sense of how impressive it must have been in 1260, when it was completed. Rodin described it as the French Acropolis, and once you've seen it, you'll be hard-pressed to disagree—especially at night between April and January, when the **Chartres en Lumières** festival (www.chartresenlumieres.com; free; daily dusk–1am) turns the cathedral's facade (along with other monuments and bridges) into beautiful, rippling screens of color.

The cathedral's facade.

❶ Royal Portal. The sculpted bodies around the portal are elongated and garbed in long, flowing robes, but their faces are disturbingly lifelike—frowning, winking, and smiling. Christ is shown at the Second Coming—his descent to Earth on the right, his ascent back to Heaven on the left.

❷ & ❸ North and South Portals. Both the North and South Portals are carved with biblical images, including the expulsion of Adam and Eve from the Garden of Eden.

❹ Choir Screen. This celebrated screen dates to the 16th century. It has 40 niches holding statues of biblical figures. Don't be so dazzled by all the stained glass (see next stop) that you overlook its intricate carvings.

❺ ★★★ Rose Windows. No cathedral in the world can match Chartres for its 12th-century glass (saved from damage during World War I and World War II by parishioners who removed it piece by piece and stored it safely). It gave the world a new color—Chartres blue—and it is absolutely exceptional. All the windows are glorious, but the three rose windows may be the best.

❻ Floor Labyrinth. Many Gothic cathedrals once had labyrinths like the one on the floor of the nave, but virtually all were destroyed over time, so this one, which dates from around 1200, is very rare. It is thought that such labyrinths represented the passage of the soul to heaven. Its 261.5m (858-ft.) path was either walked in prayer as a symbolic pilgrimage to Jerusalem or as a path of repentance, in which case the sinner would cover the distance on their knees.

❼ Crypts. Those who would like to visit the cathedral's underbelly can usually only do so as part of a

Chartres: Practical Matters

From Paris's Gare Montparnasse, trains run directly to Chartres (1 hr. to 1 hr. 15 min.). By car, take A-10/A-11 southwest from the Périphérique and follow signs to Le Mans and Chartres (about 1½ hr.). The cathedral (Cloître Notre-Dame; www.cathedrale-chartres.org; ☎ 02-37-21-59-08) is open daily 8:30am to 7:30pm (July and Aug Tues, Fri, and Sun until 10pm). Audioguides are available for 6.50€. Guided tours of the cathedral in English are offered by former Chicagoan Anne Marie Woods (annemariechartres@gmail.com; early May to end Sept Tues–Sat noon; 18€ adults, 12€, ages 13–18, free for children 12 and under). Anne Marie also offers private guided tours on request, as does Malcolm Miller, a veteran scholar who has been studying the cathedral for over 3 decades (email Malcolm Miller at millerchartres@aol.com).

Any trip to the cathedral should include a visit to the medieval cobbled streets of **Chartres's Vieux Quartier (Old Quarter),** which stretches from the cathedral down to the Eure River. **Rue Chantault,** where the 800-year-old houses have wonderfully colorful facades, is particularly lovely. Also, stop in at the **Musée des Beaux Arts de Chartres,** right next to the cathedral, at 29 Cloître Notre-Dame (☎ 02-37-90-45-80; free admission). It has an excellent collection covering the 16th through the 20th centuries. You'll find a vibrant food market Saturdays and Wednesday mornings (and also Wed afternoons) in the market hall at Place Billard, near the cathedral. There's also a flower market Tuesdays, Thursdays, and Saturdays at Place du Cygne. For lunch, try **Le Tripot,** 11 place Jean Moulin (https://letripot.wixsite.com/chartres; ☎ 02-37-36-60-11), a traditional French restaurant close to the cathedral.

guided tour (9€; ask at the desk about English language tours). What you'll see is Europe's longest crypt, medieval frescoes, and contemporary stained glass.

❽ Towers. The evolution of Gothic architecture was influenced by the cathedral's 12th-century towers, which you can climb to get sweeping views across the Beauce countryside. Architect Viollet-le-Duc considered the 105m (344-ft.) spire of the Old Bell Tower (also called the Tour du Midi) to be flawless. The flamboyant Gothic New Bell Tower is one of the tallest in France. Huff and puff your way to the top and admire the village of Chartres's tiled rooftops. *Cloître Notre-Dame. www.cathedrale-chartres.monuments-nationaux.fr.* ☎ *02-37-31-22-07. Admission 6€, free for ages 17 and under, and 25 and under for EU countries. Daily 10am–12:45pm & 2pm–5pm (May–Sept until 6pm).* ●

The **Savvy Traveler**

Before You Go

Visitor Information

The **Office de Tourisme et des Congrès** in the Hôtel de Ville (29 rue de Rivoli, 4th; www.parisinfo. com; ☎ 01-49-52-42-63; daily 10am–6pm) is the city's main tourist information office, providing information on hotels, restaurants, excursions, shopping, transport, and events. Other offices dotted around the city (closed during some major holidays) include: **Gare du Nord,** 18 rue de Dunkerque, 10th (between platforms 7 and 9; Mon–Sat 9am–5pm); **Travel Wifi,** 38 av. de l'Opéra, 2nd (Mon–Sat 11am–7pm); and **Récéption du Carousel du Louvre,** 99 rue de Rivoli, 1st (Wed–Mon 11am–7pm).

The international website for tourism in France is www.atoutfrance.fr. For comprehensive information about traveling to Paris and Île de France, including hotels, sightseeing, and notices of special events, check out www.parisinfo.com and www.visitparisregion.com.

The Best Times to Go

Paris is less crowded in **August,** when the locals traditionally take their annual holiday. This is also a time for some of Paris's best outdoor festivals. However, some shops, restaurants, and galleries close for 2 weeks at the beginning of the month (usually until Aug 15). You may want to avoid **late September/early October,** when both the annual auto and Paris Fashion Week shows attract thousands of enthusiasts. Spring in

Paris is still a good time to come, but so too is December, when many hotels have special offers on the run up to Christmas—although you might not get any sunshine. In summer 2024, Paris will be hosting the Olympic and Paralympic Games. The city will be swamped, so unless you have tickets to see the games, avoid it like the plague (for more information, www.paris2024.org).

Weather

Global warming issues haven't left Paris unscathed, and the weather is increasingly changeable throughout the year. Generally speaking, summers are hot. Although more and more hotels are adding air-conditioning to the rooms, many cheaper accommodations still get hot and stuffy. Rain is common throughout the year, especially in winter.

Useful Websites & Apps

- **www.mappy.fr**, **www. viamichelin.com**, **www.waze. com**, and **www.google.com/ maps**: Online maps and journey planner.

- **www.pagesjaunes.fr**: Online phone directory for businesses and services.

- **www.culture.fr**: Extensive listings of upcoming cultural events.

- **www.paris.fr**: The City Hall's guide to Paris, with museum and exhibition listings (French only).

Information on COVID & Travel

Check the following official websites for information on rules, regulations, and possible travel restrictions due to COVID:

- **U.S. Embassy & Consulates in France:** https://fr.usembassy. gov/covid-19-information offers up-to-date traveler information, including EU Digital COVID Certificate (Health Pass) info, entry information for France, and information for reentry into the United States after your trip.
- **French government website:** https://www.diplomatie.gouv. fr/en/coming-to-france/ coming-to-france-your-covid-19-questions-answered
- **Paris Tourist Office website:** https://en.parisinfo.com/ practical-paris/info/guides/info-disruption-paris
- **European Commission EU Digital COVID Certificate:** https://ec.europa.eu/info/live-work-travel-eu/corona virus-response/safe-covid-19-vaccines-europeans/ eu-digital-covid-certificate_en

Cellphones (Mobile Phones)

If you own a mobile phone (GSM, tri-band, or quad-band), you should be able to make and receive calls to and from France, and other countries worldwide. Check with your service provider before you leave. Charges can be high. A good way around this is getting your phone unlocked before you leave. This will allow you to buy a local SIM card from a French provider. The main ones are **Orange** (www.orange.fr), **Bouygues Telecom** (www.bouyguestelecom.fr), and **SFR** (www.sfr.fr). Or a better strategy is to download apps like WhatsApp, Facebook Messenger, and FaceTime and make free phone calls over Wi-Fi.

Car Rentals

There's very little need to rent a car in Paris, but if you must have four wheels, book a car online before you leave your home country. Try **Hertz** (www.hertz.com), **Avis** (www. avis.com), **Europcar** (www.europcar. com) or **Budget** (www.budget. com). If you're in the U.S., you should also consider **AutoEurope** (www.autoeurope.com), which is an excellent source for discounted rentals. Even better may be **AutoSlash.com**, which applies discount codes to rentals from all the major multinational firms; this can mean big savings. It also monitors prices, so if a rate drops, it re-books you automatically. You pay for the rental at the counter, not in advance. If you don't want to traipse across town to a car hire shop, try **Carlili** (https://carlili.fr/en), which delivers and collects your car, at the address of your choice, 7 days a week.

Getting **There**

By Plane

Paris has two international airports—**Orly** and **Charles de Gaulle** (**CDG**; www.aeroportsdeparis.fr; ☎ 00-33-1-70-36-39-50 from abroad or ☎ 39-50 in France). At CDG, Air France flights arrive at Terminal 2, while most other flights come into Terminals 1 and 3. At Orly, international flights arrive at Orly Sud (South) and domestic flights at Orly Ouest (West). RER B operates between the two airports, with two stops for CDG: the first for T1 and T3, the second for T2. A free train, the CDGVAL, connects the terminals and provides service to the train stations. Orly's stop is Anthony; from there, a monorail takes you to the airport. (See "From Orly," below.)

From Charles de Gaulle: RER trains leave every 15 minutes (5am to approximately 12:30am) from the station near Terminal 3, serving several of the major downtown Métro/RER stations including Gare du Nord (for Eurostar and Thalys) and Châtelet-les-Halles, the central hub (trip time: 35 min.). There's also a shuttle-bus service into Paris: **Roissybus** (www.ratp.fr; ☎ 34-24) departs every 20 minutes from the airport daily from 6am to 12:30am and costs 16.20€ for the 70-minute ride. The bus leaves you in the center of Paris, at the corner of rue Scribe and rue Auber, near the Opéra.

The **taxi** rate from Roissy into the city is now a fixed rate of 55€ to the Right Bank and 62€ to the Left Bank (supplements 4€ for immediate reservation; 7€ for advance reservation). Alternatively, Uber costs about 45€ to 55€ for an UberX car

(www.uber.com) depending on traffic and distance. Prices increase when demand is high.

From Orly: There are 2 terminals: Orly Sud and Orly Ouest. There are no direct trains to central Paris, but a **monorail** (Orlyval) from the airport takes you to the RER station Anthony, where you can catch line B into the city (trip time about 30 min.). The **Orlybus** (www.ratp.fr; ☎ 34-24), which leaves every 15 minutes between 5am and 12:30am, links the airport with Place Denfert-Rochereau, a 30-minute trip that costs 11.20€ for both adults and children. A taxi from the airport into Paris costs a flat rate of 35€ for a Left Bank destination, or 41€ for the Right Bank, not including supplements (4€ for immediate reservation; 7€ for advance reservation). It takes 25 minutes to an hour to get to Paris by bus or taxi, depending on traffic. The Uber's rates vary from 32€ to 37€ in an UberX car (more if in high demand).

Beauvais Airport (www.aeroport parisbeauvais.com; ☎ 08-92-68-20-66; 0.45€/min.) is served by low-cost airlines such as Ryanair and Wizz and lies around 80km (50 miles) from Paris. Buses to Porte Maillot leave roughly 20 minutes after flights have landed. To return to the airport, catch the bus at least 3 hours before your flight; the journey takes about 1 hour and 15 minutes. Tickets cost 16.90€ (29.90€ return ticket).

By Car

The main highways into Paris are the A-1 from the north (Great Britain and Benelux); A-13 from Rouen, Normandy, and northwest France;

A-10 from Bordeaux, the Pyrenees, southwest France, and Spain; A-6 from Lyon, the French Alps, the Riviera, and Italy; and A-4 and A-5 from eastern France.

By Train
North Americans can buy a **Eurailpass** or individual tickets online from www.eurail.com or www.raileurope.com. For details on the rail passes available in the UK, call the **National Rail** (www.nationalrail.co.uk; ☎ 03457-48-49-50). From the UK, you can travel to Paris under the English Channel via the Eurostar (trip time about 2½ hr.). Buy tickets directly from **Eurostar** (www.eurostar.com).

By Bus
Bus travel to Paris is available from London and several other cities on the Continent. The arrival and departure point for Europe's largest bus operator, **Eurolines France** (www.eurolines.fr), is a 15- to 25-minute Métro ride from central Paris, at the terminus of Métro line 3 (Galleini). Before you travel between London and Paris by bus, check the Eurostar website for offers, as train tickets sometimes dip to as little as 88€ return—a little more than a bus ticket, but you may find spending the extra cash worthwhile for the upgrade in comfort and speed.

Getting **Around**

Paris Orientation
The *périphérique*, a busy ring-road that loosely follows the city's former fortifications, circles the city. It links the city center to its suburbs and France's highway system (*autoroutes*). Everything within the *périphérique* is classified as the city center. The River Seine runs eastwest through it, splitting the city into the Right Bank (north of the Seine), and the Left Bank (south). Together, the Right and Left Banks are divided into 20 sectors called *arrondissements* with postcodes beginning with 75 (designating central Paris) and numbered from 1 to 20 (75001 to 75020; or abbreviated to 1st to 20th). The numbers spiral out clockwise, like the shell of a snail, starting at 1 (around the Louvre) and finishing at 20 (around Père Lachaise). In terms of atmosphere, arrondissements 1 to 8 cover most of the main tourist sights, from the Louvre and Notre-Dame to the Eiffel Tower and the Champs-Élysées. Literary Paris, with its cafes and the Sorbonne University, is concentrated around the 5th and 6th. The 9th to 11th and 17th to 20th are the city's trendiest areas (including the Canal St-Martin, Montmartre, and the Père Lachaise cemetery), although some parts may look shabby. Avoid La Chapelle and Barbès-Rochechouart (18th) at night. The 12th to 16th are largely residential areas but still have plenty of bars and restaurants. The 13th is where you'll find the city's main Chinese quarter. The 16th is very chic, with grand buildings and prices to match.

Getting Around by Public Transportation
The **Métro** network is vast, reliable, and cheap, and within Paris you can transfer between the subway and

the **RER** (Réseau Express Régional) regional trains at no extra cost. The Métro runs from roughly 5:30am to 12:30am Sunday to Thursday (until about 1:30am Fri–Sat and the night before public holidays; 2am on line 2). Detailed information is at www.ratp.fr.

The Métro is reasonably safe at any hour, but use your common sense and be on your guard against pickpockets; on-board beggars are also frequent. Châtelet-les-Halles RER is best avoided at night, as troublemakers tend to loiter there. For ticket advice, see below.

Buses are slower than the Métro but reliable and offer sightseeing opportunities. Most buses run from 6:30am to 9pm, after which a nighttime service (Noctilien) covers key areas until about 5:30am. Some services are limited on Sunday and public holidays. At certain stops, signs list the destinations and numbers of the buses serving that point. Bus and Métro fares are the same, and you can use the same tickets on both, but you'll need a separate ticket for each (you can't transfer from one to the other on the same ticket).

Trams are the latest addition to the network. The 12 lines (T1 to T13—strangely, there's no T12) run around the outskirts of the city, roughly following the *périphérique* (ring-road), linking the center to Greater Paris. Tram fare is the same as on the Métro and on buses. You can transfer from bus to tram on the same ticket, but you will need a separate ticket for tram to Métro (or vice-versa).

Buying Tickets
You can buy tickets from machines at most Métro entrances. The machines take coins and chip-enabled credit cards only, though at time of writing only a handful were equipped with contactless payment systems, making it nearly impossible to pay with phone pay apps like Apple Pay. If you buy at a machine, a **single ticket** costs 2.10€. Children 4 to 9 years old pay half-price; kids 3 and under ride free. But the RATP is gradually phasing out paper tickets, replacing them with plastic passes, so you may no longer be able to buy a paper "*carnet*" (a pack of 10 tickets). You will only be able to buy one with the plastic Navigo Easy card, sold at ticket booths for 2€. Once you have your card, you charge it, either on your phone with the app **Bonjour RATP** (www.ratp.fr/apps/bonjour-ratp), or at a machine. A *carnet* on the Navigo Easy pass costs 16.90€. The downside to this is that you can no longer share your *carnet* with fellow travelers. Each individual will need a card. If you plan to ride the Métro a lot, the **Paris Visite** pass (sold at all RATP machines and ticket booths in the Métro) may be worthwhile. You get unlimited rides for 1, 2, 3, or 5 days for access to zones 1 to 3, which includes central Paris and its nearby suburbs, or zones 1 to 5, which includes Disneyland (zone 5), Versailles (zone 4), and the Charles de Gaulle (zone 5) and Orly (zone 4) airports. It is valid only from the first time you use it, so you can buy it in advance (www.ratp.fr). Remember to fill in your name (and your children's names) as well as the series number on the card and the date of its first use. Prices range from 13.55€ to 74.30€, depending on the zone covered and the number of days.

By Taxi
Uber is available in Paris (minus Uber-Pop), and the smartphone

app works exactly the same way as in the U.S. (www.uber.com). Competing apps are **Bolt** (https://bolt.eu), which offers services in English, and **Heetch** (www.heetch.com) and **LeCab** (https://lecab.fr), which provide ridesharing in French—sometimes at a lower price. Or you can hail a taxi when its sign reads LIBRE or if it sports a full green or white light. The flag drops at 4.18€, and you pay 1€ to 1.50€ per kilometer (more at night). It's often easier to call a cab than to hail one: **Taxi G7** (www.g7.fr; ☎ 36-07; 0.45€/min.) is the main company. It also now has an app similar to those of ridesharing services in that you can pay without cash changing hands, which can be reassuring for travelers.

Cabs are scarce during rush hour and when the Métro closes. Unlicensed cabs (which are usually just a person with a car) may seem like a cheap alternative (especially at the airport), but don't use them under any circumstances. You could find yourself the victim of a robbery—or worse.

By Car

Driving in Paris is not recommended. Parking is difficult, traffic is dense, and networks of one-way streets make navigation, even with the best of maps, a problem. You would be much better off making use of the extensive public transport system or taking cabs.

By Boat

The **Batobus** (www.batobus.com; ☎ 01-76-64-79-12) is a fleet of boats that operates along the Seine, stopping at nine points of interest, including the Eiffel Tower, the Musée d'Orsay, the Louvre, Notre-Dame, and the Hôtel de Ville. They're more about sightseeing and less about getting quickly from place to place, though they will get you up and down the Seine. Buy a pass valid for either 1 or 2 days, each allowing as many entrances and exits as you want (20€/1-day or 22€ 2-day). See the website for exact intervals and closing hours.

By Foot

The best way to take in the city is to walk. The center is very pedestrian-friendly, and so long as you follow all the usual rules of thumb—buy a good map or phone app (or carry this guide with you), and stick to busy, well-lit places at night—you're bound to make a few unexpected and delightful discoveries along the way.

By Bike

Paris has over 1,000km (620 miles) of cycle paths. Even when you have to compete with heavy traffic, it's a fine way to sightsee.

The best deal for short journeys is the **Vélib'**, Paris's excellent self-service bike scheme, available 24/7. Buy a single journey ticket for 3€, for a 45-minute journey on either a pedal bike or an electric bike; get a 1-day pass for 5€ (pedal bike) or 10€ (electric), which gives you the right to as many 30-minute (45-min. for electric) rides as you'd like for 24 hours; and purchase the 3-day pass for 20€ (pedal or electric). If you want to go over 30 minutes, you pay 1€ for your extra 30 minutes on a pedal bike, and 2€ for the 45 minutes on an electric bike. You can take a bike from any stand (the city has around 19,000), use it, replace it, and take a new one. The bikes are fitted with a V-Box, a computer system set between the handlebars, which enables you to lock and unlock the bikes. It also lets you leave your bike in an otherwise full station; follow the instructions and park it top-to-tail with another bike. The English version of the website (www.velib-metropole.fr) explains how everything works; the assistance phone number is ☎ 01-76-49-12-34. To use the machines, travelers must have credit cards with chips, which not all cards have (especially in the U.S.). To get around it, buy your subscription online beforehand.

By E-scooter
In a similar line to Vélib', e-scooters are self-serve, two-wheeled, moped-style electric scooters (for people 18 and over only), though you can only use them on the road (not in bike lanes or on the sidewalk). The main company is **Cityscoot** (www.cityscoot.eu), costing 0.46€/min (that's 13.80€ for 30 min.). If you were born before 1988, you don't need a driver's license to use one; if you were born after 1988, you must have either a valid EU driving license or a license that was issued in your own country and translated into French by an accredited translator (plan well ahead and check with your embassy; the translation process can be costly and time-consuming). *Note:* Helmets are provided (with disposable helmet liners), but bring your own gloves, which are required.

Fast **Facts**

APARTMENT RENTALS   In Paris, **Alastair Sawday's** (www.sawdays.co.uk) lists a few apartments to rent. **My Nest Inn** also has four lovely apartments in the Latin Quarter and Marais (www.mynestinn.com). If you plan to stay for a month or more, try **Home Rental** (www.home-rental.com), which has a large collection of furnished apartments. **New York Habitat** (www.nyhabitat.com; ☎ 212/255-8018) rents furnished apartments and vacation accommodations in Paris and the south of France. And of course, there's **Airbnb** (www.airbnb.com)— a good source for private vacation rentals, offering direct contact with residents across Paris.

ATMS/CASHPOINTS   The easiest and best way to get cash abroad is through an ATM—the **Cirrus** and **PLUS** networks span the globe. Most banks charge a fee for international withdrawals—check with your bank before you leave home.

BABYSITTERS   Most expensive and some moderately priced hotels offer babysitting services, usually subcontracted to local agencies and requiring at least 24 hours' notice. You usually pay the sitter directly, and rates average 10€ to 15€ per hour. One good agency is **Baby Sitting Services,** 1 place Paul Verlaine, 92100 Boulogne, Billancourt (www.babysittingservices.fr; ☎ 01-46-21-33-16). Specify when calling if you need a sitter who speaks English. Also try the **American Church's** basement bulletin board, where English-speaking (often American) students post notices to offer babysitting services. The church is at 65 Quai d'Orsay, 7th (www.acparis.org; ☎ 01-45-62-05-00; Métro: Invalides).

BANKS & CURRENCY EXCHANGE
Most banks are open Monday to Friday from 9am to 5pm and on Saturday mornings. Most no longer keep cash on-site, offering only cash machines. If you have money to change, look for a Changegroup (formerly Travelex) counter (www. changegroup.com); there's a handy one at 49 av. de l'Opéra, 2nd. Traveler's checks are no longer accepted anywhere in France.

BUSINESS HOURS Shops tend to be open from 9:30am to 7pm, but opening hours can be a little erratic. Some traditional shops open at 8am and close at 8 or 9pm, but the lunch break can last up to 3 hours, starting at 1pm. Most museums close 1 day a week (Mon or Tues) and on some national holidays.

CONSULATES & EMBASSIES U.S. Embassy, 2 av. Gabriel, 8th (https://fr.usembassy.gov; ☎ 01-43-12-22-22); **Canadian Embassy,** 35 av. Montaigne, 8th (www.canadainternational.gc.ca/france; ☎ 01-44-43-29-00); **UK Embassy,** 35 rue Faubourg St-Honoré, 8th (www.gov.uk/world/france; ☎ 01-44-51-31-00); **UK Consulate,** 16 bis rue d'Anjou, 8th (www.gov.uk/world/organisations/british-consulate-paris; ☎ 01-44-51-31-02); **Irish Embassy,** 12 av. Foch, 16th (www.dfa.ie/irish-embassy/france; ☎ 01-44-17-67-00); **Australian Embassy,** 4 rue Jean-Ray, 15th (www.france.embassy.gov.au; ☎ 01-40-59-33-00); **New Zealand Embassy,** 7ter rue Lêonard-de-Vinci, 16th (www.mfat.govt.nz/france; ☎ 01-45-01-43-43).

CREDIT CARDS Credit cards are a safe way to carry money. They also provide a convenient record of all your expenses, and they generally offer good exchange rates. You can also withdraw cash advances from your credit cards at banks or ATMs (cashpoints), provided you know your PIN. Keep in mind that when you use your credit card abroad, most banks charge a fee.

CUSTOMS Customs restrictions for visitors entering France differ for citizens of the European Union and for citizens of non-EU countries.

For U.S. Citizens For specifics on what you can bring back from your trip to France, download the free pamphlet *Know Before You Go* online at www.cbp.gov, or contact U.S. Customs Border Protection (CBP; ☎ 877/227-5511, or 202/325-8000 from abroad).

For Canadian Citizens For a clear summary of Canadian rules, plus information on declaring purchases before returning to Canada, see travel.gc.ca. Or call the **Canada Border Services Agency** (☎ 800/461-9999 in Canada, or 204/983-3500 from outside Canada).

For UK Citizens For more information, contact **HM Revenue & Customs** (www.gov.uk/bringing-goods-into-uk-personal-use/arriving-in-Great-Britain), or call ☎ +44/300-200-3700.

For Australian Citizens The **Australian Customs Service** (www.abf.gov.au/entering-and-leaving-australia/duty-free; ☎ 131-881 in Australia, or 612/6196-0196 from abroad) has complete customs information on its website.

For New Zealand Citizens Check the website of the **New Zealand Customs Service** under "duty and allowances" (www.customs.govt.nz; ☎ 0800/428-786, or +64-9/886-4651 from outside New Zealand).

DENTISTS See "Emergencies," below.

DOCTORS See "Emergencies," below.

DRUGSTORES After regular hours, ask at your hotel where the nearest 24-hour pharmacy is. You'll also find the address posted on the doors or windows of other drugstores in the neighborhood. One all-night drugstore is **Pharmacie du Drugstore des Champs-Élysées,** 133 av. des Champs-Élysées, 8th (www.publicisdrugstore.com/en/lieu; ☎ 01-47-20-39-25).

ELECTRICITY France uses the 220-volt system (two round prongs), so you will need an adapter for all electronic equipment (cellphone, computer, etc.). If you can't find one in your home country, you should be able to pick one up at the airport or in almost any Paris supermarket.

EMERGENCIES For the **police,** call ☎ 17. To report a **fire,** call ☎ 18. For an **ambulance,** call the fire department at ☎ 18, or the S.A.M.U. ambulance company at ☎ 15. From anywhere in Europe, including France, the **general emergency number** is ☎ 112. If you need non-urgent medical attention, practitioners in most fields can be found at the Centre Médical Europe, 44 rue d'Amsterdam, 9th (☎ 01-42-81-93-33; www.centre-medical-europe.com). Also, **SOS Médecins** (www.sosmedecins.fr; ☎ 36-24; 0.15€/min. and ☎ 01-47-07-77-77) makes house calls that cost around 90€ to 130€ (prices quoted are for people without French social security). For **emergency dental service,** call S.O.S. Dentaire, ☎ 01-43-37-51-00 (www.sos-dentaire.com). **Hospitals with English-speaking staff** are Hôpital Américain, 63 bd. Victor Hugo, Neuilly-sur-Seine, 92 (www.american-hospital.org;

☎ 01-46-41-25-25), and Hôpital Franco Britannique, 3 rue Barbes, Levallois Perret, 92 (www.hopital francobritannique.org; ☎ 01-47-59-59-59).

UK nationals will need a European Health Insurance Card (EHIC) to receive free or reduced-cost health benefits during a visit to a European Economic Area (EEA) country (European Union countries plus Iceland, Liechtenstein, and Norway) or Switzerland.

The quickest way to apply for one in the UK is online (go to https://services.nhsbsa.nhs.uk/cra/start). You still pay upfront for treatment and related expenses; the doctor will give you a form to reclaim most of the money (about 70% of doctor's fees and 35%–65% of medicines/prescription charges), which you should send off while still in France (see the EHIC website for details, or see www.nhs.uk/using-the-nhs/healthcare-abroad). Non-EU nationals—with the exception of Canadians, who have the same rights as EU citizens to medical treatment in France—need comprehensive travel insurance that covers medical treatment overseas. Even then, you pay bills upfront and apply for a refund.

EVENT LISTINGS *L'Officiel des Spectacle* (www.offi.fr) provides listings of everything that's going on in the city. Or try the Télérama website (French only; www.telerama.fr/tag/sortir-paris). The Tourist Office also lists good events on their website: https://en.parisinfo.com/what-to-do-in-paris.

FAMILY TRAVEL Paris's official website (https://en.parisinfo.com/practical-paris/Paris-for-families) has sections on family travel, listing tips on transport, accommodation, and family activities, and where to rent baby gear (like cots, etc.).

LGBT TRAVELERS The center of gay and lesbian life is in the Marais, and the Pride Parade (which includes all LGBTQ+ people) takes place on the last Sunday of June. In France, the acronym is LGBT+. Paris's largest gay bookstore is **Les Mots à la Bouche**, 37 rue St. Amboise, 11th (www.motsbouche.com; ☎ 01-42-78-88-30). To find listings and events focused on Paris, try www.qweek.fr (in French).The city's tourist office website lists LGBTQ resources (events, associations, and marriage proposal services); go to www.parisinfo.com, then type LBGTQ in the search bar.

HOLIDAYS Public holidays include New Year's Day (Jan 1), Easter Monday (Mar or Apr), Labor Day (May 1), Victory Day 1945 (May 8), Ascension Day (40 days after Easter), Whit Monday (11 days after Ascension Day), National Day/Bastille Day (July 14), Assumption Day (Aug 15), All Saints' Day (Nov 1), Armistice Day 1918 (Nov 11), and Christmas Day (Dec 25).

INSURANCE Nowadays most upper-end credit cards provide some travel insurance. North Americans with homeowner's or renter's insurance are probably covered for lost luggage. If not, inquire with **Travel Assistance International** (www.travelassistanceinternational. com; ☎ 800/821-2828) or **Travelex** (www.travelexinsurance.com; ☎ 800/228-9792). These insurers can also provide trip-cancellation, medical, and emergency evacuation coverage abroad.

INTERNET ACCESS All hotels offer Internet access (sometimes at a price) and most are equipped with both Wi-Fi and a computer; alternatively, many cafes offer Wi-Fi. More than 250 free Wi-Fi spots are dotted around the city. For internet and printing services, try **Milk,** open 24/7, at 31 bd Sebastopol, 1st (www.milkclub.com; ☎ 01-42-33-68-17).

LIQUOR LAWS Supermarkets, grocery stores, and cafes sell alcoholic beverages. The legal drinking age is 18. Cafe hours vary; some even stay open 24 hours. It's illegal to drive while drunk. If convicted, motorists face a stiff fine and a possible prison term.

LOST PROPERTY If your luggage is lost, immediately file a lost-luggage claim at the airport, detailing the luggage contents. For most airlines, you must report delayed, damaged, or lost baggage within 4 hours of arrival. If you lose any belongings in Paris, declare your item online with the **Service des Objets Trouvés** (Lost-Property Bureau; https:// objetstrouvesprefecturedepolice. franceobjetstrouves.fr). If your belonging is found, you will be given instructions on where to pick it up (probably at 36 rue des Morillons, 15th, the bureau's HQ, which collects everything that is found in the city). You might be lucky.

MAIL/POST OFFICES Most post offices (La Poste) in Paris are open Monday through Friday from 8am to 7pm and Saturday from 8am to noon. However, the **main post office,** at 50 rue du Louvre (www. laposte.fr; ☎ 36-31), is open until midnight. Stamps can usually be purchased from your hotel reception desk and at cafes with red TABAC signs.

MONEY France's currency is the euro, which can be used in most other EU countries. The exchange rate varies, but at press time, 1 euro was equal to US$1.07. You can check for the most current rates at www.xe.com. The best way to get cash in Paris is at ATMs or cash-points (see above). Credit cards are accepted at almost all shops, restaurants, and hotels (although not always American Express or Diner's Club), but you should always have some cash on hand for incidentals and sightseeing admissions. Most taxis accept credit cards. Check with the driver as soon as you get in, or request a card-payment taxi when you reserve.

NEWSPAPERS & MAGAZINES English-language newspapers are dying out in paper form, but you'll still find some available from most kiosks, including *The New York Times* and the British *Times, Guardian,* and *Independent*. The leading French-language domestic papers are *Le Monde, Le Figaro,* and *Libération*.

PASSPORTS If your passport is lost or stolen, contact your country's embassy or consulate immediately. (See "Consulates & Embassies," above.) Before you travel, copy the critical pages and keep them in a separate place.

POLICE Call ☎ 17 for emergencies. The principal *Préfecture* (police station) is at 1 bis rue de Lutèce, 4th (www.prefecture depolice.interieur.gouv.fr; ☎ 34-30; Métro: Cité).

SAFETY The center of Paris is relatively safe. Look out for pickpockets—especially child pickpockets. Their method is to get very close to a target, ask for a handout, and deftly help themselves to your money or passport. Other methods to watch are card tricks (especially

at the base of Montmartre); and if someone picks up a ring in front of you, walk on by. Robbery at gun- or knifepoint is rare, but not unknown. For more information, consult the U.S. State Department's website at www.travel.state.gov; the Government of Canada at https://travel. gc.ca/travelling/advisories; in the UK, consult the Foreign Office's website, https://www.gov.uk/ foreign-travel-advice; and in Australia, consult the government travel advisory service at www. smartraveller.gov.au.

SENIOR TRAVELERS Mention that you're a senior when you make your travel reservations. As in most cities, people over the age of 60 sometimes qualify for reduced admission to theaters, museums, and other attractions.

SMOKING Smoking is now illegal in public places (including restaurants, bars, theaters, and public transportation) but is tolerated outside and on cafe terraces. Some hotels still provide smokers' bedrooms (so ask when making reservations); otherwise, they may fine you for smoking in a nonsmoking room.

TAXES Value Added Tax, or VAT (TVA in French) is 20%, but non-EU visitors over 16 can get a refund when they spend less than 6 months in France and purchase goods worth at least 100€ over a maximum of 3 days, at a retailer offering tax-free shopping *(vente en détaxe)* in the same brand or group of brands. The shops will give you a form—a "bordereau de vente"—which you and the shopkeeper should sign. You will also choose how you want to be reimbursed (card, bank transfer, or cash). The form has a bar code that you scan in a "'Pablo" terminal (or for cash head to the "detaxe" counter).

TELEPHONES Public phones are few and far between. If you can find one, it should accept credit cards. To make a **direct international call,** first dial 00, then dial the country code, the area code (minus the first zero), and the local number. The country code for the **U.S. and Canada** is 1; **Great Britain,** 44; **Ireland,** 353; **Australia,** 61; and **New Zealand,** 64. The country code for France is 33. Paris numbers usually begin with 01 (06 or 07 for mobiles).

TICKETS Paris has many theater ticket agencies, but buying tickets directly from the box office or at a discount agency can be up to 50% cheaper. Try **Kiosque Théâtre,** opposite 15 place de la Madeleine, 8th; in front of Gare de Montparnasse (place Raoul Dautry), 14th; or Paris's main tourist office (Office de Tourisme et des Congrès de Paris), 29 rue de Rivoli, 1st (www.kiosque theatre.com). Plenty of ticket discounts can also be had at **BilletRéduc,** www.billetreduc.com (in French).

TIPPING In cafes and restaurants, waiter service is included, although you can round up the bill or leave some small change, if you like. The same goes for taxi drivers. In more expensive hotels, a tip of 1€ to 2€ for having luggage carried by a hotel porter is appreciated but not an obligation.

TOILETS If you use a toilet at a cafe or brasserie, it's customary to make some small purchase. In the street, the domed self-cleaning lavatories are an option if you have small change. Be prepared—though the infamous "Turkish loo" (a porcelain hole in the floor) is largely a thing of the past, even cafe toilets can leave a lot to be desired, and are usually excruciatingly small.

TOURIST OFFICES For tourist information, try **Office de Tourisme et des Congrès de Paris,** 29 rue de Rivoli, 1st (www.parisinfo.com).

TOURS The largest tour companies are **Globus** (www.globusjourneys.com), **Cosmos** (www.cosmos.com), and **Trafalgar** (www.trafalgartours.com). Many major airlines offer air/land package deals that include tours of Paris; ask the airlines or your travel agent for details.

TRAVELERS WITH DISABILITIES Nearly all modern hotels in France (and those with 3 or more stars) now have rooms designed for people with disabilities, but many older hotels do not, so check when booking. Hotels sensitive to the issue may also have the "Tourisme & Handicaps" label, a sign that they are well-equipped. Most high-speed trains within France have wheelchair access, and guide dogs ride free. Paris's Métro and RER system does have some elevator access, but it is very difficult to use if you're in a wheelchair. There are, however, 60 wheelchair-accessible bus lines. **Paris Info** (www.parisinfo.com) has resources for travelers with disabilities, including a list of accessible hotels and attractions including museums, public swimming pools, and cinemas. British travelers should contact **Tourism for All** (www.tourismforall.org.uk) to access a wide range of travel information and resources for elderly people and those with disabilities.

Paris: **A Brief History**

2000 B.C. The Parisii tribe founds the settlement of Lutétia alongside the Seine.

52 B.C. Julius Caesar conquers Lutétia during the Gallic wars.

A.D. 300 Lutétia is renamed Paris. Roman power begins to weaken in France.

1422 England invades Paris during the Hundred Years' War.

1429 Joan of Arc tries to regain Paris for the French; she is later burned at the stake by the English in Rouen.

1572 The wars of religion reach their climax with the St. Bartholomew's Day massacre of Protestants.

1598 Henri IV endorses the Edict of Nantes, granting tolerance to Protestants.

1643 Louis XIV moves his court to the newly built Versailles.

1789 The French Revolution begins.

1793 Louis XVI and his queen, Marie Antoinette, are publicly guillotined.

1799 A coup d'état installs Napoleon Bonaparte as head of government.

1804 Napoleon declares France an empire and is crowned emperor at Notre-Dame.

1804–15 The Napoleonic wars.

1814 Paris is briefly occupied by a coalition, including Britain and Russia. The Bourbon monarchy is restored.

1848 Revolutions occur across Europe. King Louis Philippe is deposed by the autocratic Napoleon III.

1860S The Impressionist style of painting emerges.

1870–71 The Franco-Prussian War ends in the siege of Paris. The Third Republic is established, while much of the city is controlled by the revolutionary Paris Commune.

1914–18 World War I rips apart Europe. Millions are killed in the trenches of northeast France.

1940 German troops occupy France during World War II. The French Resistance under General Charles de Gaulle maintains symbolic headquarters in London.

1944 U.S. troops liberate Paris; de Gaulle returns in triumph.

1958 France's Fourth Republic collapses. General de Gaulle is called out of retirement to head the Fifth Republic.

1968 Parisian students and factory workers engage in a general revolt; the government is overhauled in the aftermath.

1994 François Mitterrand and Queen Elizabeth II open the Channel Tunnel.

1995 Jacques Chirac is elected president over François Mitterrand. Paris is crippled by a general strike.

2002 The euro replaces the franc as France's national currency.

2003–04 French opposition to the war in Iraq causes the largest diplomatic rift with America in decades.

2007 Nicolas Sarkozy replaces Jacques Chirac as president of France.

2012 Socialist François Hollande is elected president over Sarkozy.

2013 Gay marriage is legalized.

Architecture

This section serves as a guide to some of the architectural styles you'll see in Paris. However, it's worth pointing out that very few buildings (especially churches) were built in one particular style. These massive, expensive structures often took centuries to complete, during which time tastes changed and plans were altered.

Romanesque (800–1100)
Taking their inspiration from ancient Rome, the Romanesque architects concentrated on building large churches with wide aisles. Few examples of the Romanesque style remain in Paris, but the church of **Saint-Germain-des-Prés** (oldest part, 6th century A.D.) is a good example. The overall building is Romanesque, but by the time builders got to creating the choir, the early Gothic was on—note the pointy arches.

Gothic (1100–1500)
By the 12th century, engineering developments freed church architecture from the thick, heavy walls of Romanesque structures.

Instead of dark, somber, relatively unadorned Romanesque interiors that forced the eyes of the

faithful toward the altar, the Gothic interior enticed the churchgoers' gaze upward to high ceilings filled with light. The squat, brooding Romanesque exteriors were replaced by graceful buttresses and spires. **Notre-Dame** (1163–1250) is arguably the finest example of Gothic church architecture anywhere in the world. After the 2019 fire, which ravaged the roof and destroyed the spire, the cathedral was set to re-open at the end of 2024 as an identical copy of what came before.

Renaissance (1500–1630)
In architecture, as in painting, the Renaissance came from Italy and took some time to coalesce. And, as in painting, its rules stressed proportion, order, classical inspiration, and precision, resulting in unified, balanced structures. The 1544 **Hôtel Carnavalet** (23 rue de Sévigné), a Renaissance mansion, exemplifies the style. It now contains the **Musée Carnavalet,** a museum devoted to the history of Paris and the French Revolution.

Baroque, Rococo, and Neoclassical (1630–1800)
During the reign of Louis XIV (1643–1715), art and architecture were subservient to political ends.

French baroque buildings were grandiose and severely ordered—**Versailles** is the best model. Opulence was especially pronounced in interior decoration, which increasingly became the excessively detailed and self-indulgent rococo (*rocaille* in French) style. Rococo tastes didn't last long, though, and soon a neoclassical movement was raising such structures as Paris's **Panthéon** (1758), based even more strictly on ancient models than the earlier Renaissance classicism was.

The 19th Century

Architectural styles in 19th-century Paris were eclectic, beginning in a severe classical mode and ending with something of an identity crisis—torn between Industrial Age technology and Art Nouveau's organic vibe. During the reign of Emperor Napoleon III (1852–70), classicism was reinterpreted in an ornate, dramatic mode. Urban planning was the architectural rage, and Paris became a city of wide boulevards courtesy of **Baron Georges-Eugène Haussmann** (1809–91), commissioned by Napoleon III in 1852 to modernize the city. Paris owes much of its remarkably unified look to Haussmann.

Expositions in 1878, 1889, and 1900 were the catalysts for constructing huge glass-and-steel structures that showed off modern techniques. This produced such Parisian monuments as the **Eiffel Tower** and **Gare d'Orsay** (which now houses the Musée d'Orsay). However, the subsequent emergence of the Art Nouveau movement was, in many ways, a rebellion against the late-19th-century industrial zeal, peaking around the turn of the century. Architects like **Hector Guimard** celebrated curvaceous asymmetrical designs, often based on plants and flowers. It was this short period that gave us the famous Art Nouveau Métro station entrances (1867–1942); the **Porte Dauphine** (line 2) and **Abbesses** (line 12) entrances are the most intact examples today. But the city's finest Art Nouveau structure is the intricately decorated apartment block at 29 av. de Rapp in the 7th.

The 20th Century

The ravages of war stalled the progress of French architecture for many decades, but the latter half of the 20th century saw some of the most audacious architectural projects in French history—and certainly some of the most controversial. It has taken decades for such structures as the **Centre Pompidou** or the **Louvre**'s glass pyramids to become accepted by most Parisians, but now they are a well-loved part of the skyline.

The 21st Century

The face of Paris is ever-changing. The new era has already seen the arrival of the Jean Nouvel–designed **Musée du Quai Branly** (2006), an impressive angular structure whose bright colors and clever use of vegetation are a flagship for 21st-century architecture within the city center. The sleek **Passerelle Simone de Beauvoir** bridge (2006) is another new addition, linking the Bercy district to the François Mitterrand library's towers. West of Paris in the **La Defense business district,** the fight is on to give the metropolitan area a cluster of skyscrapers, and back in the center, architect David Mangin has the **Les Halles** district (including a park and underground shopping mall), which was finished in 2016. The most recent addition to the Louvre is a stark, modern structure—nicknamed the *libéllule* (dragonfly) after its undulating roof—in the Cours Visconti. Designed by Mario Bellini and Rudi Ricciotti, it houses the museum's Islamic art collections. In 2014, some futuristic edifices joined the skyline: Frank Gehry's **Fondation Louis Vuitton** (a contemporary art showcase for the Vuitton group), with soaring glass sails, like a glass and concrete ship. On its tail is Jean Nouvel's **Philharmonie de Paris** concert venue featuring an avant-garde wooden interior and a facade of Modernist bird mosaics.

Useful **Phrases**

It's amazing how often a word or two of halting French will change your host's disposition. At the very least, try to learn basic greetings, and—above all—the life-raft phrase, *Parlez-vous anglais?* ("Do you speak English?")

Useful Words & Phrases

ENGLISH	FRENCH	PRONUNCIATION
Yes/No	**Oui/Non**	wee/noh
Okay	**D'accord**	*dah*-core
Please	**S'il vous plaît**	seel voo *play*
Thank you	**Merci**	*mair*-see
You're welcome	**De rien**	duh ree-*ehn*
Hello (during daylight)	**Bonjour**	bohn-*jhoor*
Good evening	**Bonsoir**	bohn-*swahr*
Good-bye	**Au revoir**	o ruh-*vwahr*
What's your name?	**Comment vous appelez-vous?**	kuh-*mahn* voo za-pell-ay-voo?
My name is	**Je m'appelle**	*jhuh* ma-pell
How are you?	**Comment allez-vous?**	kuh-*mahn* tahl-ay-voo?
So-so	**Comme ci, comme ça**	kum-*see*, kum-*sah*
I'm sorry/Excuse me	**Pardon**	pahr-*dohn*
Do you speak English?	**Parlez-vous anglais?**	par-lay-voo zahn-*glay*?
I don't speak French	**Je ne parle pas français**	jhuh ne parl pah frahn-*say*
I don't understand	**Je ne comprends pas**	jhuh ne kohm-*prahn* pas
Where is . . . ?	**Où est . . . ?**	ooh eh . . . ?
Why?	**Pourquoi?**	poor-*kwah*?
Here/There	**Ici/Là**	ee-*see*/lah
Left/Right	**à Gauche/à Droite**	a goash/a drwaht
Straight ahead	**Tout droit**	too drwah

Index

See also Accommodations and Restaurant indexes, below.

1920s, 49
59 Rivoli, 82, 88–89
107 RIVOLI, 95

A

B

C

D

Photo Credits